# National Security in the Third World

# National Security in the Third World

## The Management of Internal and External Threats

*Edited by*

# Edward E. Azar
*University of Maryland*

*and*

# Chung-in Moon
*University of Kentucky*

EDWARD ELGAR

Center for International Development and
Conflict Management,
University of Maryland.

© Center for International Development and Conflict
Management, 1988

Published by
Edward Elgar Publishing Limited
Gower House
Croft Road
Aldershot
Hants GU11 3HR
England

and distributed in the USA by The Center for International
Development and Conflict Management, University of
Maryland, College Park 20742

**British Library Cataloguing in Publication Data.**

National security in the third world: the
   management of internal and external
   threats.
   1. Developing countries. National security.
   Policies of governments
   I. Azar, Edward E., *1938* – II. Moon,
   Chung-in
   327'. 09172'4


1 85278 079 7
1 85278 080 0 (Pbk)

Printed in Great Britain at the
University Press, Cambridge

# Contents

*Notes on Contributors*                                            vi

1. Rethinking Third World National                                  1
   Security   *Edward E. Azar and Chung-in Moon*
2. People, States and Fear: The National                           14
   Security Problem in the Third World
   *Barry Buzan*
3. Simple Labels and Complex Realities:                            44
   National Security for the Third World
   *Davis B. Bobrow and Steve Chan*
4. Legitimacy, Integration and Policy Capacity:                    77
   The 'Software' Side of Third World National
   Security   *Edward E. Azar and Chung-in Moon*
5. Ideology and Security: Self-Reliance in                        102
   China and North Korea   *Han S. Park and Kyung
   A. Park*
6. Economic Development and National                              136
   Security   *Ethan B. Kapstein*
7. Arms Acquisition and National Security:                        152
   The Irony of Military Strength   *Andrew L. Ross*
8. National Security Regimes and Human                            188
   Rights Abuse: Argentina's Dirty Wars
   *Carlos Egan*
9. Regime Legitimacy and National Security:                       227
   The Case of Pahlavi Iran   *Mark J. Gasiorowski*
10. Managing National Security: The American                      251
    Experience and Lessons for the Third
    World   *R.D. McLaurin*
11. Towards an Alternative Conceptualization                      277
    *Edward E. Azar and Chung-in Moon*

*Index*                                                          299

# Notes on Contributors

Edward E. Azar is Director of the Center for International Development and Conflict Management, and Professor of Government and Politics, University of Maryland, College Park, MD 20742.

Davis Bobrow is Professor, Dept. of Government and Politics, University of Maryland, College Park, MD 20742.

Barry Buzan is Lecturer in International Studies at the University of Warwick. Garden Flat, 17 Lambolle Road, London NW3 4HS, England.

Steve Chan is Professor, Dept. of Political Science, University of Colorado, Boulder, CO 80301

Carlos Egan is Assistant Professor, Dept. of Political Science, Williams College, Williamstown, MA 01267.

Mark J. Gasiorowski is Assistant Professor, Dept. of Political Science, Louisiana State University, Baton Rouge, LA.

Ethan Kapstein is Research Associate, Center for International Affairs, Harvard University, and an international banker. 55 Langdon St. Cambridge, MA 02138

Ronald McLaurin is President of Abbott Associates, a Washington-based consulting firm. 8600 Powder Horn Rd. Springfield, VA.

Chung-in Moon is Assistant Professor, Dept. of Political Science, University of Kentucky, Lexington, KY 40506.

Han-Sik Park is Associate Professor, Dept. of Political Science, University of Georgia, Athens, GA

Kyung A. Park is Assistant Professor, Dept. of Political Science, Mercer University, Macom, GA 31207

Andy Ross is Assistant Professor, Dept. of Political Science, University of Kentucky, Lexington, KY 40506.

# 1. Rethinking Third World National Security

EDWARD E. AZAR and CHUNG-IN MOON

National security is a Western, largely American, concept that emerged in the post-World War II period. As the burdens of the presidency of the United States grew heavier and American involvement in international affairs grew deeper, the structure and management of policy-making at the national level required new and bold approaches. As the international environment grew in complexity, and it became necessary to integrate military, diplomatic, intelligence, technological, economic and other diverse data at the apex of American decision-making, the American President in 1949 launched the national security apparatus. The nature of this apparatus has, of course, changed over the years. Despite a good deal of writing about the development of the concept and the machinery of national security in the USA and Western world, a good deal of writing has lacked solid analytical and empirical research, and thus only limited scholarly advances have been made.

In recent years, the concept of national security has attracted the attention of scholars and statesmen from the Third World both as an analytical and as a management formulation. The scarce body of literature on Third World national security is generally produced in the West and appears to suffer from relying on the Western experience to understand and apply national policy and security. This literature has focused chiefly on the military dimension, especially threat perceptions of contending elites, doctrinal responses, security resources and capabilities to meet external threats to the state (often the regime in power). This body of literature has, however, underestimated the salience and impact of domestic political structure and policy-making fragility, economic and technological underdevelopment, ethnic, religious and social cleavages in the ever expanding populations and the severe ecopolitical pressures affecting the Third World.

This book is intended to examine the utility and weaknesses of the Western conception of national security in the Third World. We address both the conceptual and functional issues involved and try to provide an alternative framework within which various dimensions of Third World national security can properly be identified and analysed, and subsequently raise theoretical and practical issues. The basic assumption here is that national security has a meaning, and that that meaning is related to threats to core national values. The nature of threats (which, behaviourally, must be perceived threats) will vary from country to country, across issue areas, and over time. It is a grievous error to fix a rigid operational meaning to national security and apply it administratively across the board. The conceptual meaning of national security must be definitively resolved, but must allow for varying operational and managerial elements, depending on the nature of the threat, just as it must allow for varying policies and actions depending on the nature of the situation.

## COPING WITH INSECURITY: TRADITIONAL VIEWS

The proliferation of new nation-states after World War II reshaped the global landscape. Their diversity notwithstanding, these new nations may be seen in some respects as a distinct collective entity in the bipolar cold war system.

Collective expression of their solidarity and perceived unifying grievances through the Non-Aligned Movement and the pursuit of a 'new international economic order' has elevated the Third World to the centre stage, or at least part of the centre stage, of world politics for the past three decades. In the shadow of flamboyant rhetoric and gestures of bravado, however, most Third World nations have suffered persistent and pervasive insecurity. About 90 per cent of the domestic conflict, regional crises, and overall international violence which has taken place in the world since World War II is concentrated in the Third World. More striking, of the 120 wars recorded since 1945, 119 have taken place in the developing countries.[1] Overt violence and conflict aside, most developing countries have become insecure places to live in because of chronic poverty, crime, pollution, famine, population expansion, and a deteriorating quality of life.

How can we understand this insecurity? A cursory review of the literature and government policy statements in the Third World indicates that they share several common features in the diagnosis of, and prescriptions for, insecurity.[2] First, the security problem is commonly understood in terms of the physical protection of the state from external threats — violent threats that are predominantly military in nature. External aggression involving war and border conflicts, espionage, sabotage, subversion, and other threats operationalized by actual or potential adversaries are the immediate concerns of national security.[3] Treating national security as military and political matters obviously reflects the realist interpretation of international politics where anarchy is pervasive and each state pursues its own national interests. In the vicious circle of action and reaction, self-help is the only rule of the game. For the weakest and most fragile Third World countries, which fell prey to colonial domination, conceiving security issues in terms of the Hobbesian *Weltanschauung* is certainly understandable.

Diagnosing Third World national security in terms of external military threats has produced a predictable prescription in an anarchic world where self-help is the name of the game. Security is measured by the ability to protect state sovereignty, to preserve territorial integrity, and to maintain autonomy. The behavioural and coercive nature of external threats demands the accumulation and exercise of the same kinds of force to resist or deter attack or other hostile behavior. Such logic dictates that each nation develop, maintain, and exercise coercive and behavioural power. Any shifts in absolute or relative coercive power, in fact or in prospect, trigger new security problems. This coercive-behavioural dimension of power is most clearly manifested in the form of military force. The capacity to coerce, kill, and destroy becomes the important source of power, and thus the pre-eminent safeguard for national security. Indeed, the military component becomes the ultimate criterion by which overall levels of power potential and national security capability are measured and judged. Human, material, and technological resources and constraints are all tied to this military power.

The primacy of military power in considerations of national security is pervasive in the Third World. Military expenditures of developing countries have increased sixfold since 1960 in real terms. In 1960 developing countries accounted for 8 per cent of global military expenditures. By 1985 their share had increased to 20 per cent. Arms imports by the Third World also increased sharply from $4 billion in 1960 to $35 billion in 1981. Over the two decades ending in 1983, total arms imports by the Third World amounted to $223 billion.[4]

Construction of a modern military establishment is not an easy task, nor an inexpensive one, and is rarely undertaken without the presence of tension in the security environment. A state surrounded by hostile adversaries typically produces a build-up of military forces. In the absence of endogenous power adequate to deter or contain external military threats, governments may rely on coalitions or tacit or open alliances. Most of the literature on Third World national security focuses on security environment issues such as threat perceptions, strategic interactions, and regional and superpower alignment and realignment.[5] The dominant theme of this security environment literature is ecological determinism. That is, Third World national security problems are treated as a mere extension of system-level or sub-system-level dynamics. Perhaps this bias results from the perception that most developing countries are clients and proxies of big powers and 'system-ineffectual' states that can never, acting alone or in small groups, make a significant impact on the system. In this view, the superpowers and medium-sized powers establish the agenda of international issues and determine directly or indirectly the parameters and the type and intensity of interactions in the international system. The rest of the world, including the Third World, is simply the backdrop for the competition of the superpowers and medium-sized powers and is relegated to the status of clients who benefit or suffer commensurately with their protectors. Consequently, it is essential to understand the dynamics of the general and local balances of power in order to describe, explain and prescribe the national security policies of developing countries.

Finally, most developing countries are burdened with policy environments and resource availabilities sharply different from those of the West. The developing countries typically suffer from fragile domestic political structures, shortages of qualified manpower, and ineffective security infrastructures. Nevertheless, policy-makers and scholars alike implicitly or explicitly promote and assume the importance of emulating and adopting Western national security management tools and techniques. Popular themes are policy guidelines, institutions, and lexicons such as:

- procedures for an effective integration of foreign and defence policy,
- strategic planning,
- military doctrines,
- defence budgeting,
- weapons-systems evaluation and choices,
- threat perception and analysis,
- intelligence capability, and
- alliance or coalition strategy.

This emulative process may reflect colonial ties or client relationships with Western powers.

The current concept of national security in the Third World manifests a set of distinct characteristics:

- defining insecurity in terms of violent external threats,
- heavy emphasis on coercive-behavioural power founded on military force,
- understanding of security environment through ecological determinism, and
- emulation of Western tools and techniques of security management.

This interpretation of, and prescription for, security issues has merit and relevance to Third World national security. It is, however, our contention that this monolithic view framed around the realist tradition of international politics is not only too narrow in scope, but also is distortive of objective reality. As we have argued before, there is no fixed concept of national security. The operational definition of national security is largely contextual. Consequently, the diagnosis of, and prescription for, security can vary from one country to another. Moreover, the idiosyncrasies of each national security situation complicate the application of the Western concept and management technique of national security to Third World.

## ALTERNATIVE VIEWS

Against the backdrop of conventional views, the articles in this volume question the validity and applicability of the concept, operational meaning, security environment, and policy prescriptions currently prevalent in the Third World. In the second chapter, Barry Buzan argues that the concepts and issues of national security are largely of Western origin, and he delineates some fundamental difficulties in applying them to Third World states. The security conditions of Western and Third World states differ on two grounds — their degree of political cohesion, and the nature of their security environments. Many Third World states are fragile political entities, and this fact introduces serious problems in identifying the referable object for a concept like national security. One danger in using national security for politically weak states is that it easily legitimates the use of force in domestic politics. Most Third World states also face a much more turbulent and unstable security environment than do most Western states. This endemic instability is of course linked to the political weakness of many Third World states, creating a vicious circle of insecurity. Buzan argues that these major differences may invalidate the use of the concept of national security for Third World conditions, or at the very least constitute an argument for considerable circumspection in applying the concept.

In 'Simple Labels and Complex Realities', Davis Bobrow and Steve Chan consider several of the conceptual issues raised by Buzan through different lenses. Imprecision and diversity in the application of the concept of national security make it difficult to conceptualise Third World national security in a meaningful way. The authors overcome these difficulties by differentiating content, actors and processes. Furthermore, they draw our attention to subjective interpretations of national security. An operational definition of national security is contingent upon policymakers' judgements about the *significance* and *probability* of some foreign act of commission or omission, and about their *leverage* in encouraging or restraining this act. Like Buzan, Bobrow and Chan make some salient distinctions between the Third World, on the one hand, and the First and Second Worlds, on the other, in terms of respective national security problems and coping capabilities. Departing from the previous undifferentiated view of the Third World, they further disaggregate the Third World into four subcategories — Achievers, Goliaths, Davids, and Weak — by using such indicators as size, economic development, and military capability. Within this differentiation, the variety of national security problems, options, accomplishments, capabilities, and management proclivities of each of these subcategories is raised and discussed. Finally, Bobrow and Chan suggest a direction for future national security studies by urging us to engage in more systematic mapping of the ecology of domestic and foreign military threats, comparative studies on actual operationalization of the concept of national security, plotting the relationship of means and ends among the major security dimensions, and overall patterns of status management by Third World countries.

While Buzan and Bobrow and Chan clarify conceptual ambiguities of national security and identify the limits and difficulties of applying Western concepts to the Third World, the chapter by Edward Azar and Chung-in Moon directs our attention to domestic political dimensions as a relevant area of national security studies. Azar and Moon delineate three dimensions of national security policies: security environment, hardware and software. While security environment is an essential indicator of external threat and alliance pattern, the hardware side of security management involves physical capabilities, strategic doctrines, force structure, and weapons choice. By contrast, the software side refers to political legitimacy, integration, and overall policy capacity. Traditional approaches have been preoccupied with security environment and hardware, which could hinder dynamic understanding of Third World national security realities. More attention is due the dynamic software side of security management, because of fragile political legitimacy, fragmented societies, incomplete nation-building, and rigid policy capacity. Moreover, the software side of security management is the crucial intervening variable linking security environment to hardware.

In 'Ideology and Security', Han-Sik Park and Kyung A. Park elaborate the importance of non-tangible domestic political factors in the non-Western world. Through a comparative study of China and North Korea, they elucidate the crucial role of ideology in influencing overall security management and performance. Maoism in China and the Juche ideology in North Korea, both of which embody the principle of self-reliance, have been instrumental in indoctrinating, mobilizing, and restructuring the popular masses and the military for national security objectives. Although China and North Korea may represent deviant cases by Third World standards, their practice and performance demonstrate clearly that ideology can be an integral part of national security.

In the conventional view, the stronger the military power, the better the security posture. Indeed military strength is often considered almost synonymous with national security in some simplistic analyses. In reality, however, the blind pursuit of military power may engender negative consequences. Ethan Kapstein's 'Economic Development and National Security' traces the link between national security policies and economic development strategies. Contrary to liberal assertions, the scope, timing and trajectory of economic development in the Third World seldom follow market principles. They are instead greatly influenced by the nature of national security policies. Through a comparative examination of South Korean, Brazilian, and Argentinian experiences, Kapstein concludes that national security considerations have played essential roles in shaping the nature and direction of economic development strategy through direct military spending and state support of military-related industries. These national security considerations have distorted the pattern of economic development, and created a classic trade-off between guns and butter.

In 'Arms Acquisition and National Security', Andy Ross substantiates limits of national security built on military strength. Conventionally, military force is the essential ingredient of national security. Military force in turn depends upon arms acquisition. In acquiring arms, national security policy-makers in the Third World usually rely on three distinct options: local production, importation, and a combination of the two. Each of these options has a different impact on national security. Ross, however, shows that even though arms are acquired with the expectation that security will thereby be enhanced, the manner in which arms are acquired may well erode security by significantly limiting policy and behavioral autonomy of Third World countries, precisely because of the resulting structure of military dependence.

Through a penetrating analysis of the Argentina case, Carlos Egan explores a complex relation involving national security and regime security. Egan argues that 'national security' in Argentina was nothing but a fig leaf for regime

security. The two Dirty Wars (of the 1920s and 1970s)
waged by authoritarian regimes in the name of national
security were to protect the interests and privileges of the
dominant class that dependent capitalism had created and
reproduced. Egan finds answers to the metamorphosis of
national security into regime security in interactions between global economic cycles and dependent capitalism. In
the trough of global economic cycles, Argentina as a
dependent capitalist state was forced to face major
economic crises. The crises politicized the popular sector
and made it more militant, which in turn threatened the
very survival of the capitalist system. To contain this
popular sector challenge, the capitalist regimes created
imaginary enemies, introduced the ideology of national
security, and launched the so called 'Dirty Wars' against the
popular sector. National security became an instrument to
justify state terrorism and human rights abuses for the
preservation of class interests.

Conventional wisdom argues that forming an alliance
with superpowers to seek their protection is an important
logic of survival for many Third World countries. Mark
Gasiorowski, however, challenges the proposition through
a case study of Iran under the Shah, and argues that such a
client relationship may be a liability to national security.
Imperial Iran was militarily strong, and claimed to be the
hegemonic power in the Persian Gulf. Iran's military
strength was furthered by its strong ties with the United
States. Ironically, it is this external source of power that not
only toppled the Shah, but also drove Iran to immense
insecurity. The Shah was returned to power through a
foreign-backed coup and built up his military strength
through a strong relationship with USA. This cliency
compelled the Shah to pursue policies distinct from the
public interest. As a consequence, the Shah's legitimacy
eroded, inviting social unrest and revolution, and eventually subjecting Iran to Soviet intimidation and an invasion
by Iraq.

Finally, the chapter by Ronald McLaurin relates problems
associated with the emulation of Western security management techniques to the uniqueness of the environment in

which the concept of national security evolved in the USA, and distinguishes this environment from that in the Third World today. The concept of national security must be related to 'threat'. In the USA, national security, employed initially to refer to the general area of politico-military affairs in relatively specific contexts of jurisdictional, budgetary, and policy disputes after World War II, increasingly took on management overtones, but continued to focus on the politico-military environment. Economic and social issues were seen as relevant to 'national security' only to the extent they impinged on the politico-military domain. Therefore, the prevailing concept of 'national security' in the United States is highly inappropriate for most Third World governments whose principal threat is economic and social. The concepts of national security management developed in the USA may well be applicable to the Third World, but if so must be modified to suit the circumstances of this very different threat.

## RETHINKING THIRD WORLD NATIONAL SECURITY: NEW DIRECTIONS

The articles presented in this volume argue compellingly that the traditional approach to national security is inappropriate to Third World countries. Four major weaknesses can be singled out. First, defining the concept of national security in terms of physical protection of nation-states from external military threats is not only narrow, but also misleading. The threats facing the Third World are diverse and complex, and so are the dimensions and content of national security.

Second, the accumulation, maintenance and development of military force is no panacea for security problems. Military strength is a necessary but insufficient guardian. The complex and multiple vulnerabilities of Third World states compel us not only to look at a deeper structure and a broader spectrum of issue-nexuses, but also to search for different resources and capabilities corresponding to each pertinent threat. Furthermore, excessive preoccupation with military power can entail extensive trade-offs with domestic social, political and economic issues, which would eventually undermine overall security posture.

Third, the security environment is important, but it does not necessarily determine or dictate the nature of security issues. Domestic factors such as legitimacy, integration, ideology, and policy capacity play equally important roles in shaping the national security posture. Security challenges in many parts of the Third World are of endogenous rather than exogenous origin. Moreover, it is fallacious to understand Third World national security from the perspective of superpower rivalry. The superpowers may affect — perhaps significantly — the parameters of national security in the Third World, but they do not determine its nature. As current developments in many parts of the Third World illustrate, the superpowers are seldom able to contain, manipulate, mute or dictate regional and country-specific security problems, whether military or economic. Furthermore, cliency with superpowers can be a security liability.

Finally, direct emulation and adoption of national security management tools and techniques also appears unwise. The search for effective management techniques should be context-bound, taking account of problems, resources, and requirements specific to each national security environment.

These observations can be applied at two levels and in two geographic domains. First, analysis of national security in Third World environments has been far too greatly influenced by the conventional order of battle military assessment. Where other considerations — human rights, economic development, ecological scarcity, social modernization and national integration — have been analyzed, no methodologies have been developed to incorporate such assessments into the national security picture. From the policy standpoint, this inability has seriously handicapped decision-makers and has forced them to *choose between* competing analyses rather than *choose from* an integrated national security assessment.

Similarly, the observations and conclusions advanced in this book apply to both Third World and the developed countries. Western analysts and decision-makers at present display no greater ability to assess and weigh the factors at play in Third World national security than their counterparts in the developing countries. Because of the impact of superpower policy on Third World security reality, this shortcoming has a multiplier effect on the Third World.

The foregoing does not suggest that the conventional approach to national security must be scrapped. The traditional concept of national security is still valid in many parts of the developing world where significant, immediate external military threats characterize the security situation. Against this background, the final chapter of this book refines and expands the concept of national security, suggests multiple dimensions of security concerns, and elucidates the complex trade-off structures associated with them.

## NOTES

[1] Ruth Leger Sivard, *World Military and Social Expenditures 1986* (Washington, DC: World Priorities, Inc., 1986), p. 27.

[2] See Edward A. Kolodziej and Robert E. Harkavy, *Security Policies of Developing Countries* (Lexington, MA: Lexington Books, 1982). For dissenting views, see Robert Rothstein, 'The "Security Dilemma" and the "Poverty Trap" in the Third World', *Jerusalem Journal of International Relations*, vol. 8, no. 4 (1986), pp. 1–38; Edward E. Azar and Chung-in Moon, 'Third World National Security: Toward a New Conceptual Framework', *International Interactions*, vol. 11, no. 2 (1984), pp. 103–35; Abdul-Monem M. Al-Mashat, *National Security in the Third World* (Boulder, CO: Westview, 1985). For an eclectic and comprehensive approach, refer to Barry Buzan, *People, States, and Fear: The National Security Problem in International Relations* (Brighton: Wheatsheaf, and Chapel Hill: University of North Carolina Press, 1983).

[3] W. Handrieder and L. Buel, *Words and Arms* (Boulder, CO: Westview, 1979), p. 79.

[4] Sivard, *World Military*, p. 27.

[5] An overview of Third World national security literature indicates that a great majority of works focuses primarily on regional security environment.

# 2. People, States, and Fear: The National Security Problem in the Third World

This chapter addresses the question of how appropriate the concept of national security is to the countries of the Third World. It compares the conditions of national security in the Third World with those in the West, and argues that the nature of the differences makes the concept much more problematic in relation to Third World states than for the states of the West. Security here is defined largely in sociopolitical and military terms. The economic dimension of the subject is ignored on grounds of lack of space, and because in many respects it does not run parallel to the military and political dimensions of security. Where it does run parallel, especially in terms of development issues, I hope the linkages and implications will be self-evident to interested readers.

National security is a Western, and particularly an American, post-1945 concept. It has therefore developed in response to the needs and conditions of a distinct group of states. The Western states mostly have strong, long-standing societies. Their civilization and economy are global in extent, and many of the states in the group, even small ones like Sweden, the Netherlands and Portugal, have great-power traditions. Since the end of World War II, the Western states have formed a security community, in that none of them fears military attack from any other state in the group outside the context of a larger war between East and West. This security community is partly a response to the common opposition of the Western states to the Soviet Union, but there is reason to think that its foundations are positive as well as negative. In the post-1945 period, the security outlook of the Western states has been dominated by the priority of preventing another major war amongst the great powers. This priority is explained partly as a reaction to the massive damage that the group inflicted on itself in two world wars, partly as the natural status quo position of the dominant states in the international system, and partly as a response to the militarily paralyzing effect of mutual nuclear deterrence on their collective rivalry with the Soviet Union.

In its Western usage, the term 'national security' is deeply imbued with this priority of war prevention. Both the term and the priority represent a significant shift of attitude from the pre-1945 period, a shift symbolized by the fact that what governments used to call War Departments they now call Departments of Defence. The term also suggests a wider concern than simply military defence. It reflects the Western response to the fundamental ideological challenge from the Soviet Union to the deeply-established principles of Western economic and political organization. Military stalemate may be a necessary condition for security within such a rivalry, but it is not a sufficient one. National security under conditions of ideological rivalry requires economic and political defences as well as military ones, and in that sense the concept links military and foreign policy into a combined response to a set of threats across a broad spectrum of military, political and economic contingencies.

The idea of national security has evolved in response not only to the particular nature of the Western States, but also to the particular nature of the international environment in which the Western States find themselves. To apply a concept derived from such specific circumstances to a quite different group of states requires that we be careful to specify not only the similarities that justify the usage, but also the differences that might confound it. The case for attempting a global application of the term rests on the near universality of sovereign states as the principal basis of political organization in the international system. Since the concept is specifically designed to apply to sovereign states, there is every reason to think that it might be successfully applied outside the Western group. And since the concept of state is itself a Western one, it does not seem unreasonable to expect that it will have carried some fundamental similarities into its many real-world manifestations, especially since the Western states themselves played such a large role in transplanting their political self-image all around the planet.

But the potent term 'Third World' is an indicator that we can expect to find very considerable contrasts. One does not describe a group of states as a separate *world* unless their nature and their environment are fundamentally different from one's own. We need also to keep in mind that national security is not the only concept on offer. One can also approach the Third World using the concept of state security favoured by totalitarian regimes. In many respects 'state security' is a less ambiguous term than 'national security'. When compared with the idea of national security it puts more emphasis on the state as a centralized governing organization, and less on the individuals and social groups existing within the state. State security is a simpler, and in some senses more primitive, concept than national security. For that reason it may be easier to apply to Third World conditions than a concept like national security, which was developed by and for states within which there is much less distance between the state organization, on the one hand, and society and citizens, on the other.

National security means the security of a whole socio-political entity. It is about countries as well as about states. It concerns the way of life of a self-governing people, including their social, cultural, political and economic modes of organization, and their right to develop themselves under their own rule. This chapter will focus on some of the difficulties of applying such a concept to the countries of the Third World. Doing so involves a necessity for gross generalization, for the Third World encompasses a great variety of states. Nevertheless, the broad contrasts between the Third World and the West as groups of states are sufficiently robust to support a general comparison. In what follows, I will concentrate on two areas of contrast that are central to the application of national security: first, the nature of states as the referent objects for the concept, and second, the nature of the environment that sets the conditions within which states have to pursue national security.

## THE NATURE OF STATES    STRONG VS. WEAK

In one important political sense, oil states are similar because they all claim the right to self rule. These declarations of sovereignty define the political structure of the international system as anarchic, or without any overarching central political authority. They make states similar in a functional sense since, as Kenneth Waltz points out, the business of self-rule imposes a host of like tasks.[2] Waltz also argues that functional similarity is a long-term consequence of anarchy, because the most effective states will either impose their own system on others or force others to copy them in order to generate sufficient power to maintain their independence.[3] The force of his latter point is clearly illustrated by the Western colonial origins of nearly all of the current states in the Third World. In a legal sense, too, states are similar because they are equal. This is especially true when it is the norm, as it now is, for nearly all states to be recognized by nearly all others as legal equals. These similarities are the basis on which a concept like national security might be applied universally in the international system since 1945.

The traditional way of differentiating states from each other in security terms has been on the basis of power. The complex fragmentation of the global political system into many states produces a very uneven distribution of power, with a few great powers clustered at the top of the hierarchy, and the rest spread out in descending order to the minor powers at the bottom. The security concerns of the great powers have always attracted more attention than those of lesser powers on the grounds that they dominated the patterns of conflict and alignment in the system as a whole. Power, however, does not give us a very interesting line of comparison in national security terms between the nature of states in the West and those in the Third World. Both groups contain a very wide spectrum of powers, and since difference in level of power does not cause difficulty in applying the concept of national security to Western states, there is no reason to think it will do so for Third World ones.

The main exception to this statement is the now quite substantial group of mini- and micro-states. These include countries like the Seychelles, Tuvalu, Nauru, Grenada, and many other mostly small island and archipelagic states in the Indian and Pacific Oceans and the Caribbean. Such states often do not command adequate economic, human and territorial resources to fulfil the basic functions of statehood. They are even vulnerable to small groups of mercenaries, and it is their weakness as powers that defines their special problems of national security.[4] Where power does make a significant general difference is in terms of the security environment, and we will explore in a later-section the significance of the fact that there are no great powers in the Third World, and that the states of the Third World are therefore nearly all in the lower parts of the global power hierarchy.

Much more interesting as a way of differentiating the nature of states in national security terms is the variable of sociopolitical cohesiveness, which gets at the very essence of what qualifies them to belong to the class of objects that we label states. I have elsewhere characterised states by their absolute degree of sociopolitical cohesion as ranging on a spectrum from weak (low cohesion) to strong (high cohesion).[5] In thinking along these lines, it is important not to confuse the strength or weakness of a country *as a state*, (i.e. its degree of sociopolitical cohesion) with its strength or weakness *as a power* (i.e. the range and size of resources and capabilities it commands). Even major powers may have significant weaknesses as states, such as the Soviet Union, and quite formidable middle powers are often quite weak as states, such as Pakistan and South Africa. Conversely, strong states may range across the whole spectrum of power from the United States, through France and Sweden, to Iceland. To avoid confusion, we will adhere to a strict usage in which the terms 'weak power' and 'strong power' will refer to level of power, and 'weak state' and 'strong state' to degree of sociopolitical cohesion.

At the bottom of the spectrum there are a few very weak states that generate almost no political cohesion of their own. Chad, Uganda and Lebanon have exemplified this condition during the last decade, and Angola, Ethiopia, Sudan, Afghanistan and Mozambique have come close to it. Very weak states possess neither a widely accepted and coherent idea of the state among their populations, nor a governing power strong enough to impose unity in the absence of political consensus. The fact that they exist as states at all is largely a result of other states recognizing them as such and/or not disputing their existence. When viewed from the outside they look like states because they have embassies, a flag, boundaries on maps, and a seat in the United Nations. But viewed from within they are anarchic, with different armed self-governing groups controlling their own territories and contesting central government by force.

Further up the spectrum we find ordinary weak states like Pakistan, Syria, Bolivia, the Philippines, Turkey and Zaire. These generally contain a governing power that is strong enough to override a domestic environment in which many people's political loyalties are more strongly directed towards tribal, ethnic, political or religious groups than they are to the state. Because their political cohesion rests more on power than on any sociopolitical consensus about the nature of the state, weak states are vulnerable to external powers willing to channel resources to particular factions within their political life.

In the middle of the spectrum we find states like India, the Soviet Union, Brazil and Argentina. These typically display

a mix of characteristics, as in India, where there is both a
widespread identification with the idea and institutions of
the state, and a set of strong local political identities that
sometimes clash violently with the central government.
And at the top of the spectrum we find strong states like
Japan, France, Sweden and the United States, whose
political life rests on a synthesis of state and society. They
have a widely accepted idea of the state, which is expressed
in stable governing institutions.

In trying to apply the variable of sociopolitical cohesion
we face one of the same problems that arises in trying to
apply the concept of power, namely, the lack of a quantifi-
able measure. Both concepts ideally require precise and
objective measures not only to differentiate states on the
spectrum of high to low, but also to enable hypotheses
about differences to be tested. The lack of such measures
restricts what we can do with both concepts, but does not
prevent them from being useful for a general analysis of the
type we are engaged in here. Both concepts have common-
sense applicability. They indicate differences that are large
enough to be obvious, and significant enough to be important. Very few people would dispute the statement that there
are large and significant differences of both power and
sociopolitical cohesion among states. Widespread agreement could even be obtained for a crude ranking system.
Who would dispute that the United States is more powerful
than France or that France is more cohesive than Sri Lanka?
Only when it comes to finer rankings are we unable to
proceed. Who can say whether France is more powerful
than China, or Italy more cohesive than Spain?

No single indicator adequately defines the difference
between weak and strong states. The following list outlines
the kinds of conditions one would expect to find in weak
states (with some recent examples), and the presence of any
of which would make one at least query whether a state
should be classed as strong:

1.  high levels of political violence (Kampuchea, South
    Africa, Ethiopia),
2.  major recent changes in the structure of political insti-
    tutions (Iran, Ethiopia, Spain, Portugal),

3. conspicuous use of force by the state in domestic political life (Afghanistan, Turkey, South Korea),
4. a conspicuous role for political police in the everyday lives of citizens (Soviet Union, Romania, Poland),
5. major political conflict over what ideology will be used to organise the state (Peru, El Salvador, possibly Greece),
6. lack of a coherent national identity, or the presence of contending national identities within the state (Nigeria, Ethiopia, Sudan, Turkey, South Africa, Yugoslavia),
7. lack of a clear and observed hierarchy of political authority (Lebanon, Chad, Uganda),
8. a high degree of state control over the media (Nicaragua, Soviet Union, China, Iran),
9. a proportionately small urban middle class (Zaire, Afghanistan, Bangladesh).

The converse of all of these conditions would indicate a strong state.[6]

Although power and sociopolitical cohesion do not correlate extensively, Richard Little has developed an illuminating way of looking at the weak–strong state spectrum in terms of the balance of power.[7] He proposes three types of state: *unified*, *fragmented* and *anarchic*. Unified states correspond quite closely to strong states. State power within them is held legitimately and on a monopoly basis — with the support, or at least without the opposition, of the governed. Little defines the relationship between legitimacy and monopoly of power as mutually supporting, but monopoly of power as the fundamental condition for a unified state. Fragmented states occupy the middle and weak ends of the spectrum. State power within them is held on a dominance rather than on a monopoly basis. Various domestic power groupings compete for control of the state, and it is success in manipulating the balance of power among them that brings control. Legitimacy in such states is also fragmented, though this fragmentation may be moderated by the existence of some overarching idea of the state which exists in parallel with sectional loyalties. Pakistan is an example, with Islam providing an overarching legitimacy, but ethnic divisions among Punjabis, Pathans,

Baluchis, Sindis, and before 1971, Bengalis, providing the basis for fragmentation. Anarchic states correspond directly to very weak states. State power within them is openly contested by the use of force, and although the state may still exist in some formal and legal sense, power within it is so fragmented, and legitimacy so weak, that it is impossible for any group to obtain the degree of dominance necessary for central governing control. Such states exist in a condition of civil war which mirrors all the worst and none of the best features of anarchic structure at the international system level.

The utility of Little's formulation of the problem of weak and strong states, is that it enables us to apply the familiar concept of a balance of power to our two basic questions about the applicability of national security as a concept for Third World countries. The balance of power is usually applied only to relations among states. In that guise, it encourages the habit of thinking of states as unitary objects, essentially alike except for their differences in power. By extending the idea to domestic politics, Little enables us not only to characterise the political nature of states, but also, as we will see in the next section, to link that nature to the state's relationship with its security environment.

Given the broad sociopolitical character of national security as a concept, the variable of sociopolitical cohesion gives us important insights as to how the concept applies to different types of state. There is no doubt that the concept is easiest to apply to the strong states for which it was originally coined. Strong/unified states provide a relatively clear referent object for national security. They have a single source of authority which commands a broad legitimacy amongst the population. Because state and society are closely linked together, indigenous domestic issues play a relatively minor role in national security concerns. Even a strong state must guard against subversive penetration of its political and military fabric by foreign agents and interests, but for strong states the concept of national security is primarily about protecting its independence, political identity and way of life from threats posed by other states, rather than from threats arising within its own fabric.

Within the externally orientated conception of national security appropriate to strong states there is still vast room for argument and contradiction about the ends and means of national security.[8] Should protection of the government and ideology have priority over protection of the population? Are nuclear threats a reasonable way to pursue military security when they might lead to national suicide? How, indeed, does one pursue national security in an age when states are increasingly interdependent in economic and environmental terms, and when the power of military technology makes them utterly dependent on the restraint of others for their survival? Can national security be pursued by individual state action or does it require co-operation? A good argument can even be made that strong states cultivate external threats as a means of maintaining their high levels of internal cohesion.[9] Not for nothing did Arnold Wolfers label national security an ambiguous symbol.[10] But despite the ambiguity of the concept in its specific applications, when the referent object is a strong state, it is at least clear that national security is primarily about defining and dealing with external threats to a sociopolitical entity that is in itself more or less free-standing and stable.

But as we move down the spectrum towards weaker states, the referent object for national security becomes harder to define, and the primarily external orientation of the concept gives way to an increasingly domestic agenda of threats. When governments rule more by power than by consensus, and when their authority is seriously contested internally by forceful means, then much of the sociopolitical meaning begins to drain out of the concept of national security. When political power and ideology within the state do not command broad legitimacy, or are contested by force, there is no clear content to such central elements of national security as political style, ideology and institutions. Even the notion of self-government can be questioned in cases where a minority dominates the majority by force: as an American diplomat allegedly described the Franco dictatorship in Spain, it was 'government without the people, above the people and against the people'. The political conditions of weak states often propel the military into government as the only organization possessing the power and/or the national legitimacy to hold the state together. Strong governments (in the sense of being dictatorial and repressive), especially military ones, usually indicate a weak state. Especially in Latin America, such governments have articulated a whole philosophy of national security specifically orientated towards the domestic conditions of weak states.[11]

In the extreme case of anarchic states, the concept of security can only be applied in its political sense to the interests of the various factions struggling for control of the state. Some basic referents for national security will remain no matter how weak the state becomes. These include territorial integrity, sovereignty, and the lives and culture of the people. But in the absence of political cohesion, even these objective referents will be viewed subjectively by contending factions. Each faction will take a different view of which lives and what territories are important, and national values of any sort will be subordinated to the struggle for power. As we move towards the weak end of the spectrum, much of the core political content of national security therefore becomes effectively void.

In practical terms, this void leads to some extremely difficult questions about the boundaries of national security as a concept. By definition, governments in weak states will have serious concerns about domestic threats to their own authority. These threats can take many forms including military coups (Argentina, Chile, Bolivia, Brazil, Pakistan, Nigeria, Liberia), guerrilla movements (Peru, the Philippines, Nicaragua, Angola, Mozambique), secessionist movements (Ethiopia, Iraq, Sri Lanka, Spain), mass uprisings (Iran, South Africa), and political factionalism (South Yemen, Afghanistan). Domestic threats are to a considerable extent endemic to states with no clear machinery for political succession. But are such threats to be considered part of the national security problem? Are they really threats to the state or to the nation, or are they just threats to the narrower interest of the incumbent ruling group? Should they be seen merely as a form of the domestic political process — a chaotic and bloody substitute for more orderly means of succession — and therefore as an expression of the

sovereign right of self-rule rather than as a threat to that
right?

Firm answers to these questions lead to awkward dilemmas either way. If domestic threats are accepted as a
national security problem, then the government is provided
with a powerful tool to legitimize the use of force against its
political opposition. In practice, this is often what happens.
As well as posing obvious moral issues, the opening up of
national security to include domestic threats raises serious
logical criticisms about the distinction between the security
of the government and the security of the state or nation.
There is an important linkage between the two, as indicated
by the fact that strong states will often fight major wars to
protect their system of government. But in weak states this
linkage is very problematic because of the narrowness of the
government's political base in relation to state and nation as
a whole. Is it really correct to see opposition to unpopular
dictators like Somoza and Duvalier as part of the national
security problems of Nicaragua and Haiti as countries? In
cases such as these, use of the concept of state security
would avoid the ambiguities raised by the broader social
and political content of national security.

But if domestic threats are not accepted as part of the
national security problem, other equally serious difficulties
arise. The fate of the government cannot be wholly separated from the issue of national security even in a weak state.
The government is both an important symbol, and a major
manifestation of the state. The fate of particular governments may not be of much account to the state as a whole,
but the congenital weakness of government brings into
question the integrity, and even the existence of the state,
and therefore has to be regarded as a national security
issue. But how does one distinguish between the sectional
interests of any particular government's claim that its own
security is a national security issue, and the broader national
security problem raised by the overall fact of weak political
cohesion? The case of Lebanon since the mid-1970s illustrates this problem clearly. Is it any longer reasonable to
consider Lebanon a state?

Domestic political fragmentation also makes the state
exceptionally vulnerable to penetration by external political

interests. In weak states, the domestic threats to the government can almost never be wholly separated from the influence of outside powers, and, in this sense, the domestic security problems of weak states are often hopelessly entangled with their external relations. This line of argument, however, takes us into the subject matter of the next section.

The relevance of all this for the national security problem in Third World countries is, of course, that most of the states in that group are towards the weak state end of the spectrum. The weakness as states of so many Third World countries, especially in Africa and Asia, stems from the process of decolonization itself. That process created states in the Western image, but it did not create nations that fit within them. The nationalism that accompanied decolonization was not the positive unity of a coherent cultural group, but the negative one of common opposition to occupying foreigners. The bond of xenophobia disintegrated as soon as the euphoria of independence died down, leaving arbitrarily defined populations occupying post-colonial states possessing no firm political foundations of their own other than the fact of their existence. The political legacy of most Third World governments was a state without a nation, or even worse, a state with many nations. It is this legacy that defines the problem of weak states in the Third World.[12] Because they are still in the early stages of the attempt to consolidate themselves as nation-states, domestic violence is endemic in such states. Under these circumstances, violence is as likely to be a sign of the accumulation of central state power as it is to be a symptom of political decay.[13]

By the arguments made above, it seems clear that applying the concept of national security to Third World states will at the very least involve making major allowances for the higher significance of domestic factors in these states. Quite how the domestic element should be treated in terms of national security is not obvious, although towards the very weak end of the spectrum, there are grounds for wondering whether the concept is useful at all given the extreme ambiguity of the referent object for it.

And as we shall now see, the high salience of domestic political security in Third World states also has considerable significance for the way in which these states relate to their security environment.

## THE NATURE OF THE SECURITY ENVIRONMENT

Whether states are weak or strong as states affects the overall constitution of the international anarchy quite profoundly. At the international level, anarchy is a decentralized form of political structure. It is not like a Hobbesian anarchy of individuals in which there is no political order. The claim of states to be sovereign — i.e. their claim to the absolute right of self-government — is what defines the political order of the modern international system. If states are sovereign, then by definition the structure of their relations is anarchic. The international anarchy is one in which political organisation and authority are vested in the parts rather than in the whole. Its claim to be a system of order at all therefore rests on the political robustness and stability of the states that are its component parts. Their ability to fulfil that claim determines in good part whether the system is orderly or not.

At the international level, anarchy does not necessarily, or even normally, imply chaos. Although it is a decentralized political system, it is none the less strongly structured, and reflects high values like national self-determination, cultural and ideological distinctiveness, historical tradition, and the primacy of local over remote interests in government. One cost of this type of political structure is that states are not restrained by any higher power or authority in their behaviour towards each other. As a consequence, insecurity is a problem for all states, and war is an ever-present possibility. It is possible to imagine anarchic conditions in which the positive values of a decentralized structure are maximized, and the negative consequences of insecurity and war minimized.[14] It is a necessary, though not sufficient, condition of any such benign image of anarchy that the system be composed of strong/unified states. To the degree that states are internally fragmented, and therefore weak as states, they contribute more to the instability and insecurity of the international system than to its order. Because they lack cohesion themselves, weak states are poorly placed to make any contribution to the order of the system as a whole. As in the case of the break-up of Pakistan in 1971, they invite, and often require, the intervention of other states, so feeding international rivalries. Anarchic states contribute no order at all: indeed, like Lebanon, they are open sores in the international system. They confront the structure of anarchy at the international level, with the chaos of anarchy at the level of individuals and groups. In terms of the international environment as a whole, we can therefore argue that strong states are a necessary, though not sufficient, condition for international security, and weak states a recipe for international insecurity.

There is some danger, as discussed in the previous section, that thinking in terms of national security generates an assumption that all states are similar in security terms except for their differences in power. But in the real world, the distribution of states in terms of political cohesiveness is all too obviously not homogeneous, and this, too, has major security consequences. In the international system as we find it, strong, unified states do not add up to more than a substantial minority of the system's members, anarchic states are usually a tiny, but persistent, minority, and a range of variously weak and fragmented states make up the majority. This mixture of types means that the character of the international security environment is quite different from that assumed in a homogeneous model of strong states, where the national security problem is primarily in terms of the classical balance of power with states perceiving mainly external threats from each other.

In a mixed system, international relations take place not only between states of the same level of political cohesion, but also between states with different levels. Strong/unified states can relate to each other as coherent political entities on a fairly detached and continuous basis. Changes in government within them do not generally cause major realignments in foreign relations, and contact is conducted primarily through a clearly defined and stable hierarchy of authority on both sides. This is not to argue that foreign relations between strong/unified states are completely separate from domestic issues. All interaction between states is to some extent a form of indirect intervention in domestic political affairs. The Soviet Union, for example, cannot help but influence American elections through the degree of hostility or détente it maintains in its relations with the United States. Strong states will also meddle directly in each other's internal affairs to some extent by supporting local factions or causes favourable to their interests. But because strong states are politically cohesive, such intervention cannot easily dominate the indigenous pattern of domestic political life. The primacy of domestic political patterns is indicated by the normally low salience of foreign affairs as a determinant of voting behaviour in the major Western democracies.

At the other extreme, a unified state cannot by definition engage in relations with an anarchic state without intervening directly in its domestic politics. Almost any contact with an anarchic state involves taking sides in its internal power rivalry, as even a brief examination of the history of Lebanon since 1976 will illustrate.[15] The same is true, although in a less dramatic form, of relations with weak or fragmented states. Contact with such a state almost automatically involves taking sides in its internal rivalries, because the state machinery itself is an expression of those rivalries. In Angola, for example, governing power in the country is about equally divided between the MPLA government in Luanda, and the UNITA movement in the bush. Even a disinterested and fair-minded foreign state seeking relations with Angola as a country cannot easily get round this fact. It cannot recognize one side without doing damage to the cause of the other, and therefore perhaps to its own interests in the longer run. Less detached foreign countries will, of course, be happy to take sides for a variety of ideological and power-political reasons. To the extent that a state lacks a clear and stable hierarchy of political authority, other states seeking relations with it therefore have to deal with its internal factions and organizations as semi-autonomous bodies. They cannot avoid direct, and sometimes strong, intervention in its internal political life.

As Little argues, the logic of relations between weak and strong states, and also between weak states, therefore leads directly to the intermingling of the international balance of power and the domestic balance of power within weak states.[16] Any state which befriends the government of a weak state almost automatically strengthens whatever faction is in control in relation to its domestic rivals. Similarly, any state that is hostile to the government of a weak state will have every incentive to weaken the faction in power by supporting its domestic rivals. When the internal balance of power within a weak state is precarious, then outside support may well be a crucial factor in domestic outcomes. Both the frequent changes of government, and the extent of the measures taken to suppress political opposition in many Third World countries indicate that their internal balance often is precarious.

For this reason, when some or all of the actors in a system are weak states, the domestic political aspects of national security become more important both to the weak states themselves, and in terms of the security relations between states in the system as a whole. In a hypothetical system entirely composed of strong/unified states, Little describes inter-state relations as fitting the classical balance-of-power model. Where relations are between strong and weak states, he describes the balance of power as 'asymmetrical'. Strong states hold substantial political advantages in such relations for they always have the possibility of shifting allegiance within the domestic balance of power of the weak state, whereas the reverse is not true. Where relations are between weak states, Little calls the balance of power 'transnational', indicating the virtual disappearance of the boundary between the domestic and international balances of power. In both asymmetrical and transnational balance of power relationships, the governments of the weak states must calculate their international relations in terms of their domestic rivalries. Examples of this behaviour can be seen in the mutual support arrangements between elitist Islamic governments in Saudi Arabia and Pakistan,[17] and in the conspicuous dependence of some Third World governments — Afghanistan, South Vietnam, Kampuchea, Chad — on outside backers. One consequence of such relationships is that the network of political alignments within and between states makes the political dimension of national security at least as important for weak states as the military one.

The variable of sociopolitical cohesion thus gives us an insight into the security environment of states as well as into the nature of national security in domestic terms. Since the character of the security environment cannot be separated from the nature of the states within it, the fact that most countries in the Third World are weak states means that their security environment will be distinct from that of the mostly strong states of the West. Amongst the strong states of the West, the security environment is dominated by traditional balance-of-power relations. But for Third World countries, the security environment is dominated by asymmetric and transnational balance-of-power relations.

The security environment of Third World states is also, as suggested in the previous section, shaped by the variable of power. In their relations with each other, Third World states are more distinctively affected by the cohesion variable than by power. Amongst the Third World states variations in power are as large as those amongst and between the states of East and West. Power differences between India and Sri Lanka or Brazil and Uruguay, for example, are of the same order as those between the Soviet Union and Sweden or Britain and Ireland, so there is no reason for us to think that the local security environment of Third World states is distinctive on these grounds. Where power does make a difference to the Third World is in terms of its position in the global hierarchy as a whole. Nearly all of the Third World states rank low in the global power hierarchy, which means that while their relations with each other may be normal in power terms, their security environment as a whole is substantially shaped by their relative weakness as powers in relation to the states of the North. The overall security environment of the Third World is thus set by a combination of factors markedly different from those in the North: a local environment dominated by weak states, and a global one dominated by an outside group of strong powers.

This combination produces a national security problem for Third World countries that is both different from, and in many respects more difficult than, that faced by states in the West. Because most Third World states are weak both as states and as powers, they are more vulnerable to the impact of their environment than are states that are strong and/or powerful. And because their environment is composed of other weak states, and vulnerable to the larger resources of outside powers, it is much less stable than an environment composed of states both strong and powerful. The potential for a vicious and self-reinforcing circle between weak states and unstable security environments is all too obvious.

A local security environment composed of weak states contains within itself many sources of instability. A state within such an environment cannot count on the political continuity of its neighbours, and therefore cannot easily build up a durable and stable set of local political relations. Changes of leadership can produce drastic changes of ideology and outlook, as in the shifts from monarchy to military government in Libya, Ethiopia and Iraq, and from monarchy to theocracy in Iran. The behaviour of states like Libya, Syria and Iraq illustrates the potential for high rates of change among weak states in amity/enmity attitudes towards neighbours. Domestic conflicts can spill over borders, as in Ethiopia, Pakistan, Uganda, Afghanistan, South Africa and Israel. Insecure rulers can succumb to the traditional temptation to consolidate their domestic position at the expense of their neighbours by cultivating external frictions or conflicts. Such stimulation of foreign threats to strengthen national unity played a strong role in the development of the European states, seems vital to the Soviet Union, and is evident in the behaviour of Third World states like Syria, Iraq, Pakistan, Argentina, and even India. In good part because Third World states themselves are unstable, conflicts between them are rife, alliances are temporary and unreliable, and security communities like ASEAN are rare.

Because relations among Third World states are mostly in terms of Little's transnational balance of power, these

what abt
on foreign policy?

environmental instabilities can easily feed into domestic
ones. The impact of Iran's revolution on the domestic
politics of the Gulf Arab states is one example of such
linkage. Others are the role of the Palestinians in the Middle
East, and the effect of the ongoing tensions in South Africa
on the frontline states. This basic indigenous instability in
the security environment of Third World states is exacerbated both by the absence of strong restraints on the use of
force amongst them, and by the effects of their vulnerability
to the influence of the stronger and more powerful states of
the North.

Restraints on the use of force by Third World states
against each other are much weaker than those on the use of
force between states in the North, and arguably even
weaker than those on the use of force by the states of the
North against Third World countries. Third World states do
not share the fear of war that most states in the North feel
both because of their memories of two world wars, and
because of the surplus capacity for destruction that nuclear
weapons have placed in their hands. For many Third World
countries, World War II was not the self-mutilation of their
civilization, but the key to their decolonization. Wars
amongst Third World countries mostly do not involve
nuclear threats and are therefore not subject to the constraint of a deterrence logic based on fear of cataclysmic
consequences. Neither do most Third World states share the
strong preference for the status quo that shapes the political
outlook of the West. Most of them have strongly revisionist
outlooks on an international order that they did not make
and which does not give them much advantage. Many also
have territorial disputes and political rivalries with their
neighbours.

Except for the few dozen states like Sierra Leone, Bhutan,
Lesotho, Tuvalu and Belize that are too weak as powers to
mount externally significant armed forces, the military
remains a useful and usable instrument of state policy for
most Third World governments. In practice, neither the
United Nations nor regional organizations like the OAU,
OAS and Arab League provide much restraint on the resort
to war. Although many Third World states use their armed

forces primarily for domestic security, there are plenty of
political and territorial disputes amongst them adequate to
justify the resort to war. Haphazard colonial boundaries
have left a rich legacy of conflict for Third World countries,
and the frequently weak political legitimacy of opponents
makes it easy to justify the use of force against them. For all
these reasons, many Third World states live in an environment in which the prospect of war is a much more
immediate part of the security problem than it is for states in
the more militarily paralyzed security environment of the
North.

The Third World's relationship with the countries of the
North does little to restrain this propensity for the use of
force, although occasional efforts at mediation like those of
the United States in the Middle East and the Soviet Union in
South Asia, and the superpowers' joint campaign against
the horizontal proliferation of nuclear weapons, should not
be entirely dismissed. But contact with the North often
exacerbates the security environment of Third World
countries by perpetuating the internal political weakness of
Third World states, and by reinforcing antagonisms
amongst them in both political and military terms. For Third
World states, contact with the North almost inevitably
involves engagement in the global power rivalry between
East and West. This rivalry means that the vastly superior
power resources of the North play competitively in the
weak political environment of the Third World. It also
means that the weak political structures of Third World
states are subjected to those power resources in terms of the
ideological rivalry between East and West.

This combination of political competition and disproportionate resources from the North can greatly complicate
the domestic security problems of Third World states.
Because resources are disproportionate, strong powers can
make big interventions into the domestic politics of weak
states/powers at very little relative cost to themselves.
Great powers like the United States and the Soviet Union
can easily make resources available on a scale that overawes
the locally available political resources in countries like El
Salvador, Afghanistan or Liberia which are weak both as

states and powers. The possibilities are illustrated by the rather exceptional case of American aid to Israel, which amounts to several hundred dollars per head of population annually. In colonial days, these disproportionate resources used to enable large powers to control the political life of a small weak state directly, but political consciousness in the Third World has long since grown past the point at which such control is easy, and in most places it is probably not possible at all.

The most common effect of disproportionate resources under current conditions is that the internal political fragmentation of weak states is reinforced and perpetuated by the competitive provision of outside resources to competing domestic factions. The workings of Little's asymmetrical balance of power not only increase the intensity of domestic rivalry, but also impede progress towards a more unified, stronger state structure by preventing the natural (in the sense of based on local resources) victory of any one unifying faction in the country. Where asymmetrical balance-of-power relations exist, external alignments can easily become the decisive factor in the domestic balance of power within the weak state. The consequence of such relations is that external political factors get injected into its domestic political life when other factions call in competitive outside support to redress the internal balance. Afghanistan, Nicaragua, Kampuchea, Ethiopia and Angola are obvious recent examples where competitive intervention has worked to sustain domestic political conflicts.

Almost the only factor that Third World states can use to counter the larger resources of the North is mass mobilization. Various forms of mass mobilization played a decisive role in decolonization, but the level of mobilization necessary to offset foreign influence is much higher than that necessary to end direct foreign control. A few states like Libya, Iran, Cuba and Vietnam have achieved substantial levels of mass mobilization, but in general there is an obvious dilemma about how to achieve mass mobilization in a weak state. Revolution is the usual tool, but an extremely hazardous one.[18] If revolution fails, the attempt simply worsens domestic fragmentation, invites more foreign intervention, and threatens to push the state from weakness to anarchy. If it succeeds, it can lead to intensification of pressure from the North, as in the case of Cuba, or to intensification of conflicts with neighbours, as in the case of Iran. Once the domestic political life of a weak state becomes entangled in the rivalries of the great powers, the pattern of perpetual fragmentation becomes difficult to break unless a major outside backer decides to withdraw from the game, as the United States did in South Vietnam.

A similar sort of fragmentation-perpetuating mechanism works in terms of the impact of the North on local regional relations between Third World states. Governments in Third World states will often trade a degree of support for one side or the other in the cold war in return for political support and arms in both domestic and local conflicts. Politically, the effect is one of adding a complicating overlay of global patterns of rivalry onto the local pattern. Thus in South Asia, India is supported by the Soviet Union, and Pakistan by the United States and China; in the Middle East, Syria and Libya are supported by the Soviet Union and Egypt and Israel by the United States; and in South-East Asia, Vietnam is supported by the Soviet Union, and ASEAN by the United States. This political overlay is often not especially significant in itself. It can be important when there are strong ideological links between the Third World country and its Northern backer, as in the cases of Cuba and Vietnam, but otherwise, as in South Asia, political links between Northern sponsors and their Third World clients are often quite minimal, and do not impinge directly on local conflicts.

The main significance of such alignments is that they provide the principal means of entry for the great powers into the regional politics of the Third World. Disputes between Third World countries make it easy for the superpowers to pursue their own rivalry, and Third World countries actively participate in this process by seeking out external support to bolster their local position. Pakistan, India, Syria, Iran before 1979, Egypt, and Morocco are all clear illustrations. By adopting this tactic, Third World countries connive at the interference in their affairs by the

North which so many of them loudly decry.[19] They also
demonstrate the destabilizing effect that weak states have
on the international anarchy when whole regions are
dominated by them. Such regions are not only inherently
conflict-prone in themselves, but also draw in and amplify
the rivalries among the great powers.

The major impact of intervention from the North is in
terms of arms supply, where the technological and material
resources of the North make a big difference to security
relations amongst Third World states. Only a few Third
World countries like Brazil, Argentina and India have much
capability to produce major modern weapons systems, and
even those three are dependent on Northern suppliers for
the more sophisticated parts and materials. Quite a few
Third World states can manufacture general infantry equipment independently, but the Third World as a whole
depends heavily on the North for its supplies of advanced
weapons.[20] This fact of dependence on outside sources of
arms supply marks one of the most significant differences
between the security environment of states in the North and
those in the Third World.

By using arms supply competitively as a source of
influence, the North collectively exerts tremendous pressure
on Third World countries. Apart from the general economic
and security pressure of having to keep up with the fast-
moving standard of military technology generated by the
Northern states, Third World countries are exceedingly
vulnerable to changes in their local security environment
resulting from the arms trade. The supply of modern
weapons to one side of a local Third World rivalry obliges
the other side to seek offsetting supplies if it is not to be
seriously disadvantaged. The classical action-reaction pattern of arms racing that results is, however, quite different
from that in a race between states that produce most of their
weapons themselves.[21] In a race between producers (a
primary arms race), the pace of competition is measured by
the relatively slow-moving and predictable factors of production capacity. But in a race between non-producers who
get their weapons by buying them or receiving them from
producers (a secondary arms race), very little limits the pace

of accumulation except the credit rating and absorption rate of the receiver. Suppliers may subsidize costs, so that the natural economic limits of the recipients no longer govern the size of their arsenals. When arms levels in the Third World are low, the supply of even relatively small numbers of sophisticated weapons can cause large and abrupt changes in the local balance of power. Secondary arms races detach both the rate of supply of arms, and the level of their sophistication, from the actual production capacities of the states in the race. As a consequence, secondary races are much less stable and predictable than primary ones, and contribute significantly to the general instability of life in the security environment of the Third World.

Both the Middle East and South Asia illustrate this process. India and Pakistan have been locked into a long secondary arms race that started when the United States supplied modern arms to Pakistan in the early 1950s as part of American containment policy against the Soviet Union. Pakistan has always directed these arms against India, twice in substantial wars, and has been able to use the generosity of its American and Chinese suppliers to sustain a rivalry with India that it might otherwise well have lost.[22] Although the Indian rivalry with China complicates the picture of this particular race, for Pakistan, politically motivated external arms supply has been a way of enabling it to sustain a rivalry with its much larger neighbour. In the absence of such supply, it seems inconceivable that the naturally greater capability and resources of India would not by now have left it much more dominant on the subcontinent than it actually is. American aid to Israel has likewise enabled it to maintain itself against large odds.

In both cases, external arms supply raised costs and enabled wars to be fought on a much larger scale than local resources alone would have permitted. But more importantly it paralleled the effect of external intervention on fragmented domestic politics by perpetuating local conflicts. Politically motivated external arms supply props up the weaker side and ensures that no local state achieves a dominant position simply by being able to marshall superior local resources. Since the superpowers are guided more by their own rivalry than by concern for local outcomes, and since their access to local influence usually depends on their taking sides in local conflicts, the natural outcome of their intervention in the Third World is to perpetuate local rivalries. If a local victory would mean the triumph of a superpower client, then the dynamics of the superpower rivalry will tend to ensure compensating movements of resources to local opponents.

## CONCLUSIONS

The concept of national security is much more problematic in relation to Third World countries than it is for the countries of the West. Although there are some fundamental similarities among all states which suggest that the concept should be universally applicable, there are also some big differences among them that profoundly affect the significance of a concept like national security. These differences are very marked as between the countries of the West and those in the Third World. Because the countries of the Third World are mostly weak states, it is much harder to identify the referent objects for the concept of national security than is the case for the strong states of the West. Furthermore, the security environment of the Third World is altogether less stable and more prone to the active use of force than is that of the West.

These differences raise the question of whether it is appropriate to apply a concept like national security to Third World states even if the difficulties of doing so can be overcome. The idea of national security is profoundly conservative. It reflects not only a status quo outlook on the international system, but also the aspirations of societies that are relatively stable in themselves. It also reflects the circumstances of states whose security environment gives them reason to think that they might achieve a considerable measure of international stability. Such states in such circumstances can reasonably aspire to a broad and ambitious objective like national security. But is such a concept appropriate for states whose immediate prospect for a stable security environment is low, whose outlook on the international system is defined by a desire for change, and whose domestic ambitions are for the wholesale transformation of development? Under such conditions, national security may define a long-term aspiration, but it is not achievable in the short term, and does not anyway capture the revisionist aspirations that govern policy in many Third World states.

In terms of measures designed to improve long-term national security conditions in the Third World, the analysis in this chapter points to two conclusions. The first is that such measures must concentrate on creating stronger states in the Third World. The existence of stronger states will not by itself guarantee security, but their continued absence will certainly sustain insecurity. Both national security in the Third World, and international security for the system as a whole, will remain problematic so long as the structure of anarchy is flawed by the presence of so many weak states. Although weak states in the Third World may serve some short-term economic, political and military interests of the great powers in the North, those gains have to be weighed against the risk that conflict in the Third World poses to the security of the North. Continued instability in the Third World is not only a matter of conscience for the North, but also a threat to its own peace. So long as the weak political environment of the Third World is a forum for superpower rivalry, the security of the North will be endangered by the risk of entanglement in, and escalation from, conflicts in the Third World. That risk is most clearly illustrated in Third World areas adjacent to the superpowers, particularly the Middle East and the Caribbean, but it is not confined to them.

For the Third World states themselves, the idea of national security borders on nonsense unless strong states can be created. Weak states simply define the conditions of insecurity for most of their citizens. In the regional context they make the formation of security communities extremely difficult, and virtually guarantee the existence of an unstable security environment. Building stronger states is virtually the only way in which the vicious circle of unstable states and an unstable security environment can be broken.

The second conclusion is that more attention needs to be given to regional patterns of security relations in the Third World. There can be no doubt that distinct and durable patterns of military and political security relations do occur in the Third World. I have elsewhere discussed these in detail under the label 'security complexes',[23] and clear examples can be found in South Asia, the Middle East and Southeast Asia. It is notable that the states within these three regions define their security problems primarily in terms of other states with which they share the same complex. Wars and alliances within one local complex have little impact on relations outside the complex, as witness the numerous self-contained conflicts in the Gulf, South Asia, and South-East Asia. These complexes are separated by boundaries of relative indifference, where local security perceptions stand, as it were, back to back.

Security complexes in the Third World are important because they define the patterns of hostility that so often provide the entry for penetration of Third World politics by the great powers of the North. They also define meaningful units, or sub-systems, that are relatively self-contained in security terms. These sub-systems must be the basis for action in any effective moves towards the development of security communities in the Third World. Too often, the states of the North define security issues in the Third World in terms of their own security priorities. This easily leads either to underestimation of the local security dynamics, as in American interpretations of the Middle East that stress the role of the Soviet Union in shaping events there, or to ignoring of the local patterns of regional security, as in American attempts to define a South-West Asian region in relation to their rivalry with the Soviet Union in Afghanistan and the Gulf.

The idea of South-West Asia illustrates the pitfalls of taking too little account of security realities in the Third World. The idea has been around ever since the United States first tried to tie Pakistan into the defence of the Middle East during the early 1950s. By tying Pakistan to the Gulf it ignores the reality of quite distinct local security complexes in the Gulf and South Asia, and turns a boundary of indifference into the centre of a regional problem. Conceptually unsound thinking along these lines underlay the American supply of arms to Pakistan that had such disastrous effects on the real focus of Pakistan's security interests in South Asia. Moves made against the grain of local security relations serve the interests neither of the local states nor of the intervening power. American insensitivity to the local security complex in South Asia contributed materially to the obsessive insecurity of India and Pakistan in relation to each other, and opened the way for Soviet influence in the dominant power of the region. If the concept of national security is to be applied to the Third World, then it will need to be accompanied by other concepts like security complexes that define Third World security issues in terms rooted in local realities, and distinct from the preoccupation of the superpowers with their own rivalry.

## NOTES

[1] This chapter is based on Chapters 2 and 4 of Barry Buzan, *People, States and Fear: The National Security Problem in International Relations* (Brighton: Wheatsheaf, and Chapel Hill: University of North Carolina Press, 1983).

[2] Kenneth N. Waltz, *Theory of International Politics* (Reading, MA: Addison-Wesley, 1979), pp. 93–7.

[3] Ibid., pp. 127–8.

[4] Report of the Secretary-General, *Study on Concepts of Security*, UNGA Document A/40/553 (26 August 1985), paras. 91–4.

[5] Buzan, *People, States, and Fear* pp. 65–8.

[6] Barry Buzan and Gerald Segal, 'Comparative Defence Policy', unpublished manuscript (1986), pp. 7–9.

[7] Richard Little, 'Political Realism and the Universal Balance of Power', paper presented to the BISA Theory Group, City University, October 1985, as draft chapter of *The Balance of Power: Metaphors, Models and Myths* (London: Allen & Unwin, 1987).

[8] Buzan, *People, States, and Fear*.

[9] John Burton, *Global Conflict: The Domestic Sources of International Crisis* (Brighton: Wheatsheaf, 1984).

[10] Arnold Wolfers, *Discord and Collaboration* (Baltimore, MD: Johns Hopkins University Press, 1962), ch. 10.

[11] Robert Calvo, 'The Church and the Doctrine of National Security', *Journal of Interamerican Studies and World Affairs*, vol. 21, no. 1 (1979), pp. 69–88.

[12] I am grateful to my colleague Gowher Rizvi for this point.

[13] Youssef Cohen, B.R. Brown, and A.F.K. Organski, 'The Paradoxical Nature of State-Making: The Violent Creation of Order', *American Political Science Review*, vol. 75, no. 4 (1981), pp. 901–10.

[14] Buzan, *People, States, and Fear*, pp. 94–100; *idem*, 'Peace, Power, and Security: Contending Concepts in the Study of International Relations', *Journal of Peace Research*, vol. 21, no. 2 (1984), pp. 109–25.

[15] *Strategic Survey* (London: IISS) annually since 1976.

[16] Little, 'Political Realism'.

[17] B. A. Roberson, 'South Asia and the Gulf Complex' in Barry Buzan, Gowher Rizvi *et al*, *South Asian Insecurity and the Great Powers* (London: Macmillan, 1986), ch. 6; and W. Howard Wriggins, 'South Asia and the Gulf: Linkages, Gains, and Limitations', *Middle East Review* (Winter 1985), pp. 25–35.

[18] Barry Buzan, 'Security Strategies for Dissociation' in John Ruggie (ed.), *The Antinomies of Interdependence: National Welfare and the International Division of Labour* (New York: Columbia University Press, 1983), pp. 417–19.

[19] Barry Buzan and Gowher Rizvi, 'The Future of the South Asian Security Complex' in Buzan and Rizvi, *South Asian Insecurity*, ch. 9.

[20] Andrew J. Pierre, *The Global Politics of Arms Sales* (Princeton, NJ: Princeton University Press, 1982), Part 3.

[21] Barry Buzan, *Strategic Concepts in the Nuclear Age: An Introduction* (London: Macmillan for the IISS, forthcoming 1987), Part 2, Conclusions.

[22] Buzan and Rizvi, 'The Future of the South Asian Security Complex'.

[23] Barry Buzan, 'A Framework for Regional Security Analysis' in Buzan and Rizvi, *South Asian Insecurity*, ch. 1; *idem, People, States, and Fear*, pp. 105–15.

# 3. Simple Labels and Complex Realities: National Security for the Third World

DAVIS B. BOBROW and STEVE CHAN

We begin this chapter with a simple question — what is the essence of national security for Third World countries and of its military aspects in particular? In thinking about it, we quickly came to the conclusion that the question as stated was inherently unanswerable since it assumed some obvious clarity about and homogeneity of what national security and Third World refer to. Those conditions are not met in our view. Accordingly, we report some modest efforts to clarify these concepts and to decompose their real-world referents. The distinctions we draw are then explored briefly with regard to military threats as targets and sources.

## A GENERALIZED CONCEPTION OF NATIONAL SECURITY

We clearly need a conception of national security that can accommodate alternative content in terms of the problems addressed and the means considered for dealing with them. We want a conception useful for comparative analysis which calls for the capacity to treat common features and categorize differences in some orderly fashion. One approach would be to take the essence of national security for one or more First World countries as a starting point. That is not an unusual choice for American analysts.[1] We reject that approach because of a number of major distortions that will result when it is applied to the Third World.

If one were to use the American conception of the last three decades as a framework, what would one in fact be doing? One would be treating national security as calling for levels of military and economic capability far beyond the Third World's financial, organizational, and technological capabilities. One would be focusing on threats that are overwhelmingly external and military in nature, and on policy instruments of a like kind. One would be defining sources of threat as primarily centred on Moscow. One would be analysing military strategic themes that emphasize deterrence, alliance cohesion and nuclear weapons. And one would be assuming military institutions as reliably subordinate to civilian authorities and primarily concerned with external threats.

As others have argued well,[2] proceeding along these lines would involve enormous errors of commission and omission. That is, it would lead to emphasizing what many Third World governments pay scant attention to and ignoring what many of them concentrate their national security endeavours on. Even less excusably, this particular form of ethnocentrism would make conformity to American practices the yardstick for treating Third World regimes as well informed and wise about national security.

Instead of taking that easy path, we suggest a less biased and partial framework — one that is compatible with multilateral diplomacy, complex interdependence, and sharp status discrepancies and shifts. We think that this framework readily accommodates differences in security content (military, economic, and sociopolitical), in security actors (the number and identity of key domestic and foreign actors), and in security processes (how actors and content interact). It seems to us to allow for security relations to involve different mixes of constant- and non-constant-sum games, where outcomes may be zero-sum, negative-sum, or positive-sum. Further, the relevant 'games' may be played in bilateral isolation or embedded in a much larger set of strategic interactions.

We conceive of national security for a political system as the joint product of three baskets of judgements by policy-makers. National security is then in the eyes of the operationally-involved beholder more than it is a matter for some 'objective' quintessential definition or academic consensus. We recognize that there is a significantly common general vocabulary for this concept (e.g., 'threats to vital interests'). Yet we also know that across policy systems, and even within them at different points in time, enormous differences exist in the salience accorded to particular problems and the means considered to deal with them. The three baskets of judgments are the immediate cause of those differences. The judgements deal respectively with the *significance* of some foreign act of commission or omission to the achievement of the perceiver's goals; the *probability* of that act; and the *leverage* that the perceiver has on those who can take or refrain from the pertinent act.

Cardinal national security matters are those topics — issues, developments, actors — perceived to involve great significance, high probability, and substantial leverage. Topics at the opposite extremes have at most a ritual, lip-service place on national security agendas. The joint product of the three sets of judgements is of central importance, and each can up to some point reinforce, offset or substitute for the others. For example, great significance and substantial leverage (controllability) can compensate for initial low probability and indeed can contribute to subsequent changes in perceived probability. National security fears are most intense when perceived significance and probability are high and leverage low. National security tranquillity is best established when the opposite is the case. National security effort on a sustained basis depends on the leverage that policy-makers and would-be policy-makers feel they have and can have. After all, to concentrate policy resources and attention on problems that one can do nothing about is hardly rewarding. And for all but the most affluent, it makes little sense to throw additional resources into the pursuit of excess leverage. We call attention to the possible and reasonable co-occurrence of acute national security vulnerabilities and very little national security effort. In any event, the issues that emerge centre on what countries can do and are doing to gain leverage on the probability and gravity of external acts of commission or omission.

The relevant foreign acts of commission or omission can involve a wide range of phenomena that can affect goals. For our purposes, the goals in question need not be typecast as 'national', 'class', 'regime', or even those of an influential individual. In practice, these blur together to the point where the lines are not clear even to the holder of the goals in question. The pertinent acts may involve supplying or withholding tangibles (e.g., money, personnel, weapons) or intangibles (e.g., status, prestige, moral support). They may involve direct significance for the perceiver or indirect significance via third parties (i.e. steps that alter the relevant behaviour by allies, adversaries, or neutrals that in turn affect the perceiver's goal pursuit). The pertinent perceptions of significance very much include second-order effects. The acts in question involve both the provision and withholding of 'goods' and 'bads'. Goods might include peace, access to export markets, foreign investment, weapons supply, alliance protection, prestige-conferring declarations, and even photo opportunities. Bads are illustrated by political interference, diplomatic isolation, trade sanctions and war. The pertinent acts are not restricted to the military domain but also include economic, ecological, and communally significant types of provision and withholding. What matters is that the act in question is taken or avoided by an external party and that it impacts on what the perceiver cares about. Policy elites usually care about domestic outcomes as well as foreign policy objectives. Therefore, foreign acts matter even when they only affect the former (e.g., internal control, regime maintenance, domestic stability).

This conception of national security may seem too encompassing. Our intent is to be encompassing in general while enabling in specific ways that are appropriate to the differences between cases. The narrowing down comes in two ways. The first is by the perceiver's choice of goals that are held to be central for the survival and well-being of the political and social system to which it is committed. If, for example, those goals include eliminating internal dissent, foreign acts that foster such dissent pertain to national security. Otherwise, they may not be. This aspect of narrowing addresses only national security relevance, but not national security priorities.

Priority-focusing can be dealt with in terms of a supply-and-demand metaphor we have suggested elsewhere.[3] Priority goes to those foreign acts seen to determine the existence of a grave shortfall of supply relative to demand. The conviction of a current or potential shortfall and thus of the significance accorded to particular foreign acts comes to reflect (1) varying distribution of domestic assets and liabilities across countries, (2) varying evaluation in different countries of what are the pillars of an acceptable political and social order, (3) asymmetries in national sensitivities and vulnerabilities to externally-provided bads, (4) cross-national asymmetries in the elasticity of demand for externally-provided goods, (5) differential substitutability of those goods, and (6) foreign providers that differ in identity, number and incentives.

Our thinking converges with that of W. Harriet Critchley in focusing on perceived *scarcity* and *dependence*.[4] With perceptions of massive current or impending scarcity, a high premium comes to be placed on those foreign acts that can alleviate that scarcity or block efforts to alleviate it. The point is to offset what are viewed as major comparative disadvantages or domestic shortages. Even when the shortfall is not currently massive, priority goes to sustaining foreign inputs should these be the reason for the lack of a pressing shortfall.

The likelihood of particular foreign behaviours (i.e. probability) is also a subjective estimate. Extremely potent acts tantamount to the extinction of the perceiver's political and social system may receive substantial attention even when the probability is thought to be low. Most acts with significance are filtered by relative likelihood because of the constraints of material and human resources (e.g., expertise, information, policy-makers' time). For most relevant acts, their place in the pecking order of policy attention is a function of the expected utility or disutility provided by the combination of significance and probability judgements. Nations and groups under especially severe human and material resource constraints can be expected to be under special pressure to prioritize — or at least to select a very small number of significant acts to focus on. Probability judgements contribute to doing so. As we know, those judgements are often profoundly affected by the most salient recent experience — in this case, highly positive or negative foreign acts.[5] Also, we know of a general tendency to be particularly sensitive to acts that seem to threaten deprivations of what the perceiver already has or thinks that it will soon come to have. *Ceteribus paribus*, these tendencies create a bias that exaggerates the probability of a repetition of the last substantially depriving foreign act of commission or omission, especially if that act impinged on what the perceiver now views as its primary success. One would therefore expect post-colonial national elites whose only success is formal political independence to pay exaggerated attention to foreign acts that would reintroduce external control. By the same token, one would expect a national elite whose formative experience was shaped by war and whose major achievement was military capability to exaggerate the probability of war and to be hypersensitive to foreign acts that seem to impinge on its military capability.

Policy elites, as we conceive of them, behave not just on the basis of the problems they perceive (i.e. significant acts and their likelihood), but also on the basis of perceived efficacy — that is, what they can do something about. The third or leverage basket of judgements deals with this last part of our conception. Leverage refers to the perceiving policy elite's ability to control, influence, or manipulate foreign acts that would impact in any of the ways mentioned above on goals. Gross limitations on leverage, a common Third World phenomenon, have several implications that merit consideration. First, they motivate a continuing, assiduous search for direct and indirect means of leverage well beyond conventional statecraft. Second, they induce sharp constriction of national security agendas to a few parties and problems, unless some leverage windfall occurs or the search is both unusually creative and fortunate. Third, they can create a situation in which the *de facto* agenda gives priority to what are not the gravest foreign acts or the most likely ones, but rather ones that seem possible to be influenced. Finally, severe limitations on leverage can well lead to eventual lassitude, fatalism, and a hollow facade of policy which is little but bluff. These points may be more persuasive by contrast. We would expect the superpowers, to take an extreme, to be relatively lazy and uncreative in their search for leverage means, to have open-ended national security agendas, to exercise less discrimination in allocating policy attention on the basis of supposed significance and probability, and to continue to believe that policy efforts will pay off in the face of prior set-backs.

Leverage is a highly non-uniform product of a country's endowments, world position, and policy capacity. It varies from issue to issue, place to place, and time to time. Saudi Arabia is in a better position to influence the supply of oil than that of wheat; it is better able to shape events in the Emirates than in Eastern Europe, and it finds its influence rising and falling with global developments in energy supply and demand. For most Third World countries, whatever leverage they have is sharply limited in content and geography, and is susceptible to serious changes due to events often outside their control.

Like significance, leverage can be direct or indirect. Linkage politics can enable a country to increase its control of a topic (issue, development, or actor) by promising or threatening to use its leverage in distributing goods or bads in another area. Relatedly, it is useful to recognize that in managing national security, the denial or balancing of an adversary's leverage is sometimes as relevant as the preservation of one's own influence or that of one's allies. Just as in the case of significance, leverage suffers by being thought of unilaterally in isolation. Instead, a comparative and multilateral perspective helps. The pursuit of indirect leverage is illustrated by efforts to build transnational interest groups, to persuade third parties that they should provide the needed leverage, and to pool resources with others via formal clubs (e.g., OPEC, ASEAN) or *de facto* joint action (e.g., the policy collaboration efforts of some 'pariah' states).

Leverage may also be sought by shaping others' images. In this regard, two rather opposite strategies adopted by some Third World countries merit mention. On the one hand, there is the face of almost devil-may-care risk-taking in the sense of making credible the willingness to engage in leverage actions that seem to involve extreme costs (e.g., Israel, Libya, Vietnam). On the other hand, there is the face of helpless weakness. Some countries may go to great pains to demonstrate their lack of leverage as a means to attain two intermediate ends. These are, first, to make it apparent that others who value them at all must provide them with positive inputs and shield them against negative ones and, second, to picture those who resort to negative actions against them as indeed extremists with no reasonable justification. Illustrations of attempts to pursue these lines of manipulation are familiar to even the cursory follower of Third World developments. On vulnerability, consider the gambit of dramatic presentations to the foreign media of domestic fragility by means of 'spontaneous, surprise' mass demonstrations that show the regime's need for foreign buttressing. On the extremism of enemies, consider the effort made to seize the symbolic high ground and attribute to the enemy acts that evoke general condemnation.

Finally, it is important to keep in mind the distinction between leverage in the form of bargaining power and that in the form of structural power.[6] The former refers to specific advantages in influencing the outcomes of a particular game or topic. The latter refers to general advantages in influencing the nature or the rules of the game to be played. Third World countries, individually or collectively, can have bargaining power in specific situations. They lack structural power. Bargaining power (e.g., OPEC's ability to manipulate energy prices during the 1970s) can be nullified by superior structural power (e.g., the United States' ability to change the rules of international trade, bring other suppliers on line, or 'call' a new game of military take-over of Middle

East oilfields). In the hierarchy of international power, Third World countries usually must play by the rules established by others, or risk severe sanctions.

The preceding discussion suggests several obvious strategies to improve national security. For the significance element, a country can try to increase its positive value in contributing to others' goal attainment (i.e. an enticement or bonus policy), or its negative value in blocking others' goal attainment (i.e. a denial or deterrent policy). It can try to decrease the significance of others' positive inputs to its goal attainment (i.e. a policy of seeking self-reliance and autarky), or that of others' negative inputs to its goal attainment (i.e. a policy of reducing vulnerability to external shocks). These policies are not mutually exclusive and in fact tend to overlap considerably, with the implication that they can be pursued concurrently. Also, their feasibility is influenced by a country's objective capabilities and assets, and by their global scarcity and distribution.

A country can also try to manipulate others' perception of the probability that it will carry out sanctions or rewards in such a way as to influence others' actions. It can, for example, try to increase the credibility of its deterrent threats in line with the image of a risk-taker mentioned earlier. Alternatively, it can try to foster its image as a reliable supplier (e.g., of oil or military protection) as a means to discourage the recipient from seeking autarky (e.g., energy independence, armament development) or alternative suppliers. Given their pressing material and human resource constraints, however, many Third World countries are apt to resort to their weakness and the probability of collapse or instability as a means to recruit the desired foreign acts.

As for leverage, it is inherently a function of *both* what a country has to offer to others and what others want for their own purposes. Both the supply and the demand conditions matter. As stated earlier, these conditions are affected by the global distribution of the goods (or bads) in question, their scarcity and substitutability, and the incentives and appetites of foreign recipients. The discrepancies between supply and demand produce differences in national sensitivities and vulnerabilities.[7] For the Third World, these asymmetries mean that they are usually 'price takers' rather than 'price givers' in economic as well as non-economic transactions. The resort to collective action, linkage politics, and image-shaping strategies mentioned earlier suggests some feasible efforts to improve their marginal leverage.

To summarize this section, we suggest that (1) national security agendas are the product of three sets of judgements about the significance of foreign inputs, their probability, and one's own leverage; (2) national security judgements are not restricted to foreign military threats; (3) national security judgements will often be made in the light of a many-actor setting rather than in purely dyadic terms; (4) national security judgements change as a result of altered domestic as well as foreign conditions; and (5) various policy instrumentation choices and management styles can be employed to pursue national security, including ones of great complexity even by countries with limited military hardware.

## IDENTIFYING THE THIRD WORLD

If 'Third World' has any clear connotation, it is that of a certain separateness from the two dense networks of international relations centered on Washington and Moscow. That is, it refers to countries that are relatively peripheral to these two core security communities.[8] Relative integration — cultural affinity, political empathy, common institutions, frequent governmental interactions, active exchange relationships and communicative ties, and collective arrangements for joint action — among members of these communities distinguishes them from the non-members (i.e. the Third World).

For our purposes, full membership in the Organization for Economic Cooperation and Development or in the Council for Mutual Economic Assistance provides a reasonable surrogate measure of this integration and, thus, for identifying countries that are not part of the Third World. Note that formal alliance ties (e.g. a security treaty with either of the superpowers), official ideology, and actual or potential national capability are not part of our criteria. We put Finland, Austria, and Switzerland outside the Third World, and Israel, South Korea, India, and China inside it. Our criteria emphasize the less tangible considerations of mutual responsiveness, shared concerns, and subjective identification with the First or the Second World.

It is obvious that Third World countries are a highly mixed lot. In the next section we shall try to distinguish among them in ways pertinent to national security differences, and the military aspects in particular. Before doing so, it seems important to point out relatively common general characteristics that bear heavily on our topic. By common we do not mean universal but rather features that contrast Third World countries as a class from the classes of the First and Second Worlds.

One commonality is that of endemic internal political instability. Ruling groups tend to lack a wide and deep base of support in the general population. There is little in the way of widely accepted rules for peaceful power transitions that are part of a continuing political order. The blurring of the distinction between regime security and national security means that more foreign acts are apt to be seen as threats to the office holders and not just the nation than is the case in the First and Second Worlds. Another commonality of Third World countries is limited state capacity — for resource extraction, for domestic mobilization, and for information search and bonding activities in international affairs. For example, it is not unheard of for central authorities charged with national security in the Third World to be unaware of what is happening at their national borders, let alone to move forces to their borders. Again in relative terms, Third World countries often have less in the way of usable national instruments of power than their aggregate profile would suggest. Yet another commonality is the lack of role specialization by coercive institutions and by the military in particular. In gross terms, Third World military establishments are less focused on external threats, less reliable instruments of state policy, and more prone to internal fragmentation.

The implications of these common tendencies can be brought out in the terms of scarcity and dependence suggested earlier. Compared to the First and Second Worlds, the countries of the Third place a premium on foreigners acting in ways that strengthen incumbents and refraining from acts that weaken them. They are extraordinarily dependent on foreign inputs to provide surrogate state capacity, whether it be intelligence, communications, weapons, capital, transportation, or food stocks. And these foreign inputs often have to be secured on a non-market basis. Since whatever image of capacity they have may well be inflated, they are highly dependent on foreigners acting in ways that do not put it to an acid test on any sustained basis. Finally, they are dependent on foreign behaviour to shape a less domestically interventionist ethos on the part of their military, to bribe or pressure it into subservience or at least restraint, and to help it to stay somewhat unified. These are the side of the coin that implies weak leverage. They often have another face.

The variety of limitations and fragilities does provide foreigners with some incentives to ignore them. Being incapable often of significant action, they offer few carrots or sticks. That does little to cope with the internal aspects of national security though it may help with some of the external ones. The problem is getting everyone to ignore them at the same time. Everyone obviously includes both superpowers. It also includes, to an extent that is rare in the First and Second Worlds, other countries in their region. The importance of regional threats *per se* as distinct from an opposing superpower-centred alliance tends to distinguish Third from First and Second World countries. The potentially grave foreign acts are those of neighbours, and not just of the Soviet and American giants and their proxies. Whether regional threats carry a particularly heavy need for foreign support (i.e. dependence) varies among Third World countries. The centrality of regional relations in their national security agendas does not.

Suppose that there is an active need for security-conducive foreign actions. The extent to which they will be forthcoming depends on foreigners' perceptions of the worth of the Third World country to them. The Third World country usually has little intrinsic value except that provided by its place in more general concerns. These may include resource provisions that are hard to replace, historical associations with national grandeur or, for the superpowers in particular, the perceived utility to the other superpower. The first ground is surely unstable and open to radical change through economic and technological adaptation (e.g. OPEC's recent experience). The second ground is not available to all Third World countries, but is rather limited to those who are viewed to be at the heart of a still cherished sphere of influence and therefore those who strike a respondent chord in the desire for international assertion. Examples include Francophone Africa for France, the Falklands for the UK, and Central and South America for the USA. As for the third basis, the interest of one superpower hinges less on the behaviour of the Third World country and more on judgements about the importance that the other superpower attaches to it. Thus, even a country of China's size and assets finds itself being portrayed by the USA as a card to be used for disciplining the Soviets. All three bases for supportive foreign action rest on factors that the Third World country can only encourage in some marginal way — but not instill or unilaterally perpetuate. Nevertheless, when they are operating powerfully, the widespread Third World 'scarcities' or weaknesses can provide leverage. They make it credible that without supportive foreign actions, including ones to prevent or compensate for negative foreign inputs, the Third World country will 'fall' or be 'lost' or even disappear. This remedy for inherently limited leverage has its own risks. Dependents are only supported out of self-interest or because they behave as gratefully as they are expected to. Should either condition no longer be met, all reasons for supportive foreign actions soon evaporate.

In other words, the security problems and thus the leverage needs of Third World countries are more acute than those of First and Second World countries, because they do not have the benefit of the doubt with regard to the justification for foreign support. Taiwan and South Korea differ from Norway and Belgium not so much in their size, military vulnerability, level of external threat, or even in their regimes' persuasive ability. Rather, being securely integrated in a superpower's core domain, the latter countries can be assured of a greater coincidence of their military security interests and those of the USA. This does not deny that occasional differences, even sharp ones, may arise among these allies. We merely argue that Washington, being motivated by its own military security interests, is more apt to supply those facilitative inputs that enhance Norwegian and Belgian defence capabilities. That is, these inputs tend to take on the aura of collective goods. In contrast, Third World countries generally have more diffi-culty in recruiting such foreign support, because they hold only marginal or derivative interests to those in the First and Second Worlds.

This support often can only be obtained by accentuating or exaggerating the linkage between the supplicant's fate and the policies or status of the rival superpower (e.g. Soviet aggression, Communist Victories setting off a domino chain). The more successful Third World countries in this regard (e.g. Israel, South Korea) have been able to carve out for themselves a special niche in the strategic conceptions, political doctrines, and domestic opinions of their chief ally. But even then, the sponsor's defence contributions entail a heavier cost in national autonomy, and are more apt to be suspended or disrupted in the Third World context than in the First World or Second World contexts. Consequently, those Third World countries that are faced with severe regional military challenges and unfavourable balance of forces have constantly to guard against the possibility of somehow being left in the cold and required to fend for themselves. They can less afford to take foreign support for granted.

In short, the military capabilities of Third World countries are such that they cannot hope to counter the threat from a determined superpower no matter what they do in domestic armament. The best they can do in deterring and balancing this threat is by recruiting help from the other superpower. In these respects, they are no different from the other countries in the First and Second Worlds. What tends to distinguish them is that they are generally in a poorer position to recruit this aid, given their tangential status in the superpowers' strategic calculations, domestic political agendas, and elite and public opinions. Most of them would add or subtract little materially to or from the strategic assets of either side in the East–West competition, and many would have attracted even less attention were it not for their symbolic value in the core countries' domestic politics and a flourishing desire to deny them to the opposing side. Moreover, their military security agenda may be significantly different from that of their core sponsors. The sources of their threat perception, whether from regional rivals or domestic adversaries, may not correspond with their foreign allies' targets of concern. Given their general lack of centrality in their foreign allies' political culture and military plans, support for them is also more apt to generate domestic disagreement within the aid-giving countries. Consequently, they face these additional difficulties in obtaining and retaining foreign contributions to their military security goals.

The almost universal national security dilemma of the Third World is to balance several paradoxes. Failure to strike the difficult balances implies losing the leverage needed to get foreigners to act in ways that have positive impact and refrain from those with negative impact. One paradox is that of weakness (i.e. need for help) but not hopelessness (i.e. there cannot be enough help). Another is that of demonstrating a capacity to acquire and wield leverage without appearing to have an independent agenda counter to that of the foreign provider. Failure on the first paradox leads to others 'washing their hands of the whole mess' as in Lebanon. Failure on the second paradox leads to 'graduation'. The achievements that often trigger a verdict of graduation are usually not enough to eliminate more fundamental discrepancies between the impact of foreign acts and the leverage of the graduated actor. Graduation unaccompanied by incorporation into a core security community may be a mixed national security blessing. A third paradox relates to the shaping of foreign images about one's vulnerability and the need for support. Its solution calls again for a delicate balancing of enticing the desired foreign buttressing without being taken for granted or treated as a pawn in superpower rivalries. Policy steering therefore requires avoiding the Scylla of being neglected by others and the Charybdis of attracting too much foreign attention to the point of suffocating national independence.

## DISAGGREGATING THE THIRD WORLD

Valid categories are an obvious prerequisite for sound generalisation and meaningful measurement.[9] Analysis of quantitative differences in degree should come after recognition of qualitative differences in kind. From this perspective, we are dissatisfied with the undifferentiated notion of the 'Third World'. It seems to us to have lost much of whatever analytic usefulness it once had. It now ignores the polycentric nature of much of international affairs and blurs major distinctions between the rapidly growing newly industrializing countries, the resource-rich raw-materials exporters, and the developmental laggards (the so-called Fourth World) that continue to suffer relative and even absolute economic and in many cases political decline. We suspect that the differences in the national security problems and agendas of the long list of countries assigned Third World status are in many respects at least as great as those between most of them and most of the First and Second World members.

If therefore seems useful to make a very preliminary effort to subdivide our universe of Third World countries in ways that can further clarify their national security problems and policies. We want some sorting variables that seem to matter for what governments do in foreign affairs and that seem central to perceptions in many cultures of national security capabilities.

Survey data indicate that there is a striking congruence ($r > 0.9$) in mass publics' assessments of those factors that contribute to national power. The most important attributes seem to be per-capita wealth and population size. Military factors — such as the size of armed forces and the level of defence expenditures — also figure heavily in mass perceptions of national power in the USA, Finland, Japan, and Canada.[10] Two of the factors just mentioned are included in James Rosenau's well-known attempt to develop a country typology. He suggested that physical size, economic development, and political accountability are the key variables that affect governments' conduct of foreign policy.[11] Subsequent empirical assessments found that these variables were able to explain better a variety of foreign policy behaviours than did other variables that had often been suggested.[12]

As a crude start to developing subcategories of Third World countries, we examine their distribution on three aspects of national power — size as measured by population, economic development as measured by per-capita GNP, and military capability as measured by defence spending. These measures all have their problems, and obviously many other measures merit consideration and use. Nevertheless, each seems to tap an important dimension relative to national power in general and military power in particular. None of them is of course automatic in its national security implications. Large population size may be a burden more than an asset. Great wealth may be a temptation for exploitative behaviour by foreigners more than anything else. Spending on the military account may be for chrome and flash rather than for muscle, and it can drain resources away from other foundations of national strength. These negative aspects are not in our view reasons to reject these measures. Instead, they make the relations among these measures in a variety of combinations of special interest. Large population size combined with high per-capita GNP has a different power implication than large population size combined with low per-capita GNP, and so forth. The importance of the three dimensions of the profile is then one of power holdings as well as one of the variety of pressures associated with status congruence or the lack thereof in the international system.

The global distribution of countries on our three-power measures is extremely skewed. The top ten countries (about

3 measures for "Third Worldness" of a State

6 percent of all countries in the world) have about 64 percent of the globe's population, 71 percent of its aggregate economic output, and 80 percent of its arms expenditures.[13] No country that we have defined as being in the Third World stands above the global means for all three of these variables. Only four do so for two out of the three power measures. They are China and India for population size and military spending, and Israel and Saudi Arabia for per-capita GNP and military spending. If we are to discriminate between Third World countries in terms of our power measures singly and in combination, it seems more appropriate to view them relative to the global medians rather than means. The results are reported in Table 3.1.

In Table 3.1, national profiles on population size, per-capita GNP, and military spending (columns A, B, and C respectively) are used to arrive at the three groupings shown and a residual category. The countries in Group I, the *Achievers*, score above the global median on all three power measures. These countries occupy the semi-periphery of the world economic system. Either recently or some decades ago, they have ridden the wave of raw-materials exports and/or export-led industrialization to relative wealth. In relative terms, they have substantial human, economic, and military capabilities. The Group II and Group III countries are characterized by the common feature of asymmetry in their standings on the different dimensions of national power.[14] Those in Group II — the *Goliaths* — stand substantially above the global median in population and military spending, but below it in per-capita wealth. Those in Group III — the *Davids* — stand substantially above the global median in per-capita wealth and military spending, but below it in population size (and, in most cases, spatial size as well). Both groups thus suffer some weakness in national power. Each also has some substantial strengths.

The fourth and residual grouping — the *Weak* — includes all the Third World countries not listed in Table 3.1. They tend to rank low on all three dimensions of power. They are at best bypassed and at worst buffeted by international events. Most of them face chronic stagnation. The lucky few may be pulled upward, or at least avoid being pushed

Table 3.1 **National profiles of Third World countries**

| | A | B | C | D | E | F | | G | | H | | I | |
|---|---|---|---|---|---|---|---|---|---|---|---|---|---|
| World Total | 4,700 | 2,725 | 811,900 | | | | | | | | | | |
| Global Mean | 32.4 | 2,725 | 5,640 | | | | | | | | | | |
| Global Median | 7.5 | 1,224 | 300 | | | | | | | | | | |
| **Group I: The Achievers** | | | | | | | | | | | | | |
| Algeria | 20.7 | 2,269 | 1,334 | OPEC | U | 0.44 | (344) | 0.08 | (1) | 0.0 | (0) | 0.000 | (0) |
| Argentina | 29.7 | 1,824 | 1,523 | NIC | U | 0.20 | (155) | 0.00 | (0) | 0.0 | (0) | 0.000 | (0) |
| Brazil | 131.3 | 1,987 | 1,769 | NIC | U | 0.22 | (175) | 0.00 | (0) | 0.0 | (0) | 0.000 | (0) |
| Chile | 11.5 | 1,886 | 1,021 | | U | 0.39 | (311) | 0.00 | (0) | 0.0 | (0) | 0.000 | (0) |
| Colombia | 28.3 | 1,342 | 456 | | F | 0.00 | NA | 0.00 | (0) | 8.3 | (1) | 0.001 | (0.3) |
| Iran | 42.5 | 2,485 | 5,500 | OPEC | U | 0.49 | (383) | 0.00 | (0) | 2.8 | (1) | 0.011 | (4.5) |
| Iraq | 14.5 | 1,667 | 11,900 | OPEC | U | 0.53 | (421) | 0.03 | (1) | 8.3 | (3) | 0.026 | (3.8) |
| Korea, South | 41.4 | 1,870 | 4,717 | NIC | U | 0.70 | (552) | 0.00 | (0) | 40.6 | (2) | 1.256 | (520.0) |
| Malaysia | 15.0 | 1,746 | 1,432 | | U | 0.20 | (155) | 0.18 | (3) | 0.0 | (0) | 0.000 | (0) |
| Mexico | 75.7 | 1,997 | 872 | NIC | U | 0.23 | (179) | 0.00 | (0) | 0.0 | (0) | 0.000 | (0) |
| Saudi Arabia | 10.4 | 10,314 | 27,192 | OPEC | U | 0.55 | (438) | 0.03 | (1) | 2.8 | (1) | 0.001 | (0.1) |
| South Africa | 30.9 | 2,240 | 3,132 | | U | 0.25 | (201) | 0.00 | (0) | 0.0 | (0) | 0.000 | (0) |
| Syria | 9.8 | 1,609 | 2,138 | | U | 1.30 | (1,025) | 0.24 | (6) | 9.4 | (3) | 0.117 | (11.5) |
| Taiwan | 18.8 | 2,663 | 3,925 | NIC | F | 0.27 | (215) | 0.00 | (0) | 0.0 | (0) | 0.000 | (0) |
| Venezuela | 16.8 | 3,977 | 920 | OPEC | U | 0.18 | (141) | 0.00 | (0) | 0.0 | (0) | 0.000 | (0) |
| Yugoslavia | 22.8 | 2,594 | 2,309 | | U | 0.56 | (442) | 0.07 | (1) | 0.0 | (0) | 0.000 | (0) |
| **Group II: The Goliaths** | | | | | | | | | | | | | |
| China | 1,020.9 | 376 | 34,500 | | U | 2.82 | (2,225) | 0.41 | (12) | 31.3 | (4) | 0.089 | (913.5) |
| Egypt | 45.8 | 674 | 2,679 | | U | 3.82 | (3,017) | 0.28 | (8) | 19.4 | (5) | 0.055 | (25.0) |
| India | 730.6 | 248 | 6,546 | | F | 1.43 | (1,126) | 0.30 | (8) | 17.6 | (5) | 0.002 | (14.0) |
| Indonesia | 165.8 | 541 | 2,649 | OPEC | U | 0.39 | (309) | 0.16 | (4) | 18.1 | (1) | 0.006 | (10.0) |
| Morocco | 22.9 | 673 | 1,318 | | U | 0.20 | (158) | 0.11 | (2) | 0.0 | (0) | 0.000 | (0) |
| Nigeria | 85.2 | 782 | 1,723 | OPEC | F | 0.41 | (323) | 0.00 | (0) | 0.0 | (0) | 0.000 | (0) |
| Pakistan | 94.1 | 373 | 1,984 | | U | 1.05 | (826) | 0.15 | (4) | 5.9 | (2) | 0.007 | (6.8) |
| Thailand | 50.7 | 746 | 1,539 | | U | 0.53 | (421) | 0.00 | (0) | 27.8 | (2) | 0.004 | (1.8) |
| Vietnam | 57.6 | ~180 | NA | | U | 6.66 | (5,262) | 0.05 | (1) | 59.3 | (3) | 2.016 | (1,161.0) |
| **Group III: The Davids** | | | | | | | | | | | | | |
| Israel | 4.0 | 5,144 | 6,229 | NIC | F | 5.66 | (4,465) | 0.23 | (6) | 21.2 | (6) | 0.189 | (7.6) |
| Kuwait | 1.7 | 16,444 | 1,173 | OPEC | U | 0.22 | (173) | 0.08 | (1) | 6.0 | (0) | 0.000 | (0) |
| Libya | 3.5 | 6,608 | 4,223 | OPEC | U | 0.48 | (379) | 0.00 | (0) | 6.9 | (1) | 0.014 | (0.5) |
| Oman | 1.1 | 6,084 | 1,944 | | U | 0.00 | NA | 0.00 | (0) | 0.0 | (0) | 0.000 | (0) |
| Singapore | 2.5 | 6,319 | 955 | NIC | U | 0.00 | NA | 0.00 | (0) | 0.0 | (0) | 0.000 | (0) |
| | 1.3 | 18,067 | 1,867 | OPEC | U | 0.00 | | | | 0.0 | (0) | 0.000 | (0) |

Notes

A: Population in 1983 (in millions).

B: GNP per capita in 1983 (in 1983 US dollars).

C: Military expenditures in 1983 (in millions of 1983 US dollars).

D: Type of country. All OPEC countries, except Ecuador and Gabon, are included in this table. Also, all newly industrializing countries (NICs) identified by Park and Teng are included, except Hong Kong, Portugal, Spain, and Turkey.

E: Freedom status in 1982. All countries given a rating by the Freedom House of 1 or 2 on political rights were given F for free, and all countries rated between 3 and 7 were given U for unfree.

F: Involvement in international affairs as indicated by the World Events Interaction Survey (WEIS) during 1966–75. The first figure is the number of events initiated by a country as a percentage of the total number of events recorded by WEIS. The second figure, in parentheses, is the raw number of events initiated by a country.

G: The first figure is the number of involvements in international crises per year since 1945 or since a country became a member of the inter-state system (if later than 1945) during the 1945–73 period. The second figure, in parentheses, is the number of crisis involvements. During 1945–73, there were 72 international crises recorded by the CACI project, with 163 national participations in them (several countries can be involved in one crisis).

H: The first figure is the percentage of years since 1945 or since a country became a member of the inter-state system (if later than 1945) with at least one international war under way (for the 1945–80 period). An international war can be either an inter-state war or an extra-systemic war as defined by the Correlates of War project. Civil wars are not included in this column, nor are wars resulting in fewer than 1,000 military deaths. The second figure, in parentheses, is the raw number of international wars experienced by a country during 1945–80.

I: The first figure is the percent of all military deaths suffered in international wars (as defined by the COW project) in terms of a country's 1983 population. Civilian deaths are not included. The second figure, in parentheses, is the raw number of military deaths during the same period of 1945–80.

Sources:
The data in A, B and C are from US Arms Control and Disarmament Agency, World Military Expenditures and Arms Transfers: 1985 (Washington, DC: USACDA, 1985), pp. 42–88.
The identification of NICs in D is based on Tong-whan Park and Chung-chian Teng, 'Between the North and the South: Foreign Policy of the Newly Industrializing Countries', paper presented at the 1983 International Studies Association meeting at Mexico City, pp. 33–4 (Table 2).
The data in E, on freedom status, are based on Raymond D. Gastil, Freedom in the World: Political Rights and Civil Liberties (Westport, CT: Greenwood Press, 1982), pp. 39–47.
The data in F, on international events, are based on Charles A. McClelland, 'Warning in the International Events Flow: EFI and ROZ as Threat Indicators', International Interactions, vol. 5 (1978), pp. 199–202.
The data in G, on international crisis involvement, are based on James A. Moore, 'Crisis Inventory', mimeograph (Washington, DC: CACI, 1975).
The data in H and I, on war involvement and military deaths in battles, are based on Melvin Small and J. David Singer, Resort to Arms: International and Civil Wars, 1816–1980 (Beverly Hills, CA: Sage, 1982), pp. 167–73.

downward, by attaching themselves to the more powerful in the Third or the First and Second Worlds. Most of them are seemingly destined to be pawns in international rivalries or, at best, objects of benign neglect. For the fortunate, their lack of indigenous capabilities for monitoring and managing external affairs is somewhat offset by their remoteness from the centres of action and by their generally perceived irrelevance to others' interests. Abstention, passivity, and compliance tend to characterize their approach to the international aspects of their national security problems. Even among the Third World countries, they generally take a backseat and adopt a low profile in collective action such as with regard to the Group of 77's proposals to establish a new international economic order. Indeed, the great dependency of these countries on their respective core sponsors more severely reduces their decisional autonomy and policy latitude relative to those in the other three groups. As a consequence, national security management in the sense of charting and steering a policy course to bring about a more conducive foreign environment is far more elusive and illusory for them than for the other subcategories of Third World countries.

## NATIONAL SECURITY VARIETY

We now turn to the first three subcategories of Third World countries in order to examine the extent to which they pose different patterns of national security scarcity and dependence, and thus suggest differences in impacting foreign actions and in their own leverage. We do not expect the Achievers, Goliaths, and Davids to conform fully to completely distinct profiles in these respects. We do expect some relative differences which are only partly modified by differences in history, location, and the characteristics of neighbouring states. We introduce some additional experiential variables in columns F through I of Table 3.1: involvement in international affairs, involvement in international crises, involvement in international wars, and war deaths.[15]

It is obvious from Table 3.1 that some countries in each of

the three subcategories have had much more experience with military contingencies than others. The incidence and severity of those experiences will affect the probability estimates made by their officials in a way that may override our subcategory differences. Accordingly, concerns with external military threats should be more salient in the minds of the officials of countries such as China, India, Egypt, Syria, Israel, and South Korea. These concerns are buttressed not only by a perception of the possible reoccurrence of past conflicts, but also by the severity of past battle casualties. The latter aspect of negative significance is apt to be especially sensitive to countries that have suffered comparatively heavy military casualties relative to their population size. The Koreas, Vietnam, and Israel are such countries. Note that these countries fall between the 'cracks' or at the overlapping intersections of the historic domains of several contending core powers, and that they are generally quite dependent on foreign support to buttress their regional positions.

The Achievers all possess substantial power stocks. At the same time, they face particularly complex problems of national security management. They manifest a modest level of international event initiation, and most of them have avoided involvement in international crises and wars. In these respects, they seem relatively inactive compared to the Goliaths. While few would argue that they can dominate the global or regional political-military balance, most would view the Achievers as important in regional distributions of power and control.

The complexity of the Achievers' national security situation derives primarily from the interacting factors of involvement in the international economy and challenges to the internal control and legitimacy of the prevailing political order. Their military problems derive from regional rivalries and claims by powerful external actors of 'rights' to limit what they do internally as well as abroad. Their leverage lies in economic assets, regional military significance, and the precedential implications of their movement into or out of the camp of one or another superpower. Like the Davids and relatively unlike the Goliaths, the Achievers' assets and vulnerabilities are usually extraordinarily sensitive to foreign acts of commission and omission. Unlike the Davids, they do have significant economic leverage.

National security policy for the Achievers is therefore a pressure cooker, and national security performance often resembles a roller-coaster, rising and falling with great rapidity. The policy process is under great pressure to be nimble, but is at the same time committed to those institutions that reduce that very nimbleness. Some of those institutions are military which, in most cases, hold *de facto* veto power over most aspects of public policy.

Facilitative foreign inputs are crucial for the Achievers' attempts to maintain internal control in the face of communal tension (e.g., Iran, Iraq, Syria, Malaysia, South Africa, Yugoslavia), economic and political demands (e.g. Argentina, Brazil, Chile, South Korea, Mexico), external challenges to regime legitimacy (e.g. Taiwan, South Korea), or domestic insurgency (e.g. Colombia, South Africa). Those inputs include political endorsement to dissipate opposition, military hardware to appease the armed forces, and investment capital, loans, and access to overseas markets to provide the wherewithal for domestic economic benefits. Entangled in the world economy as many of these countries are, they are prone to rapid growth, inflation, and austerity imposed by foreign developments. The speed of change in these economic factors clearly compounds problems of internal control.[16] The Achievers are therefore driven to a variety of strategies to buffer themselves from external shocks. At the same time, there are obvious elements of regional interaction and competition among these countries — most obviously in Latin America and the Middle East. These elements coexist uneasily with incentives for joint action to manage foreign behaviour, again most notably for the Latin American and Middle Eastern Achievers.

Economic linkage to the First World has been one common strategy of the Achievers. That is, through the provision of raw materials, exports of consumer products, imports of agricultural and capital goods, and hosting of the First World's direct investment, the Achievers have tried to give others (especially the USA) a stake in their security.

Some have gone so far as to sweeten the stake by offering themselves as a surrogate for their protector's policies in the region or elsewhere in the world. Another strategy has been to impose tight and indeed coercive control of internal pluralism and dissent. A third strategy has been to lay the foundation for their own military autonomy as well as a spoiler capability to affect military relationships in the region and elsewhere in the world. This strategy has involved the development of substantial arms industries for domestic and foreign markets (e.g. Argentina, Brazil, South Korea) and advanced nuclear technologies with a weapons potential (e.g. Argentina, Brazil, Iraq, South Africa, South Korea, Taiwan). This last strategy clearly fits with a drive for a deterrent capability against regional enemies and rivals — often the other Achievers.

The dilemma faced by the Achievers is that all of the strategies are doubled-edged in their implications. Economic linkage carries with it extraordinary vulnerabilities and sensitivities to others' economic policies and conditions. Internal control absorbs resources, reduces flexibility, and may even lead to increased foreign pressure and decreased foreign provision of facilitative inputs. Success in economic performance, internal control, and military autonomy may all lead to a foreign perception of graduation and thus a reduced willingness to provide facilitative inputs except for a clear quid pro quo. It may also induce countervailing competitive or defensive efforts by the Achievers' regional rivals to contain their influence.

Regional rivalries among roughly-matching powers both contribute to leverage and detract from it. They contribute so long as one superpower sees the achieving country as a check on the other superpower's clients in the region or as worth bribing to avoid disruption to its own clients in the region. They detract from leverage as the superpowers recognize that there are alternative Achievers to affiliate within a region, and that there is a danger of conflict escalation should they take sides in regional rivalries between the Achievers. Collective action among the Achievers also has double-edged implications. On the one hand, the pooling of their leverage can help to offset the foreign vulnerabilities of individual Achievers as has been tried with oil prices and debt relief. On the other hand, it clearly erodes their claims for facilitative foreign contributions as rewards for ostensibly loyal followership.

Faced with this array of pressures, it is hardly surprising that many Achievers have placed great emphasis on military institutions, yet have been unable to solve any of their national security problems through military action. They have the wherewithal, or think they do, for conspicuous military consumption. They do not have the wherewithal for decisive military victory. In this as in other respects, their pursuit of national security leads to substantial activity without achieving a new and more stable plateau.

The Goliaths, our second group, are perceived to have almost a permanent importance in global or at least regional political and military affairs. Their perceived importance rests less on what they have done in any sphere (i.e. their achievement) and more on what they are (i.e. their sheer size) and where they are. There is then a gap between the importance attributed to them (by themselves and by others) and reality.

The aspirations or self-proclaimed importance of the Goliaths tends to outstrip their actual policy performance whether in terms of political influence (e.g. the leadership of the Arab, Muslim, black African, or non-aligned world by Egypt, Morocco, Pakistan, Nigeria, or India), economic development (e.g. the use of petrodollars for domestic modernization by Indonesia and Nigeria), or military effectiveness (e.g. China's 'punitive' expeditions against Vietnam, and the Egyptian and Moroccan military engagements with Israel and the Polisarios respectively). Status discrepancy theory informs us that frustrated countries are more apt to start or get involved in wars.[17] The focus of this theory is on states which feel that their achievements have not been given due recognition by the international community (e.g. Germany prior to both world wars), whereas the Group II Third World countries tend to experience the opposite situation of having their reputation exceeding their actual accomplishments. Yet as shown in Table 3.1, the Goliaths conform to the status discrepancy theory's prediction of greater conflict proclivity. With the exceptions of the superpowers, they have been involved in the largest number of international crises. They have, as a group, also fought more wars than other countries. And, they have generally been much more active in international relations than the other Third World countries in Groups I and III (except for Syria and Israel).

Furthermore, there is a significant gap between the Goliaths' endowments, on the one hand, and their accomplishments, on the other. They generally rank quite high in the global hierarchy on inherited attributes such as territorial size, population base, and natural resources. By comparison, they score much lower on social, economic, and military achievements. This failure to match actual achievements with inherited endowments suggests a certain 'paper tiger' quality in these countries' foreign military postures. The tendency to abet attributions of importance in excess of objective capabilities, as noted earlier, can be seen in this light as an effort to offset deficiencies in performance. It is at the heart of the foreign policy management styles of these countries to attract foreign attention and to deter foreign hostility. At the same time, the Goliaths typically allocate a large percentage of their available economic and human resources for military purposes. This allocation policy is in a sense part of the premium imposed to maintain their claimed importance in international affairs. Given their compelling internal socioeconomic needs and slower economic growth, the opportunity costs for spending on guns as opposed to butter are especially high. That is especially true because of the massive population burden that they must struggle to carry. The combination of enormous population, lagging economic performance, grand self-image, and historical domination of their respective regions makes the Goliaths as a class our prime Third World candidates for experiencing shrinking internal carrying capacity, mounting lateral pressure to expand externally, and thus more frequent international conflicts.[18]

This conflict temptation is only imperfectly disciplined. In part this is because of the internal importance of their military establishments and their lack of other leverage instruments. In part it is because of their indeed being military superiors to many but not to all. That is, they tend to be militarily superior in some but not other dyadic situations, and to be potentially inferior in situations where they alone face a coalition that includes members of the First or the Second World. For example, Thailand is militarily stronger than most of its neighbours, but is outmatched by Vietnam. Similarly, Pakistan has one of the most professional armed forces in the Third World and ranks as a leading military power in the Muslim world. But it is militarily much inferior to India, which is in turn fearful of a stronger China. The Chinese, however, are themselves extremely vulnerable to and ill-prepared for a Soviet conventional or nuclear attack. Accordingly, the management of military security by these countries tends to be complicated. First, they are perceived as threats by their smaller neighbours and become the targets of the latter's attempts at deterrence and containment (with the aid of outside powers). Second, their own weakness and vulnerability *via-à-vis* even stronger adversaries call for counterbalancing policies through the recruitment of outside help. That in turn must come from the powerful, that is, countries of the First or the Second World.

This foreign aid is likely to be extended if the providers believe several things about the receiving Goliath. It must be threatened directly or indirectly by another major power or Goliath in the service of another major power. It must indeed be credible as a Goliath in spite of its manifest current and historical weaknesses. The problem, of course, is that the Goliaths really do not relish the idea of relying heavily on First or Second World powers in their region of claimed supremacy. This dependence undermines their standing. And they can only go to the well so often with the bright prospects of overcoming historical socioeconomic and political weaknesses before these promises lose credibility. The prospects are especially hard to achieve should the Goliaths feel it necessary to keep acting along the lines we attribute to them. That is, they will have to start acting like an achiever or risk coming to be seen as fakes. In the latter event, they may still be able to extract facilitative foreign inputs, but only in the context of the foreign contributors' national security agendas and not those of the Goliaths. The resulting dependence clashes with the status that the Goliaths traditionally claim and opens their ruling elites to internal attacks.

The national security consequences are an intriguing combination of strength and weakness, and activism and isolation. As for weakness, the large military establishments of the Goliaths are generally incapable of effective and sustained force projection beyond their immediate border areas. That is, these countries lack the logistic capability, the command-control-communications system, and the appropriate arsenals to pose an offensive threat to distant others in either the conventional or the strategic sense. Instead, their 'offensive' strategy lies much more in the use of unconventional means, such as sponsoring or supporting insurgent movements in neighbouring countries (e.g. in Afghanistan, Kampuchea, the Ogaden), or in undertaking direct but limited (in action, objectives, and duration) campaigns to harass nearby adversaries (e.g. in the Sinai, Kashmir, and the Sino-Vietnamese border).

As for strength, the huge population and territory of the Goliaths buttress a significant capacity to absorb military punishment and setback, and a substantial 'staying power' to outlast their opposition. A large-scale foreign attack aimed at taking physical control of the population or territory of a Group II country is quite improbable. The more realistic threat facing them involves border incursions, even over a relatively large span of land (e.g. the Ogaden, Sinai, Kashmir, Inner Mongolia, Manchuria). It is with respect to this kind of threat that the Goliaths need most help from their foreign allies for deterrence and containment. Their sheer size and strategic depth tend to serve as a protection against foreign aggressions that are in any sense comparable to the Japanese attempt at conquering China during World War II. Internal fragmentation (e.g. those already experienced in the wars for Bengali and Biafran independence) appears to be a more genuine threat to the national survival of some Goliaths.

It would seem, therefore, that the Goliaths have no

external security problems if they just want to be left alone. The problem is that the combination of self-image, economic weakness, population pressure, and perceived importance in power alignments, all makes being left alone a national security failure in the broadest sense. In this chronic bind, they do what they can do with considerable ambivalence. It amounts to a declaratory policy of independence and assertiveness, an attempt to extract status as well as economic and military resources from the East and the West, an enticing posture to attract those foreign contributions by holding out the allure of potential alignment and base rights, and intermittent efforts to concentrate on becoming Achievers as a springboard to becoming Goliaths in fact as well as in image. Along the way, they often try to mask from themselves and others the hollowness of their power of assertion by modest contributions to members of our fourth subcategory — the Weak.

The Davids, by contrast, do not have a defensive option of falling back into their hinterland. Going it alone probably means disappearing as an independent entity. They tend to have an extraordinarily small and concentrated demographic, territorial, and economic base. Given their severely limited absorptive capacity for military setbacks and 'staying power' for protracted military struggles, a strategy of territorial defence in depth or wars of attrition are recipes for disaster. Economically, they are also not much better qualified to withstand external pressure and to survive on their own. Their domestic markets are too small to consume or exploit indigenous riches in natural or human resources. For different reasons — historical enmity, economic booty, or critical bottleneck location — they cannot expect to be left alone in the absence of foreign backing. Acute threat is a relative constant. It is hardly surprising, therefore, that their military establishments tend to be of high combat quality marked by an emphasis on militancy and readiness.

Given the almost universal inferiority in their inherited endowments in geography and population, the Davids of our analysis tend to pursue two common strategies. First, they seek maximum effectiveness in mobilizing, extracting, and utilizing indigenous resources, including ones of emotion. Wealth, education, and mass organization all contribute to this effectiveness. Second, they place themselves under the protection of First and Second World powers as well as that of regional Achievers and Goliaths when possible. They seek especially deep and tight official and unofficial ties with their foreign protectors, in order to reduce the danger of abandonment and to increase the deterring perception that an attack on them is an attack on their protector. All of this places an emphasis on loyalty, be it to a superpower protector (e.g. Israel, Libya), a regional protector (e.g. Kuwait, the UAE), or a larger regional grouping (e.g. Singapore in ASEAN). The ability to secure such protection hinges on the perception by others that the Davids are worth it. As with the Goliaths and Achievers, that judgement of worth may rest on geographic location such as key access to a potentially or currently 'hot' region, or chokepoints that connect transit between regions (e.g. Singapore, Oman). It also rests on perceived effectiveness in wielding some instruments of power, be it capital, arms, or raw materials. Like the Goliaths, the Davids must foster an image of significance. However, they must do so through acts rather than just words. Accordingly, they can particularly ill-afford setbacks or any appearance of internal disarray.

The grave dependency of the Davids on foreign support for coping with their military threats and on foreign transactions for their economic survival carries with it extreme vulnerability. They are therefore especially susceptible to heavy pressure to compromise their national sovereignty in order to maintain that support and those transactions. Faced with unusual challenges to their autonomy, it is hardly surprising that they have pursued rather unusual means to cope with those challenges. These include supporting the enemies of their enemies who may also be hostile to them, indirect and masked trade, and covert action. Anything that will divert external pressure and increase internal resources merits pursuit. The knack is to do so in ways that neither alienate primary protectors nor lead them to take the Davids for granted.

## CONCLUSION

The distinctions we have made in the problems and coping behaviours of our three subcategories of Achievers, Goliaths, and Davids are admittedly both fuzzy and oversimplified. All of the subcategories, as well as the largest one of the Weak, manifest the general properties of Third World countries noted earlier. We do hope that our discussion will generate more thorough work to make national security a less ethnocentric concept. What is the agenda for analysis that follows from our preamble?

We see four major tasks. First, empirical studies should be undertaken to map more systematically the ecology of domestic and foreign military threats faced by the various country types suggested, and to assess whether there are indeed systematic differences in their strategies and behaviours in coping with these threats. Second, comparative case studies should be pursued to show how the officials of different countries actually go about operationalising the concept of national security. Are the judgemental baskets of significance, probability, and leverage the central themes of policy-making? Third, much more work is warranted to plot the relationships of means and ends among the major security dimensions — military, economic, ecological, and communal — at both theoretical and practical levels. Finally, it is obvious that countries can to a significant extent move from one to another of our subgroups. Only detailed analyses of transitional cases will clarify to what extent changes in national security conception lead or lag movement from one to another subcategory and for what reasons.

## NOTES

[1] See, for example, Douglas J. Murray and Paul R. Viotti (eds), *The Defense Policies of Nations* (Baltimore, MD: Johns Hopkins University Press, 1982).
[2] For example, Edward Azar and Chung-in Moon, 'Third World National Security: Toward a New Conceptual Framework', *International Interactions*, vol. 11 (1984), pp. 103–35.

[3] Davis B. Bobrow and Steve Chan, 'Understanding Anomalous Successes: Japan, Taiwan, and South Korea' in James N. Rosenau, Charles F. Hermann, and Charles C. Kegley, Jr. (eds), *New Directions in the Comparative Study of Foreign Policy* (Boston: Allen & Unwin, 1987).

[4] W. Harriet Critchley, 'Defining Strategic Value: Problems of Conceptual Clarity and Valid Threat Assessments' in Robert Harkavy and Edward A. Kolodziej (eds), *American Security Policy and Policy-Making: The Dilemmas of Using and Controlling Military Force* (Lexington, MA: D.C. Heath, 1980), pp. 45–65.

[5] See, for example, Amos Tversky and Daniel Kahneman, 'Judgement under Uncertainty', *Science*, no. 185 (27 September 1974), pp. 1124–31.

[6] This distinction was proposed by James A. Caporaso, 'Introduction to the Special Issue of International Organization on Dependence and Dependency in the Global System', *International Organization*, no. 32 (Winter 1978), pp. 1–12.

[7] These concepts were first proposed by Robert O. Keohane and Joseph S. Nye, *Power and Interdependence: World Politics in Transition* (Boston: Little Brown, 1977).

[8] The classic formulation of the concept of security community was by Karl W. Deutsch, Sidney A. Burrell, Robert A. Kann, Maurice Lee, Jr., Martin Lichtenman, Raymond E. Lindgren, Francis L. Loewenheim and Robert W. Van Wagenen, *Political Community and the North Atlantic Area: International Organization in the Light of Historical Experience* (New York: Greenwood Press, 1957).

[9] Giovanni Satori, 'Concept Misformation in Comparative Politics', *American Political Science Review*, vol. 64 (December 1970), pp. 1033–53.

[10] Charles F. Doran, Kim Q. Hill, Kenneth R. Mladenka, and Kyoji Wakata, 'Perceptions of National Power and Threat: Japan, Finland, and the United States', *International Journal of Group Tensions*, vol. 4 (December 1974), pp. 431–54.

[11] James N. Rosenau, 'Pre-Theories and Theories of Foreign Policy' in R. Barry Farrell (ed.), *Approaches to Comparative and International Politics* (Evanston, IL: Northwestern University Press, 1966), pp. 27–92.

[12] Some of the other independent variables used by analysts to explain foreign policy behaviour were, for example, geographic distance, cultural similarity, and the capability balance between nations. The results of empirical tests of Rosenau's country

typology can be found in James N. Rosenau and Gary D. Hoggard, 'Foreign Policy Behaviour in Dyadic Relationships: Testing a Pre-Theoretical Extension' in James N. Rosenau (ed.), *Comparing Foreign Policies: Theories, Findings, and Methods* (New York: Sage, 1974), pp. 117–49; David W. Moore, 'Nation Attributes and Nation Typologies: A Look at the Rosenau Genotypes' in ibid., pp. 251–67; and Maurice A. East and Charles F. Hermann, 'Do Nation-Types Account for Foreign Policy Behaviour?' in ibid., pp. 269–303.

[13] Steve Chan, *International Relations in Perspective: The Pursuit of Security, Welfare, and Justice* (New York: Macmillan, 1984), p. 35.

[14] The Goliaths and the Davids score at least three times the global median on two of the three power measures used by us. The adoption of a cut-off point of three times the global median has led to the exclusion of some countries (e.g. North Korea) from Table 3.1. The decision is inherently arbitrary.

[15] The distributions of the 'dependent variables' in columns F through I are even more extremely skewed than those for the 'independent variables' in columns A through C. The global means and medians approach zero for these variables. Consequently, these figures are omitted in Table 3.1.

[16] Mancur Olson, Jr., 'Rapid Growth as a Destabilizing Force', *Journal of Economic History*, vol. 23 (December 1963), pp. 529–52.

[17] See, for example, Johan Galtung, 'A Structural Theory of Aggression', *Journal of Peace Research*, vol. 1 (1964), pp. 95–119. An empirical test of this theory was provided by Michael D. Wallace, *War and Rank Among Nations* (Lexington, MA: D.C. Heath, 1973).

[18] See Nazli Choucri and Robert C. North. *Nations in Conflict: National Growth and International Violence* (San Francisco: W.H. Freeman, 1975); and Melvin Small and J. David Singer, *Resort to Arms: International and Civil Wars, 1816–1980* (Beverly Hills, CA: Sage, 1982).

[19] See, for example, A.F.K. Organski and Jacek Kugler, 'Davids and Goliaths: Predicting the Outcomes of International Wars', *Comparative Political Studies*, vol. 11 (July 1978), pp. 141–80.

# 4. Legitimacy, Integration and Policy Capacity: The 'Software' Side of Third World National Security

EDWARD E. AZAR and CHUNG-IN MOON

The conventional assessment of national security management has been framed around two important clusters of variables: security environment and the availability and readiness of hardware. Security environment refers to external threat and alliance pattern, whereas the hardware side of security management involves physical capabilities (e.g. military and economic power) and tangible policy infrastructure comprising strategic doctrine, force structure, intelligence, weapons choice, and so on. The preponderance of the 'realist' paradigm in international politics has made them the key to the understanding of national security concerns as a whole.[1] We argue, however, that the blind emphasis on security environment and hardware may be a hindrance to a proper assessment of the overall security posture. Attention needs to be paid to the *software* side of security management, which involves the political context and policy capacity through which national values are defined, threats and vulnerabilities are perceived and assessed, resources are allocated, and policies are screened, selected and implemented.

The concept of 'software' is not new. Traditional realists have subjected it to extensive scholarly enquiries focusing on such variables as national will, national morale, regime type, and government structure.[2] But the realist approach is limited on two accounts: conceptual ambiguity and analytical mislocation. National will and national morale can hardly be operationalized , while regime type and government structure are merely institutional arrangements devoid of content. One cannot describe and explain national security dynamics by relying on such ambiguous and porous concepts. Second, the conventional usage of the above software items suffers analytical mislocation. In our conceptualization, the software refers to the conversion mechanism linking security environment and hardware to the final policy outcomes and the overall security performance. In the traditional usage, such software items are treated either as components of hardware (i.e. intangible sources of power) or as part of security environment (i.e. input variables).

We suggest that legitimacy, integration, and policy capacity are more useful components of security management software. We shall demonstrate below that these variables are especially germane to the Third World national security context.[3] Legitimacy is an integral part of the software because it shapes the macropolitical context of the national security management system. It determines to a large extent the national will, morale and character, and conditions all levels of security management ranging from threat environment to policy capacity. Even the relevance of regime type and authority structure to security performance can be meaningfully captured by examining the nature of legitimacy involved.

Integration, on the other hand, molds the social and cultural infrastructure of a security management system. Both the formulation of national interests and the overall software mechanism are conditioned by the level of integration. The failure to integrate diverse social groups into a unified political force brings about new security threats, fragments macropolitical infrastructures, and weakens policy capacity. The integration variable is of great significance in the Third World context because of the pervasiveness of political and social disintegration. Many developing countries still suffer a colonial legacy by which diverse communal (ethnic, linguistic, religious, and cultural) groups were forced to merge into a single territorial and administrative body. Ironically the tide of modernization has accelerated the process of communal fragmentation, elevating integration as a unique and important dimension of the Third World national security management.[4]

While legitimacy and integration shape the contextual framework of the software, policy capacity constitutes its dynamic core, operational modes and contents. The detection and processing of information (or threats), the choice and articulation of policies (e.g. defence, foreign and public), control, allocation, and mobilization of resources and capabilities, and their implementation characterize policy capacity.[5] Policy capacity steers the security management system by determining the scope and range of internal and external behaviour. In the Third World, where the security environment is relatively fluid and the provision of hardware is difficult, effective and adaptive policy capacity is vital to the overall security performance.

In this chapter we examine the nature of the software side of the Third World security management by elucidating how legitimacy, integration, and policy capacity relate to the overall security performance. The first section discusses the nature of legitimacy and its relationship with national security. The second section addresses security dimensions of political integration and disintegration focusing on communal cleavages and political disintegration. The third section delineates the dynamics of policy capacity and its impact on the security posture. The final section presents a preliminary comparative assessment of the Third World national security by examining the relationship of threats, hardware and software.

## LEGITIMACY CRISIS AND SECURITY MANAGEMENT

In his recent work on world power assessment, Cline argues that 'national will is the foundation upon which national strategy is formulated and arrived through to success'. By defining national will as 'the degree of resolve that can be mobilized among the citizens of a nation in support of government decisions about defense and foreign policy', he identifies as its component parts the effective strength of leadership, relevance of national strategy to national interests in the perception of citizens, and the degree of cultural integration.[6] Cline is right in pointing out national will as an important determinant of national security, but his explanation and conceptualisation are incomplete. Where does the effective leadership come from? Under what conditions does the relevance of national strategy increase, and what facilitates or inhibits cultural integration? The concept of national will or morale, without the elucidation of its ultimate determinants, becomes ambiguous and abstract.

The form of government or regime in power is also often cited as an essential part of the domestic security coping mechanism. Morgenthau asserts that good government increases intangible sources of national power and therefore strong security posture because good government is able to maximize popular support and vice versa. The criterion which Morgenthau uses in judging the 'bad' and the 'good' is the form of government. Open democratic governments are good while autocratic and totalitarian ones are bad.[7] This view is dominant in much of the research and theories of linkage politics or national attributes. Henry Kissinger, for example, classifies three different types of leadership structure (bureaucratic, revolutionary and charismatic), and argues that revolutionary and charismatic politics are more prone to provoke conflictual external behaviour and therefore by implication to experience insecurity.[8] Even though empirical researches have tried to test the linkage between regime type and external conflictual behaviour, we still do not have conclusive evidence that external behaviour and insecurity are directly linked to institutional arrangements *per se.*[9] What really matters is the content not the form of government and regime.

A missing link here is the role of legitimacy. The effective leadership strength, the people's perceived relevance of national strategy, and social and cultural integration derive from the level of legitimacy which a government or regime in power enjoys. It is also legitimacy that shapes the contents of institutional arrangements. National security performance may be enhanced more by 'benevolent' dictatorship with high legitimacy than by the fragile and incompetent pluralist regime with low legitimacy. For legitimacy relates to whether citizens are loyal and willingly support state policies — whether they accept the authority of the state and believe existing institutions are functionally competent, legally right, and morally proper.[10] Indeed legitimacy affects all levels of national security management. High levels of legitimacy help the regimes in power establish easily national consensus on ends and means of security management. Popular support and acceptance facilitate the smooth mobilization and allocation of domestic resources and allow speedy and effective implementation of security policies.

Unlike advanced industrial countries, most developing Third World countries suffer from acute legitimacy crises which severely constrain security performance. Those regimes which have built up their legitimacy by appealing to traditional values and norms are endangered by the rising tide of modernization and increasing social mobilization. On the other hand, some regimes have responded to the crisis of legitimacy with the exercise of personal charisma and ideological manipulation. Such manoeuvres, however, rarely sustain political legitimacy. Structural rigidity, economic backwardness, and most importantly resource scarcity pervasive in Third World developing countries seldom allow regimes in power to enjoy functional competence and legal appropriateness, which are essential to the creation and maintenance of legitimacy in modern societies. Failure to meet the basic needs of the people, suppression of increasing citizens' demands for participation, jobs, justice, and so on, are both determinants and

resultants of this crisis of legitimacy. Moreover, irregular
political changes such as military coups, palace coups, and
hereditary political succession, along with repressive and
arbitrary political rule based on the personal whim of rulers,
deepen the legitimacy crisis and reinforce the vicious cycle.[11]

The deprivation of structural sources of legitimacy raises
several critical implications for the Third World national
security. As the linkage theorists implicitly assert, chronic
crisis of political legitimacy and resulting social and political
instabilities can alter the overall security environment in the
direction of increased external threats. The defiance of
political authority and dwindling popular support amidst
increased domestic social instabilities lead to changes in the
perception of the adversary. Domestic instabilities become a
sign of weakness and an inducement for adversarial military
provocation and domestic sabotage. Increased hostile
behaviour by adversaries, which results from diminishing
levels of legitimacy and domestic stability, threatens the
core values of a nation. The recent Iran–Iraq war is an
example of the link between internal weakness, crisis of
legitimacy, and changing threat environment. In terms of
conventional power configuration, Iran has been the top
dog, Iraq the underdog. But the Shah's excessive emphasis
on the military power build-up based on a client relationship with the USA and uneven economic development in
that oil-rich country led to the loss of his political legitimacy.
The Shah's undisputable authority was shattered, and the
Revolution soon followed. In the wake of this revolution
and the consequent domestic instability and chaos, Iraq's
images of Iran's strength were altered. The Iraqi ruling elite
went to war with Iran over issues which were presumed to
have been settled. In this case, the legitimacy crisis in Iran
succeeded in inviting external threats.[12]

The trade-off between regime security and national
security is another manifestation of the legitimacy crisis.
Faltering legitimacy and the erosion of political authority
increase internal threat to regimes in power in the form of
political protests, sabotages, revolts and rebellions. As
regimes in power try to respond to and control these threats
in the name of national security, they employ several

methods. The troubled political leadership may invent a new national security ideology and attempt to indoctrinate and contain those who oppose the regime. This approach comprises the creation of real or imaginary enemies and threats, which would allow the 'legitimate' use of repression and coercion for the purpose of reducing internal threats to the regime. Perhaps the worst part of this trade-off manifests itself in the situation where imaginary threats are translated into real ones in order to help foster regime security, but which eventually fails and ends up weakening and destroying national security *per se*. The Argentinian military regime in the wake of the Falklands crisis exemplifies the trade-off amidst a legitimacy crisis. President Galtieri and his junta members suffered severe domestic crisis preceding the event. Rampant inflation and sagging economic growth rapidly worsened the quality of life in Argentina. Deepening economic crisis accelerated political instability, threatening the survival of the junta regime. The military junta responded to the threat by precipitating a new national security crisis, namely, the use of the Argentinian military forces to regain the Falklands from the British. Of course, the Falklands has been a persistent security issue for Argentina, but there is a different consensus that the timing of the invasion was motivated largely by the survival of the regime. The gamble did not work. As a result, national security was further endangered, national morale lowered, and the regime eventually collapsed.[13]

In the Third World, the dilemma between regime security and national security is ubiquitous. In many parts of the world where nation-building is in its infancy, regime security, not national security, is the dominant game. All Arab states tend to ensure regime security by provoking national security concerns. While Qadhafi of Libya tries to camouflage internal functional failures and political repression by inventing both real and imaginary external threats, President Assad of Syria maintains the Alawite minority's precarious but dominant power by championing on Arab 'militant' foreign policy behaviour. South Korea under Park Chung-Hee is another classic example in which national security is equated with regime security amidst

eroding legitimacy.[14] What is common in these situations is
the precipitation or amplification of external threats to
national security, the use of political repression, the consolidation of power and mass mobilization as means for regime
security. However, the consequences of these political
tactics are the increase in 'real' threats to national security
and the demise of regime security *per se*.

Legitimacy is not limited to the reshaping of the ecology
of threats, but extends to the substance of security management. Weak legitimacy exhausts domestic capabilities and
turns the overall policy capacity rigid and ineffectual. As a
regime attempts to ensure its survival through the use of
force or by co-optation and appeasement of the opposition,
it begins rapidly to deplete the nation's capabilities and
scarce resources. For example, the protracted war of
Morocco with the Polisario, which was partly motivated by
internal legitimacy factors, has placed the Moroccan economy on the brink of virtual bankruptcy and lowered the
morale of soldiers and civilians. The futile efforts of
Ferdinand Marcos to crack down on the New People's Army
in the Philippines consumed enormous military and
economic resources, and eventually led to his fall from
power.

Among the serious side-effects of the erosion of domestic
policy capacity are: a sharp decrease in the people's loyalty
and confirmity to, and compliance with, government policies and decisions; a decrease in the government's ability to
mobilize material and human resources in the event of
national security crisis; diminution in the accountability or
the virtual termination of the steering function of the
government; and a serious reduction in the co-ordination
and implementation of policies. History is full of such
situations. The defeat of the nationalist Kuomintang
government by Mao's Communist Party is a classic in this
regard. Fragile legitimacy caused by political incompetence
and the failure to cope with economic crises prevented the
Kuomintang government from steering effective policies.
The fall of Saigon is another example. The Thieu government fell prey to North Vietnam, not because of inferiority
in hardware, but because of the paralysis of the regime's

policy capacity caused by its decreasing legitimacy. All of this suggests that no government can sustain a sound security posture for any length of time if its population and bureaucracy have grown apathetic and indifferent.

Another significant security implication of the legitimacy crisis involves the actual and perceived increase in internal and external threats brought about by the pattern of external links under the condition of declining legitimacy. Fragile regimes with limited domestic popular support usually seek and eventually find themselves involved in a web of external alliances to deter external threats and to ensure regime survival. Such efforts, which entail military alliance between the weak and the strong, are inherently asymmetric. The weak and fragile regime's dependent and client ties with the strong pay off up to a certain point in terms of military protection of the regime and nation, but eventually deprive the weak of autonomy and independence. The current international bloc politics dramatizes this aspect. Several regimes facing weak legitimacy tend to invite political and military involvement in the form of bilateral defence treaties and technical and economic assistance. But such external links plunge the weak into the vortex of superpower rivalry, making the global insecurity their own insecurity. Being trapped in the inexorable balance of power determinism, weak regimes find themselves devoid of any meaningful autonomy and independence. Cuba, Afghanistan, Angola, Ethiopia and South Yemen from the Soviet bloc and the Philippines, South Korea, Oman, and imperial Iran from the American bloc tend to experience insecurity stemming from superpower competition.[15]

In principle, legitimacy shapes the macropolitical context of the software side of security management as shown in its impact on the policy capacity. In the Third World countries, however, this situation exercises a more sweeping influence on the overall security performance not only by determining the parameters of security environment, but also by exhausting domestic capability and resources. Indeed the legitimacy variable affects all levels of security management, necessitating itself as an important unit of analysis in the study of Third World national security.

## INTEGRATION CRISIS AND SECURITY DILEMMA

The issue of integration as a national security concern has not received adequate attention particularly because the conventional way of defining national security assumes a unitary national-state actor with the existence of commonly shared national values. Few scholars have questioned the essence of unified national values, although the difference of opinion on hierarchical ordering of national values has always existed.[16] Integration as a prerequisite for nationhood is viewed as an irreversible process of historical change accompanied by the global diffusion of modernization. Furthermore, when social and cultural disintegration disrupts domestic stability, it tends to be seen as temporary and transitory. Industrialization, structural differentiation, urbanization, increased literacy and mass media weaken the forces of traditional divisiveness, and lead to a more wholesome society and secure political system.[17]

This optimistic vision does not, however, dovetail with the reality. According to Walker Connor, of a total of 132 states in 1972, only 12 could be said to be essentially homogenous. About 90 per cent was characterized by communal diversity. In 53 states (40.2 per cent) the population was divided into more than five significant groups. In some instances, the number of communal groups within a state ran into the hundreds. One and half decades later, such communal division continues to exist.[18] On the contrary, subgroupism has further proliferated against the tide of modernization, and political violence associated with communal fragmentation has been intensified.[19]

The fragmentation and disintegration of a nation-state into several communal groups adds new dimensions to the complex Third World national security question. Perhaps the most visible is the failure of developing countries to produce a feeling of covariance or commonly shared national values and interests. Deep-rooted communal cleavages do not allow the aggregation of national needs, values or interests any more than they permit a priori any unified values and interests. Each communal group develops its own collective identity based on communal values and interests instead of national ones. The governments' efforts to assimilate, accommodate, and contain them seldom work, often resulting in violent secessionist or partition movements.[20] For example, despite the Iraqi government's consistent endeavours, Kurds have pursued their nationalist goals of territorial integrity and political autonomy. Kurdish values and interests therefore contradict with those of Iraq, although the former is contained in the Iraqi territorial jurisdiction. Lebanon demonstrates another dramatic example. Commonly shared national values cannot be found in today's Lebanon. Instead one finds only the confessional interests and values of the Shi'a, Sunni, Maronite, Druze, and Greek Orthodox. In Sri Lanka, to Tamils, national values and interests are those of Singhalese, not theirs.

Contending communal values often erupt into explicit political actions, especially in the form of secessionist or separatist movements demanding separate territorial identity in terms of independence or autonomy from a larger territorial unit. Such political moves then pose immediate threats to the core values shared by the majority of the national population. They endanger the territorial and political integrity of the state. Thus, in addition to the reduction in order and stability, threats from communal division and political disintegration constitute the core of 'internal insecurity'. Kurds in Iraq and Iran, Muslims in the Philippines, Tamils in Sri Lanka, Muslims in Thailand, Karens in Burma, Eritreans in Ethiopia, and the Southern Sudanese are in this sense national security issues.[21]

In many instances, however, communal conflicts blur the demarcation between internal and external threats. In the initial stage, most separatist movements tend to be confined to the domestic realm. However, as governments fail to accommodate their demands, needs and grievances, and try to repress them by coercion and force, they induce these communal groups to look for external patrons, mostly neighbouring countries and groups with overlapping communal ties. The alliance between dissatisfied communal groups and external actors produces more complications for the internal and external threat system, thus making its management more difficult. In Lebanon, communal conflicts have gone beyond the national boundary: Maronites have had a loose alliance with some Western states and Israel, Sunni, Shi'a, and Druze communities have formed delicate patron–client ties with Syria, Iran, and several Arab groups. The invited intervention of foreign powers by contending communal actors produces a complex matrix of external and internal threats. As Table 4.1 demonstrates, most communal conflicts involve some delicate and volatile linkage politics, which complicate the security environment.

The integration crisis as a whole exhausts the domestic capabilities and resources and cripples a country's policy capacity. Azar *et al.* have shown that communal conflicts are too costly and exhaustive because they are protracted in duration and fluctuate in intensity and frequency over time with no clear termination point. There are more than 60 ongoing communal conflicts in the Third World, all of which are characterized by the longer duration and the constant oscillation between overt and covert violence.[22] Arabs in Israel, Muslims in the Philippines, blacks in South Africa, and Tamils in Sri Lanka have all engaged in protracted violent confrontation with those in power. Communal strife in Lebanon is a more dramatic instance. The costs of such conflicts are high in human and material terms. Protracted conflicts not only destroy human, physical, and social infrastructure, but also deplete the economic resources and military capabilities of states and organized communities. All parties to protracted social conflicts become victimized, by being trapped in the vicious spiral of hostility and violence.

Equally devastating is the virtual paralysis of the policy capacity of the state. Countries inflicted with protracted communal conflicts become incapable of steering the national security management system. Military and bureaucratic recruitment along communal lines fails to form a broad policy consensus and effective implementation. Communal power sharing and the resulting composition of policy-making machinery increase bureaucratic fragmen-

*Table 4.1* **Protracted social conflicts: a selection**

| Situation | Issues | Violence Pattern | External Parties |
|---|---|---|---|
| Kashmir | communal-secession | covert-overt | Pakistan/India/China |
| Arab-Israel | communal-strategic-territorial | overt | USA/USSR/UK/and many others |
| Cyprus | communal-secession | covert-overt | Turkey/Greece NATO |
| Ogaden-Somali | communal-territorial | covert-overt | Ethiopia/Somalia/Arab States/USSR |
| Eritrea | communal-secession | covert-overt | Ethiopia/Arab states |
| Lebanon | communal-strategic | overt | Arab/Israel/USA USSR/UK/France |
| Cambodia-Vietnam | ethnic-territorial | covert-overt | China/USSR/ASEAN |
| Kurds | communal-secession | covert-overt | Iran/Iraq |
| Mindanao-Muslims | communal-secession | covert-overt | Philippines/Malaysia/Libya |
| Polisario | communal-secession | overt | Morocco/Algeria/Libya |
| South Moluccans | communal-secession | covert-overt | Indonesia/Dutch Australia |
| South Africa | racial-class | covert-overt | Neighboring African states |
| Afghanistan | ideology-class | overt | USSR/Pakistan/Arab states |
| Sri Lanka | communal-secession | overt | India |

tation, create costly redundancies, politicize all micro and macro decisions and delay their implementations. Conflicting images of national values and interests make it almost impossible to undertake objective threat assessments, to allocate resources efficiently, and to produce a workable consensus on policies and strategies. For example, in Lebanon, the cabinet, which is represented by various confessional factions, becomes a battlefield for ministers and high civil servants who are caught between several loyalties — the bureaucracy, the community and the nation. As a result, co-ordination and articulation of policies are minimized. Constitutional provisions notwithstanding, neither defence minister nor president have the full authority of command and control over the Lebanese Army. While the defence minister controls certain segment, the sphere of Presidential influence is limited to the Maronite contingent in the Army. The Shi'a unit is usually beyond the command, control, and communication of the Lebanese government. As a result, Lebanon is devoid of any meaningful policy capacity and suffers from perpetual internal and external insecurity. Examples such as that of Lebanon exist throughout the Third World and demonstrate how communal cleavages and political disintegration paralyze the policy capacity of a country.

Our discussion reveals that the integration variable is an important part of national security management. The more integrated a nation-state, the more stable its security posture. It is, however, presumptuous to argue that the crisis of integration leads to protracted communal strife and to perpetual insecurity. Not all communally pluralistic societies face the same fate. The case of Israel proves the point. Israel is not homogeneous at all. Jews and Arabs are under constant tension and confrontation. Even Jews themselves are divided into Shepardis and Ashkenazis. Communal division is often intermeshed with ideological cleavages. Nevertheless, the Israeli national security posture is relatively solid. This may be attributable to the very existence of acute threats. As Coser asserts, external threats might have promoted internal unity and cohesion.[23] But more important is the government's efforts not only to integrate Jews of different locational and social origins but also to contain Arabs even by force.[24]

## POLICY CAPACITY AND SECURITY PERFORMANCE

A striking aspect of the literature on Third World national security is that while the security environment, hardware and even parts of software such as regime type and the form of government have been analysed in depth, very little attention has been paid to issue of the policy capacity. Policy capacity comprises the planning, formulation, and implementation of national security policies. Furthermore, threat assessment, decisions, articulation and enforcement of policies, and mobilization and allocation of resources all belong to the realm of policy capacity. In other words, the policy capacity is a crucial link between security environment, hardware, and the overall security posture. No clear consensus exists on the criteria with which to judge on the nature and scope of the policy capacity. But we can consider the following three factors as the prerequisites of the ideal policy capacity: 'favourable policy mood'; comprehensive and coherent decision-making; and speedy and flexible implementation.[25]

Policy mood refers to the degree of national consensus about ends and means of security policies. The conversion of segmented attention to threats and endless argument about vague principles and policy instruments into harmonious consensus, however, requires more refined operational skills than merely favourable macropolitical context shaped by legitimacy and integration. The choice of goals and means of implementation need to be widely shared. Informal networks of consultation among elites, along with sensitivity to public opinion, are a definite asset to the formation of a favourable policy mood. For creating a sense of recognition, approval, and attention strengthens the common bond and increases the sharing of accountability among actors.

A favourable policy mood needs to be followed by comprehensive and coherent decision-making. Decisions, which are made either through the politics of muddling through amidst contending political and bureaucratic prerogatives or through the arbitrary personal whim of political leaders, are apt to be incremental and short-sighted, or rigid and deformed. Decision-making environment of this sort constrains the policy capacity of a country and eventually undermines its security posture. On the other hand, effective and adaptive policy capacity flourishes in the absence of frequent and excessive societal (or legislative) intervention and of artificial compartmentalization of bureaucratic agencies. It requires some degree of the centralization of decision-making in the executive branch. One caveat, however, is in order. Incompetent executive dominance would result in arbitrary, precarious and rigid policy outcomes. To avoid this pitfall, executive centralism must be backed by an able technocratic and meritocratic bureaucracy, with a minimum of corruption or 'capture' by social groups so as to reduce the costs of clientelism and patronage and to increase policy effectiveness.[26]

The global diffusion of communication and innovation exposes elites of developing countries to a basket of fresh and innovative ideas and plans, fancy strategic doctrines, neat tactical plans, and sweeping mobilization policies. But the issue is how to make use of these ideas and plans. Defence, foreign and domestic public policies need to be articulated and integrated into national security policies. Implementing this involves the mobilization of resources, which should be allocated speedily and efficiently. This should be supported by the constant monitoring of the results and the continuous adjustment of policy decisions. Thus, pragmatic learning and flexible feedback mechanisms are essential to achieving the desired outcomes.

Speedy, efficient, and flexible implementation is a rare phenomenon in the Third World context. As Myrdal points out, most developing countries are 'soft' or 'weak' states. They are seldom able to impose collective costs and enforce obligations on their people.[27] While the rigid distribution of political power bars flexibility, efficiency, and speed, the scarcity of resources and political currency does not allow for a pragmatic learning process. Repetition of trial and error, which is a necessary part of any flexible policy implementation, becomes a high political risk to those in power.

Apart from these structural barriers, the very process of satisfying the ideal conditions of policy capacity is paradoxical and contradictory. Flexible and pragmatic adjustment may undermine the long-term coherence of security policies. Centralization of decision-making power in terms of executive dominance may erode the policy mood because it is apt to ignore the formal or informal conversion of contending opinions into a harmonious national consensus. Speedy and forceful implementation may invite domestic opposition, thus costing public support.

Nevertheless, some developing countries show consensual, adaptive, and effective policy capacity and therefore good security performance. Israel is a case in point. The overall policy mood in Israel is extremely favourable to national security management. There is a strong national consensus on ends and means of security policies. The survival of the Jewish state is the undisputable goal shared by the entire nation, transcending communal and ideological cleavages. The uniformity of the goal prevents segmented attention to internal and external threats. Although the choice of instruments to achieve the goal is often subjected to heated political and bureaucratic debates (e.g. between the Likud and Labour Parties or between Gush Emunim and Peace Now), the open and far-ranging consultative mechanism is able to filter such differences institutionally and to produce consensus. The strong national consensus in turn facilitates comprehensive decision-making and effective implementation. Precarious coalitional politics increase inter-party and inter-agency disharmony and fragmentation. Security policies, however, are insulated from these constraints. The relative autonomy of the Israeli Defence Force and the executive dominance in security policy-making allow Israelis to enjoy effective decision-making and forceful implementation. The Israelis' alliance management, handling of terrorism, and performance in wars reveal this aspect.

Israel is not perfect, however. The intelligence failure to detect the Egyptian surprise attack in the wake of the

October 1973 War and the invasion of Lebanon that fragmented national consensus illustrate the limits of effective policy capacity in Israel. In relative terms, none the less, Israel's performance has been impressive. The country's skill to translate security liabilities into assets and its ability to articulate defence, foreign and domestic public policies into an integrated security policy are very rare in the modern world. Several factors explain the unique policy capacity of Israel: the historical origin of the Jewish state; the unity of purpose framed around Zionist ideology; the presence of clear and high tension and threats; and finally, the high level of legitimacy stemming from open democratic modes of governance.[28]

South Korea is often cited as a country with effective policy capacity and good security performance.[29] But this observation needs some clarification. While consensus on ends of security policy (i.e. threat from North Korea) is relatively high, there is ample fragmentation over means. The domestic political use of security policy instruments for regime security lowers the people's consensus on the means the government chooses and sometimes jeopardizes the existing national consensus on the ends *per se*. Moreover, the lack of institutional mechanisms to accommodate public opinion and to translate it into harmonious consensus is another barrier to the formation of a policy mood favourable to security policies.

Nevertheless, South Korea scores high on the decision-making and implementation side. An extremely homogeneous domestic population and the traditional executive dominance facilitate the formation of relatively comprehensive security policies and their speedy implementation. As in Israel, on the matter of security policies, there are neither segmented views, nor artificial bureaucratic compartmentalization. Domestic resources are well extracted and fully mobilized for security purposes. Ironically, however, the excessive concentration of decision-making power in the hands of the executive branch, especially the military, tends not only to undermine national consensus, but also to produce rigid policy outcomes.

Israel and South Korea provide an interesting contrast. In

Israel liabilities stemming from political and communal pluralism are overcome by high political legitimacy, leading to adaptive and effective policy capacity. In South Korea, on the other hand, lower levels of political legitimacy appear to affect its policy capacity negatively, thus decreasing the value of assets derived from the unusually high level of social and cultural integration. The Israeli and South Korean experiences demonstrate that countries which lack both integration and legitimacy may face the worst policy capacity. Lebanon provides a case in point. Political disintegration and the weak legitimacy of the Lebanese government make it impossible for the government to form any meaningful national consensus about goals and instruments of national security. While perceived goals vary from an unconditionally unified Lebanon and confederalism to partition, the assessment of threats is highly segmented along communal lines. The decision-making machinery is totally fragmented, making it impossible to have any co-ordination or articulation of policies across different government agencies. In the absence of consistence and coherence, implementation is virtually an impossibility. The government has been deprived of authority to extract and mobilize resources (e.g. tax collection and military deployment) and has been unable to impose any collective obligations on the people. This fractured policy capacity along with high threat and low capability makes Lebanon one of the most insecure nations in the world.

## TOWARDS A NEW TYPOLOGY OF
## THE THIRD WORLD NATIONAL SECURITY

We have argued that it is misleading to judge one's overall security posture solely on the basis of threat environment and the hardware side of security management. Any meaningful assessment of security performance in the Third World should be based on the elucidation of the dynamic interactions of security environment, hardware, and software. Ignoring the software side of security management weakens our understanding of the complexity of the relationships between input variables of threat and domestic capabilities to overall policy outputs and security performance. As we have shown, the software is an important unit of analysis in the Third World context not only because of its conversion function, but also due to its dynamic interactions with the security environment and domestic resources and capabilities.

*Figure 4.1* is an analytical illustration of possible security posture of developing countries. While the security environment is operationalized in terms of threat, the hardware side is indicated by capability. The software side is represented by policy capacity because two other components (i.e. legitimacy and integration variables) are usually crystallized in the form of policy capacity. In contrast with the conventional way of dichotomizing Third World countries into the weak and strong, we show eight different clusters (see *Figure 4.1*)

*Figure 4.1*

---

*A*: high threat, strong capability, adaptive policy capacity (Israel, Taiwan, and South Korea);

*B*: low threat, strong capability, adaptive policy capacity (most ideal case — no Third World countries fit this category);

*C*: low threat, strong capability, rigid policy capacity (Argentina, Brazil, Mexico);

*D*: high threat, strong capability, rigid policy capacity (Egypt, Iraq, Iran, Morocco);

*E*: high threat, weak capability, adaptive policy capacity (Kuwait, Thailand);

*F*: low threat, weak capability, adaptive policy capacity (Singapore, Malaysia);

*G*: low threat, weak capability, rigid policy capacity (Ghana and most developing countries);

*H*: high threat, weak capability, rigid policy capacity.

---

According to our typology, the most secure countries are those which belong to group B (low threat, strong capability and adaptive policy capacity). In reality, however, no such countries exist. Group F represents the second most secure group. Despite its weak capability, it is characterized by low threat and highly adaptive policy capacity, ensuring sound security posture. Singapore and to some extent Malaysia may be classified in group F. Countries belonging to groups A and C are good candidates for acceptable security posture. For group A, the high threat environment is managed by strong capability and adaptive policy capacity (e.g. Israel, Taiwan, and South Korea). For group C, rigid policy capacity reduces the effectiveness of national security management, but low levels of threat and strong capability allow a stable security posture. In our classification, Brazil, Mexico and Argentina belong to this group. Group E represents a cluster of countries with a precarious security position. High threat environment and weak domestic capability make them vulnerable. None the less, their adaptive policy capacity may allow them to enjoy some degree of security. Buffer states such as Switzerland and Austria are good examples of this group. However, Third World countries such as Kuwait and Thailand may also fall into this category.

Countries belonging to both groups D and G are relatively insecure. For group D, strong capability is a definite asset to national security, but rigid policy capacity makes it difficult to translate such an asset into effective management of high tension and threats. Most Arab states engaged in regional conflicts belong to this category. Group G typifies most developing countries which do not have any immediate and clear external threats. Scarce resources, weak capabilities, and fragile policy capacities make them extremely vulnerable in the event of crisis. Moreover, structural rigidity often leads to increased internal insecurity. Group H represents the worst case of insecurity. High threat amidst weak capabilities and fragile policy capacities make group H countries virtually defenseless. Lebanon is a case in point.

The above typology is by no means a precise one. Many countries do not fall into these analytical clusters, but somewhere between. Moreover, the operationalization of indicators of threat, capability and policy capacity is subjective. Context plays a major role in defining and redefining security and insecurity. Our classification, however, helps us in capturing the relative distance and variety of the Third World national security realities in a more holistic, yet dynamic and disaggregated, manner.

## NOTES

[1] See Edward A. Kolodziej and Robert E. Harkavy (ed.), *Security Policies of Developing Countries* (Lexington, MA: Lexington Books, 1982), pp. 16–19. For the general context, see Daniel J. Kaufman, J.S. McKitrick and T.J. Leney, *U.S. National Security: A Framework for Analysis* (Lexington, MA: Lexington Books, 1985), pp. 3–26.

[2] For example, see Ray S. Cline, *World Power Trends and the U.S. Foreign Policy for the 1980s* (Boulder, CO: Westview, 1980), pp. 143–69; and Hans Morgenthau, *Politics among Nations* (New York: Alfred A. Knopf, 1985), pp. 146–69.

[3] These variables are seldom discussed in the context of national security. They have been rather linked to the issue of domestic instability and internal insecurity. There are exceptions, however. See Barry Buzan, *State, Fear and International System* (Brighton: Wheatsheaf, and Chapel Hill: University of North Carolina Press, 1983); Robert L. Rothstein, 'The Security Dilemma and the Poverty Trap in the Third World', *Jerusalem Journal of International Relations*, vol. 8, no. 4 (1986), pp. 1–38; Edward E. Azar and Chung-in-Moon, 'Third World National Security: Toward a New Conceptual Framework', *International Interactions*, vol. 11, no. 2 (1984), pp. 103–35; Abdul-Monem M. Al-Mashat, *National Security in the Third World* (Boulder, CO: Westview, 1985).

[4] Kal Holsti, 'Changes in the International System: Interdependence, Integration and Fragmentation', in K. Holsti *et al.*, *Changes in the International System* (Boulder, CO: Westview Press, 1980), pp. 22–54.

[5] We owe the concept of policy capacity to Davis Bobrow and Steve Chan. See their 'Learning from Success: Japan, Taiwan and South Korea' (mimeo, 1985), and 'Assets, Liabilities and Strategic Conduct: Status Management by Japan, Taiwan and South Korea',

*Pacific Focus: Inha Journal of International Studies*, vol. 1, no. 1 (1986), pp, 23–56.

[6] Cline, *World Power Trends*, pp. 143 and 166.

[7] Morgenthau, *Politics among Nations*, pp. 146–169.

[8] Henry Kissinger, 'Domestic Structure and Foreign Policy' in James Rosenau (ed.), *International Politics and Foreign Policy* (New York: Free Press, 1969), p.267.

[9] Dina Zinnes and J. Wilkenfeld, 'An Analysis of Foreign Conflict Behavior of Nations' in W.F. Handrieder (ed.), *Comparative Foreign Policy* (New York: David McKay, 1971), pp. 193–208; Rudolph J. Rummel, 'The Relationship between National Attributes and Foreign Conflict Behaviours' in J. David Singer (ed.), *Quantitative International Politics: Insights and Evidence* (New York: Free Press, 1968), p. 205; Patrick J. McGowan (ed.), *Sage International Yearbook of Foreign Policy Studies*, Vol. 1 (Beverley Hills, CA: Sage, 1973).

[10] Hans Gerth and C.W. Mills (ed.), *From Max Weber: Essays in Sociology* (New York: Oxford University Press, 1958), pp. 77–83; Seymour Martin Lipset, *Political Man: The Social Base of Politics* (Garden City, NJ: Doubleday, 1960), p. 77; Richard M. Merelman, 'Learning and Legitimacy' *American Political Science Review*, vol. 60, no. 3 (1966), p. 548.

[11] For an overview of legitimacy crises in developing countries, see Leonard Binder, *et al.*, *Crises in Political Development* (Princeton, NJ: Princeton University Press, 1972); Samuel P. Huntington, *Political Order in Changing Societies* (New Haven, CT: Yale University Press, 1968); Michael Hudson, *Arab Politics* (New Haven, CT: Yale University Press, 1978).

[12] See Chapter 9 in this volume.

[13] For the issue of national security and regime security in Argentina, see Chapter 8 in this volume.

[14] For security and foreign policy behaviour of Arab states, see Bahgat Korany and Ali Dessouki (eds), *The Foreign Policy of Arab States* (Boulder, CO: Westview Press, 1984); and R. McLaurin, L. Snider and D. Peretz, *Middle East Foreign Policy* (New York: Praeger, 1982). For South Korea, see Azar and Moon, 'Third World National Security'.

[15] See Mohammed Ayoob, 'Security in the Third World: The ‛Worm About to Turn?' *International Affairs*, vol. 60, no. 1 (Winter 1983–4), pp. 41—51.

[16] On contending interpretations of national value, see Arnold

Wolfers, *Discord and Collaboration* (Baltimore, MD: Johns Hopkins University Press, 1962), p. 150; Ian Bellamy, 'Toward A Theory of National Security', *Political Studies*, vol. 29, no.1 (1981), p. 102; F. Trager and P.S. Kronberg (ed.), *National Security and American Society* (Lawrence, KS: University Press of Kansas, 1973), p. 36; Kaufman, McKitrick, and Leney, *U.S. National Security*, p. 6; Robert Osgood, *Ideals and Self-Interest in American Foreign Relations* (Chicago: University of Chicago Press, 1953), p. 443.

[17] Karl Deutsch, *Nationalism and Social Communication* (Cambridge, MA: MIT Press, 1966); Samuel Huntington, 'Modernization, Development and Politics', *Comparative Politics*, vol. 3, no. 3 (April 1971), pp. 283–322.

[18] Walker Connor, 'Nation-Building or Nation-Destroying', *World Politics*, vol. 24, no. 3 (1972), p. 321.

[19] Lewis Snider, 'Political Disintegration in Developing Countries: Theoretical Orientations and Empirical Evidence', *International Interactions*, vol. 11, no. 2 (1984), pp. 137–66.

[20] Donald L. Horowitz, 'Patterns of Ethnic Separatism', *Comparative Studies in Society and History*, vol. 23 (April 1981), pp. 165—95.

[21] See Ronald McLaurin (ed.), *The Political Role of Minority Groups in the Middle East* (New York: Prager, 1979); Cynthia H. Enloe, *Ethnic Conflict and Political Development* (Boston: Little, Brown, 1973).

[22] Edward E. Azar, Paul Jureidini and Ron McLaurin, 'Protracted Conflicts in the Middle East', *Journal of Palestine Studies* (Autumn 1978), pp. 41—69; Edward Azar and Steve Cohen, 'Peace as Crisis and War as *Status Quo*', *International Interactions*, vol. 6, no. 2 (1980), pp. 159–84; E. Azar, R. Marlin and Chung-in Moon, 'Protracted Social Conflicts: Some Empirical Findings' (mimeo, 1985).

[23] Lewis Coser, *Social Functions of Conflict* (New York: Free Press, 1958).

[24] For the issue of national security as an instrument of integration, see Avner Yaniv, 'Integration and National Security: The Case of Israel', *International Interactions*, vol. 11, no. 2 (1984), pp. 193–217.

[25] On the discussion of policy capacity in the Third World context, see Merilee S. Grindle (ed.), *Politics and Policy Implementation in the Third World* (Princeton, NJ: Princeton University Press, 1980).

[26] Stephen Haggard and Chung-in Moon, 'Industrial Change and

State Power: The Politics of Stabilization in South Korea' (mimeo, 1986).

[27] Gunnar Myrdal, *Asian Drama: An Inquiry into Poverty of Nations* (New York: Pantheon, 1968), pp. 66–7.

[28] S.N. Eisentstadt, *The Transformation of Israeli Society* (Boulder, CO: Westview Press, 1985); Amos Perlmutter, *Military and Politics in Israel: Nation-Building and Role Expansion* (New York: Praeger, 1982).

[29] See, for example, Cline, *World Power Trend*.

# 5. Ideology and Security: Self-Reliance in China and North Korea[1]

HAN S. PARK and KYUNG A. PARK

National security is as much a psychological concept as it is a physical one, a fact that is clearly evident in the politics of the nuclear arms race between the superpowers. The idea of 'deterrence' itself is primarily a psychological phenomenon, involving as it does calcuations of the behavioural dispositions of an adversary state. In this sense, a complete understanding of a nation's security cannot be based solely on estimations of its military capability. Nor is the need to include the psychological dimensions in conceptualizing national security limited to the superpowers. In fact, the need might be more acute in the study of Third World countries as many of them, especially those in the non-aligned bloc, have declared self-reliance to be a vital component of their national security.

In this context, Azar and Moon appropriately point out that 'an exclusive military strategic approach to the study of national security is not only narrow but also misleading'.[2] Their contention that national security should be defined to include non-military components such as economic vulnerability, ecological scarcity, and ethnic fragmentation is a healthy departure from the conventional monolithic definition based on a military strategic orientation. However, we would go further and add that a more serious problem lies in the tendency to define national security only in quantitative terms; even though those terms may go beyond computations of military might. The military and economic 'power commodities' that are considered as requisite conditions for national security are evaluated and measured exclusively in terms of quantities of military and economic assets, and from this perspective more is always better. However, contemporary national security issues in the Third World cannot be completely accounted for by such quantitative assessments alone. It is all too obvious that morale is a vital element of an army, especially when there is a dearth of conventional 'power commodities'. This tendency is especially evident in the 'revolutionary' armies of socialist states, such as China under Mao Zedong and North Vietnam under Ho Chi Minh.

The non-material aspects of national security are evident in the doctrine of self-reliance in two ways. First, the doctrine itself constitutes an integral part of the goal of national security. Self-reliance, conceived of as an absence of any reliance on other nations for the economic or military assets necessary for national survival, is itself considered a valuable component of national defence, along with more conventional power commodities such as military strength and economic capability. This sacred goal of national self-reliance is promoted as an ideological precept that serves to unify the nation in the face of foreign threats, as we have seen in China's Maoism and North Korea's *Juche*. Second, self-reliance works as a criterion for assessing other components of national security. In assessing military preparedness, for example, it is not only the size of the nation's military forces and the amount of available weapons, but also the mental quality of its military personnel and the nation's control over the supply of military hardware that makes it more secure. The same idea may be applied to the economic sector in that a self-reliant economy is valued highly in consideration of national security. In short, being reliant on others for military personnel, weapons, and the economic requisites of national security can render a nation's security rather precarious, even though the foreign-supplied weapons may be of better quality than those that the nation could provide itself.

This chapter is specifically designed to examine the relevance and role of self-reliance in national security in the Third World with specific reference to China and North Korea as the exemplary cases. These two Asian countries, although dissimilar in size and geopolitical characteristics, are similar in that both have effectively incorporated the doctrine of self-reliance into their ideological systems. To Kim Il Sung, national self-reliance is not merely a political slogan but also a central policy guideline, as it was to Mao. We shall examine the way in which the idea of self-reliance has affected domestic and foreign policies in the two countries. But we shall first examine theoretical and conceptual issues pertaining to the doctrine of self-reliance.

## SELF-RELIANCE FOR NATIONAL SECURITY

### Self-Reliance as Ideology

As long as an ideology is a belief system that affects every aspect of social life, the belief construct of self-reliance has to be seen as an ideological doctrine intended to justify certain policy orientations. Self-reliance as a belief system is essentially ethnocentric in that it promotes a *Weltanschauung* that a people have a unique character and a superior heritage that enables them, as a nation, to nurture their own existence in relative autonomy from other societies. In this way, the self-reliance doctrine can lead to spiritual or ideological determinism of political life. Even when this occurs in 'Marxist' societies, such as Mao's China and Kim's North Korea, the socialist premise of economic determinism is superseded by an ideological voluntarism that is also manifest as a guiding principle for building national security.

### Self-Reliance and Dependency

While self-reliance may be viewed as a form of nationalism, it is rather specific in defining national interests to be served only by the ability to sustain economic self-sufficiency, political sovereignty, military self-defence, and cultural independence. Thus, proponents of self-reliance argue that national security will be jeopardized when the country is unable to control its own destiny or its reliance on other nations for any or all of these assets. Accordingly, they maintain that it takes more than sheer military power or economic capability to preserve the country and its people from external threat; it will ultimately require the ability and the will of the people to resist domination by superior powers. And domination is conceived of here not only as military threat but also as economic, political, and cultural dependence.

Obviously, it is difficult for a Third World country that is incapable of producing weapons necessary for its own defence to implement the idea of self-reliance in the conventional sense. As a way of offsetting this problem, many Third World countries have opted to make up for a lack of technological sophistication in weaponry with a strong sense of ideological commitment on the part of their troops and their citizenry. For instance, the idea of a people's militia, which has been popular in many socialist systems, may be seen as an effort to convert the 'people' into valuable military asset against technologically superior forces. In fact, the concept of citizens' militias has been widely accepted in the non-aligned countries as a viable alternative to the conventional military preparation. The militia army can be advantageous when there is no combat frontline and the conflict is characterised by a guerrilla warfare.

Economic self-reliance is a central idea embedded in the various forms of dependency theory. This theory attributes the economic poverty of the Third World to the systematic and continuous exploitation of resources and human capital by the developed industrial world. Thus, economic growth through the promiscuous invitation of foreign investment is viewed a sure way to dependency and neo-colonialism that ultimately cripples the economy and impoverishes the people. Proponents of self-reliance argue that it is imperative for a Third World country to be self-sufficient at least in the area of basic necessities, especially food, that an export-orientated economy drives the country further into foreign dependency, and that a desirable development strategy is to diversify production through a balanced growth of all sectors of the economy. Of course, these ideals of economic self-reliance are often unrealistic in many countries whose only assets are cheap labour and raw materials.

To compensate for the military and economic disadvantages inherent in the policy of self-reliance, many Third World countries emphasize the importance of ideological and spiritual commitment, which, in the extreme, can lead to fanatic ethnocentrism. For example, many Chinese foreign policy measures during the Cultural Revolution were irrationally ideological. A dramatic example was evidenced by the fact that China even refused to accept relief goods from the West for earthquake victims in 1976 because it would have violated the noble cause of national self-reliance. During the Vietnam War, it was clearly demonstrated, however, that the spiritual and ideological preparedness of an army, manifested in high morale and determination, can make a vital contribution to the outcome of a military conflict.

The concept of national security entrenched in the doctrine of self-reliance rejects the simplistic measurement of military strength in numerical terms. When weapons are provided by external sources over which the nation has little control, possessing large quantities of equipment in the country does not necessarily enhance national security. The nation in this case can be subservient to and constrained by the 'donor' country. The same analysis can be applied to the economic sector. It is suggested that vital national security interests will be served by economic independence more so than by the sheer quantitative value of economic output.

In this way, self-reliance can be a powerful ideology which enhances the impact of conventional national security assets. How important, then, is the value of self-reliance in a nation's 'hierarchy of values'? Is the nation's self-reliance, for example, more important than the basic human rights of the people? That is, can the persistence of economic poverty and the denial of civil liberties be justified in defence of self-reliance? Azar and Moon suggest that the structure of 'vital' values for a given society is not constant, and conclude that 'during periods of acute economic depression or external economic disturbances, the hierarchy of 'vital' values may shift in favour of economic ones, and thereby outpace other core values previously perceived and agreed upon'.[3] In an attempt to answer these crucial questions, we shall present a set of contextual and political characteristics of a nation that might promote the value of self-reliance. Accordingly, when those conditions are more evident, the value of self-reliance is expected to be more crucial.

## Conditions for Self-Reliance

Several national characteristics may promote doctrines of self-reliance. First of all, the experience of colonialism or other forms of foreign domination may encourage a self-reliance ideology. Such an experience produces a profound sense of national humiliation for many colonies. When national independence results from a prolonged anti-colonial struggle, the leaders of a new regime can become passionately antagonistic against their former colonial masters. These Third World leaders often retain mass support by prolonging the anti-foreign sentiment. In this sense, self-reliance becomes a nationally accepted ideology by perpetuating the anti-colonialism of bygone days, and by urging continued vigilance against external aggression.

Another factor contributing to self-reliance might be found in the geopolitical conditions of the nation. Self-reliance can be encouraged when the nation is surrounded by one or more hostile nations that are either supported by hegemonic powers or are such powers themselves. A hegemonic power here can become directly linked to a 'surrogate' nation through military, economic, and cultural assistance. Where action through a surrogate proves to be infeasible, the hegemonic power can attempt to overthrow the regime by sponsoring a resistance movement within the country. Indeed, the USA and the Soviet Union have consistently been criticized for aiding insurgent forces in

Third World countries, as has been the case recently in Angola, El Salvador, Nicaragua, Afghanistan, and Kampuchea, to name a few.

Such foreign intervention, whether direct or indirect, can awaken nationalist sentiment in the population and can provide the regime with a convenient excuse to suppress political opponents and dissidents in the name of national security.

Thirdly, the ideal of self-reliance can be promoted most effectively in a nation with an ethnically homogeneous population. When a nation's population contains significant ethnic groups whose origins can be traced to other countries, a doctrine of self-reliance can be counter-productive, especially when its policies threaten to jeopardize the links between the indigenous ethnic group and their compatriots abroad. Relatedly, a self-reliance doctrine that includes hostility towards nations in which large numbers of that ethnic group reside could likewise antagonize indigenous members of the ethnic group and thereby undermine their support for the regime and its doctrine of self-reliance. Therefore, national self-reliance is far easier to implement in a nation with a population that is relatively homogeneous and isolated from the external world.

Fourthly, we might point out that the political doctrine of self-reliance can be facilitated by the presence of strong national pride and even ethnocentrism in the heritage of the people. In this case, the people may feel that their cultural achievements are superior to those of other nations, even if the latter may enjoy economic and military superiority. Here, the principle of self-reliance serves such a proud people as a remedial solution to the problem of the incongruence between their cultural achievement, on the one hand, and economic/military backwardness, on the other. Thus, the ideology can work as a compensatory force for the inability to achieve the conventional 'power commodities' of national security.

Finally, the doctrine of self-reliance is most likely to appear in a nation that is striving for political integration, having already achieved the initial stage of regime formation. A nation in this stage is expected to secure ideological solidarity in order for the regime to consolidate its power base among the masses. This nation is most likely to be a pre-industrial society, and, therefore, lacking in the conventional 'power commodities'. In such circumstances, the less costly, intangible elements of self-reliance are more attractive. However, when policy goals shift to industrialization and resource expansion, the doctrine could prove to be counter-productive. In this sense, self-reliance can be seen as a principle with varying degrees of utility depending upon the stage of socioeconomic and political development.[4]

Thus far, we have identified a few salient characteristics of a nation that might facilitate the emergence of the self-reliance doctrine. These characteristics appear to be not only empirically germane to many non-aligned countries that have adhered to the principle of self-reliance as a policy objective, but they are theoretically plausible as possible conditions for the principle.

## Policy Implications of Self-Reliance

Once the principle of self-reliance is adopted as a policy goal, specific policy actions will follow. Given the above-mentioned conditions that are conducive to adoption of this principle, we can infer a set of specific policy directions that are expected and commonly observed in many Third World countries.

In order to generate popular support while denying the people substantial improvements in material well-being, the government needs to make extraordinary efforts to legitimize its power. In these efforts, the leadership invariably adopts an official ideology with which to indoctrinate and mobilize the people. With the help of such an ideology, a regime that is incapable of providing the people with material incentives and economic opportunities can solidify its power base by means of mass mobilization. It is, in this sense, the mass mobilization that provides justification for political purges. Mass mobilization here is made possible by political indoctrination of the people with

intense measures of ideological education. A most effective
ideology for this purpose is some variety of passionate
nationalism. The above-mentioned conditions of colonial
experience and ethnic homogeneity can be especially help-
ful in the politicization and mobilization of the masses.

The politicization of the people requires active involvement of the government in all social institutions in which
political socialization takes place. At schools of all levels,
textbooks and other required readings will be written by the
government and the content of curricula will be uniform
throughout the country and designed to perpetuate the
official norms and values in the mass belief systems. In the
curricula, scientific and technological education will generally be secondary to political and ideological education. The
government will also penetrate into the religious sector. It is
highly unlikely for the regime to tolerate religious diversity
or freedom of religious activities, especially when these are
of foreign origins. However, if religion is a fundmental
element of national identity, and if its precepts are not in
conflict with the goals of the regime, it may be adopted as a
foundation upon which to build a new political culture that
is supportive of the regime and its policies of self reliance.

Another area of government control for mass politicization are the mass media. It is more likely that the
government itself publishes newspapers and operates the
radio and television broadcasting services, seldom allowing
private operations. It is absolutely essential for the government to be able to manipulate the content of the message
transmitted through the mass media if it is to indoctrinate
the people effectively. The uniformity of political socialization can be easier in an ethnically homogeneous nation
with a common cultural heritage that itself, as pointed out
earlier, is a condition conducive to self-reliance.

As yet another strategy to promote self-reliance, the
regime often maintains a closed system, tightly insulated
from the external world. By preventing direct contact with
other societies or withholding information about them, the
regime can operate to socialize the population more effectively into beliefs that are supportive of it and its goals.
Additionally, when a closed system interacts with other

societies it will use mainly the official channels of the government. Economic and cultural exchanges with other societies will be extremely limited and controlled, especially when they are with those professing ideologies incompatible with the regime's own. A neo-political situation in which the nation is surrounded by hostile neighbours can work as an impetus for maintaining such a closed system. Thus, the closure of the society and the doctrine of self-reliance can reinforce each other, as the latter is essentially an anti-foreign and ethnocentric doctrine.

Finally, for a regime in an economically backward country to implement policies that are not designed to alleviate economic difficulties immediately, it is often imperative to employ the policy measures of a dictatorial police state. Such a state will utilize what is referred to as the 'politics of fear', in which government surveillance and political sanctions against 'impure' elements are commonplace. In this way, the leadership can maintain its power position by physically suppressing opponents and dissidents. However, a police state cannot prolong its stability without the ability to generate emotional support from the masses. This emotional popular support can be most effectively mobilized by a charismatic leader, who, by virtue of his own personal appeal, can rally considerable popular loyalty and, in time, transfer this loyalty to the institutions of the regime. A charismatic leader in this case is most likely to have been personally involved in the national independence struggle and the formation of the nation itself. Thus, the colonial experience as a facilitator of self-reliance becomes very essential to this kind of leadership. To such a leadership, the principle of self-reliance is a legitimate and useful ideology.

Thus far, we have discerned some policies that are likely to be adopted by a regime that proclaims self-reliance as a guiding doctrine. We shall shift our analysis to the concrete cases of China and North Korea in an attempt to examine empirically the policy directions and security implications of the self-reliance principle. The two countries not only manifest the conditions conducive to self-reliance but in fact pursued it.

## SELF-RELIANCE IN OPERATION: CHINA AND NORTH KOREA

### Conditions of China and North Korea

Of all the Third World nations that have proclaimed self-reliance, few have incorporated the principle as thoroughly as have Mao's China and Kim's North Korea. A cursory examination of the two countries indicates they have all the social, political, and cultural attributes that are conducive to the doctrine of self-reliance.[5]

Both countries have experienced in their recent history a profound sense of national humiliation: China since its defeat in the Opium War (1839) had been subjected to continuous foreign intervention that had forced it to make humiliating concessions. Later, the Japanese imperial forces dominated much of China and completely annexed Manchuria. In this respect, Mao's revolution was a nationalist revolution against foreign domination. As such, his ideology is a form of developmental nationalism, more than Marxist-Leninist socialism. Korea was liberated from Japanese colonialism as a result of Japan's defeat in World War II. Japanese colonial policies in Korea during its 36 years there (1910–45) were intensely exploitative and dehumanizing, as their imperial forces drained Korea's resources and labour force. Furthermore, Japan attempted to wipe out the identity of Koreans by forcing them to adopt Japanese names. This was a most profound experience of national humiliation which undoubtedly facilitated the adoption of a Korean ideology embodying the value of self-reliance.

These two Asian countries have also found themselves surrounded by hostile powers, reinforcing the appeal of the doctrine of self-reliance: China has invariably felt a threat from both hegemonic superpowers, especially during the Cultural Revolution (1966–76). North Korea's fear of external threat from the American-backed South Korea has never been allayed since the Korean War (1950–3), especially with the stationing of American troops in South Korea. When Sino-Soviet tension intensified during the Chinese Cultural

Revolution, North Korea was unable to secure economic and military assistance from either neighbouring Communist power, leaving Pyongyang even more fearful of this external threat.

Furthermore, North Korea, and especially China, have shown a pervasive sense of national pride in their cultural heritage, while their economic and material achievements have remained exceptionally backward. In fact, the Chinese notion of *Ch'ung Kuo* (centre of the universe) has always remained an integral part of China's belief system. In the case of Kim's North Korea, the extent to which national superiority is embedded in the political culture remains unmatched by any other country in contemporary world, as will be shown later.

Both countries are also highly homogeneous in the ethnic characteristics of their populations: despite the fact that there are some 55 minority nationalities in China, they make up less than 7 per cent of the total population, indicating that China is basically a nation of ethnic homogeneity, with the Han comprising more than 93 per cent of the population and sharing a common language and cultural heritage. North Korea's ethnic composition enjoys a universal homogeneity. In fact, according to George Kurian's *Book of the World Rankings*, North Korea is one of only two purely homogeneous ethnic nations in the world, the other being, not surprisingly, South Korea.

Finally, the condition of pre-industrialization is clearly evident in both countries. When Mao and Kim introduced the principle of self-reliance in their respective nations, both countries were in the stage of political integration where they were struggling with the task of power consolidation. Neither country was in a position to pursue industrialization and economic expansion.

It is quite obvious that both China and North Korea had all the sociocultural, geopolitical and economic attributes thought to encourage the adoption of the doctrine of self-reliance as an ideological construct and security measure. Both Mao and Kim made deliberate efforts to formulate their ideologies in accordance with the indigenous conditions. In defining Chinese socialism, Mao asserted that:

If we have only read the [Marxist] theory but have not used it as a basis for research in China's historical and revolutionary activity, have not created a theory in accordance with China's real necessities, a theory that is our own and of a specific nature, then it would be irresponsible to call ourselves Marxist theoreticians.[6]

In the process of adapting Marxism-Leninism to the unique Chinese conditions, Mao's ideology had to deviate profoundly from the orthodox socialism to the extent that it can best be characterized as a form of developmental nationalism.[7]

Kim Il Sung is in agreement with Mao in this regard. As early as 1955 he said:

It is important in our work to grasp revolutionary truth, Marxist-Leninist truth, and apply it correctly to the actual conditions of our country. There can be no set principle that we must follow the Soviet pattern. Some advocate the Soviet way and others the Chinese, but is it not high time to work out our own?[8]

Mao and Kim's perceptions of their countries were most pragmatic and they were candid in admitting to a backward economy, feudalistic social order, and underdeveloped technology. Furthermore, both used their colonial experience as the foundation for ideological articulations. We shall now examine the political implications of the doctrine as they have been exhibited in the political orientations and policy directions of China and North Korea.

## Self-Reliance and Ideology

The principle of self-reliance has been the backbone of the ideological systems in China and North Korea. Despite the fact that the two countries experienced different courses of regime formation, they have shown such a remarkable degree of similarity in their ideological expositions that North Korean ideology and the accompanying policies may be viewed as an emulation of the Chinese experience. Both Maoism and Kimilsungism may best be characterized more as specific varieties of developmental nationalism than as variants of Marxist Communism. To them, it is imperative that Marxism-Leninism be applied 'creatively' in line with historical conditions and national characteristics.

Mao's conception of 'joint dictatorship', for instance, undermines the centrality of 'proletarian dictatorship' in that all 'classes' in China were regarded as creative forces useful in eliminating foreign domination. The idea that a nationalist revolution must precede a socialist revolution, which was clearly imbedded in Maoism, was alien to orthodox Marxism-Leninism. In fact, the entire theory of a people's democracy that Mao advanced successfully in China is radically inconsistent with the party-based elitism of Lenin and, especially, Stalin. As to the nationalist aspect of North Korean ideology, one cannot say enough about the extreme ethnocentrism advocated by the heralded belief system of *Juche*. In fact, *Juche* (commonly translated as 'self-reliance') itself epitomizes the centrality of national self-reliance, and Kim Il Sung is claimed to be its inventor. According to the North Koreans, *Juche* is an ideology that represents a perfected, and therefore more advanced, version of Marxism-Leninism. They further maintain that only North Korea could create such an ideology for it alone had all the necessary 'subjective and objective' conditions.[9] Unlike China, North Korea has never gone through a revolutionary process to establish a socialist system. Since its inception, the 'revolutionary task' has been geared to the promotion of Kim's charismatic leadership on the ideological premise of nationalism and self-reliance.

Other evidence of Maoism's and *Juche*'s deviation from Marxist socialism is in their treatment of spiritual and ideological elements as a force of revolution. Despite their lip-service to Marxism-Leninism, they reject the fundamental socialist premise of economic determinism. It is not the Marxist economic base but the ideological 'superstructure' that guides the course of a revolution. China's ambitious Cultural Revolution itself was intended to create a 'new socialist man' as a prerequisite for building the material basis of a socialist state. The Chinese attempted to achieve this through political education rather than by changing the economic structure. North Korea's *Juche* is more directly rooted in a human determinist conception of social change: 'The *Juche* idea raised the fundamental question of philosophy by regarding man as the main factor, and elucidated the philosophical principle that man is the master of everything and decides everything'.[10] Thus, *Juche* promotes the view that it is ideological consciousness that determines and regulates all actions of man.

In both China and North Korea, political ideology has indeed been a powerful instrument of mass mobilization without which neither regime would have survived as long as it has. Such mass mobilization would not have been successful without the ideologies' appeal to the nationalist sentiment already widespread and deeply ingrained in the mass political culture. Mao initiated his mass mobilization movement through the mechanism of the Mass Line campaign. By appealing directly to the grassroots, Mao's leadership was able to consolidate its power-base more effectively. Political purges, especially those during the Cultural Revolution, were given legitimacy on the grounds of ideological purity. The Mass Line campaign was largely effective in mobilizing support for the regime, indoctrinating the people, and integrating the political system until its abuse by the radicals during the Cultural Revolution. North Korea's mass mobilization campaign was more direct and intensive due in part to the social dislocation and political turmoil following the Korean War. The process of political integration was more swift and complete in the small and ethnically homogeneous nation. Political consolidation was carried out forcefully by the authoritarian leadership of Kim Il Sung. With the presence of hostile enemies just across the demilitarized zone, the regime has been in an ideal position to mobilize the masses around the doctrine of *Juche*. This process was accelerated by the growing frictions between Beijing and Moscow in which North Korea had to maintain a policy of neutrality (i.e. self-reliance) because for obvious reasons she could not afford to antagonize either of the neighbouring Communist superpowers. The extent to which *Juche* has become pervasive in North Korea is evident in the description of the country as a 'nation of *Juche*'. Political indoctrination at all levels of the educational system, including 'on-the-job-training', has been uniformly intensive, and in all cases it is *Juche* that is taught.[11]

The principle of self-reliance has been effectively incorporated in policies of both nations, largely due to government manipulation of the mass media. All institutions of the mass media are closely censored, and often operated by the government, and any deviation on the part of journalists from the official line is subject to severe action, as we witnessed during the Cultural Revolution in China. In North Korea, the government operates all forms of mass media: it is particularly attentive to the radio because of the difficulty in controlling the short wave broadcasts from other countries, especially South Korea. In fact, the radio is an item not available in department stores for public purchase. There are only a limited number of publications made by government organs, and there is no way that the public can get information about the external world.

The manipulation of information by the government is further facilitated by keeping the society closed. China did not allow its 'bamboo curtain' to open to the West until the advent of 'ping-pong diplomacy' in 1971 and the ensuing pragmatic development after Mao's death. A cursory examination of Chinese foreign relations indicates that Beijing's political, economic, and cultural activities with other countries were severely restricted during the Cultural Revolution. The case of North Korea is even more extensive and thorough as her diplomatic relations were limited to the Soviet Union, China, and the Eastern European countries until the early 1970s.[12]

The principle of self-reliance ultimately helped both Mao and Kim cultivate their charismatic leaderships. Mao, as a nationalist leader who led a revolution against Japanese colonial power and the American-backed Chiang Kai-shek regime, gained the people's overwhelming support for his devotion to national independence and self-reliance. The Sino-Soviet split helped Mao's campaign for self-reliance and strengthened his charisma. In fact, Mao's reputation and recognition by the international community, especially the non-aligned world, attained pre-eminence because of his self-reliance ideology. To many Third World countries, Maoism represented a new world outlook that was seen as a genuine alternative to the 'hegemonic' ideologies of the superpowers. It was Maoism that appealed to the non-aligned world because of its premise that no alien ideology should be adopted without critical evaluation of its applicability to the unique national characteristics of the Third World.

Kim Il Sung's charismatic leadership surpasses even Mao's. It is more intensive, thorough, and pervasive in the North Korean political culture than was Mao's in China. Kim Il Sung, who has been in power continuously since the formation of the regime in 1948, built his charisma on the scenario that he, as a commander of guerrilla forces against the Japanese troops, had brought national independence. Without his heroism, so the North Koreans have been told, Korea would not have gained its independence (a point utterly inconsistent with the reality that Korean independence was a result of Japanese defeat in World War II). Kim is credited as the creator of the 'immortal *Juche*', a doctrine designed to free all the oppressed peoples of the world. As such, Kim is perceived by his people not only as their Great Leader but a global leader destined to save humanity from all forms of imperialist domination. In this sense, Kim has been elevated to the level of a religious founder with 19 million followers.

In short, China and North Korea have shown ideological constructs that are discernibly different from Marxism and, to a large extent, the difference can be attributed to their aspirations for national self-reliance. The ideologies have been thoroughly integrated into the belief system of both countries, especially North Korea, and profoundly affect virtually every aspect of social life. The self-reliance principle as the foundation of the ideologies has set the 'hierarchy of values' in the society and determined the direction of policies especially the policies of national security. We shall now examine the way in which the self-reliance principle has affected policy priorities pertinent to the national security of the two countries.

## Self-Reliance and National Security

As discussed earlier, the concept of national security in China and North Korea has been perceived in more inclusive terms than the 'power commodities' of military strength and economic power. Furthermore, the two countries have consistently maintained that a self-reliant defence and economic independence are indispensable components of national security.

### Military Self-Defence

The idea of self-defence has been incorporated into a number of policy measures in China and North Korea. According to *Juche*, 'the implementation of self-reliance in national defence is a military guarantee for the political independence and economic self-sufficiency of a country'.[13] Thus, military self-defence capability is a necessary condition for other areas and, therefore, it deserves top priority in policy-making. Without peace guaranteed by a strong military, economic planning and implementation are considered not feasible. Chang-ha Kim reiterates the North Korean official stand on this matter: 'When one relies on others in national defence, he is bound to study their faces and moods and cannot say freely what is in their minds. Any sensible man can easily find such cases in the events taking place on the international arena today'.[14] The rhetorical North Korean pronouncement, however, does not necessarily measure up with the actual performance, especially in Pyongyang's reliance on the Soviet Union for sophisticated weapons.[15]

*The Military Industry* In principle, it is imperative for any country's self-defence to be able to produce its own weapons. This requires economic resources and technological skills that most Third World countries are lacking. It is therefore necessary for them to concentrate disproportionately larger amounts of available assets in the military sector. This phenomenon is clearly evidenced in North

Korea's military spending over the years. When the doctrine of self-reliance was accentuated following the Sino-Soviet tension during the Chinese Cultural Revolution, North Korea spent nearly one-third of its national budget on the military sector (Table 5.1). According to the World Bank, Chinese military expenditure in the years 1961–83 has been between 31 and 48 per cent of total government expenditure. Although Chinese official sources show substantially less amounts, it is clear that the heavy burden of military spending has plagued other sectors of the economy, especially during the Cultural Revolution.[16]

The development of a military industry requires concurrent growth in the heavy industrial sector. Since China's Great Leap Forward programmes in the late 1950s, heavy industry has consistently outperformed other areas of the economy, though political slogans seldom neglected the agricultural sector in order to appease the overwhelmingly agrarian population. The successful testing of the atomic bomb in 1964, when the nation's economy was in the primitive stage, needs to be seen as evidence of China's determined effort to build a self-reliant defence capability, after the Soviet Union withdrew its nuclear weapons technicians and blueprints from China in 1960.

The North Korean military industry has been disproportionately strong in view of her overall economic stagnation, especially in the 1960s and 1970s.[17] In fact, since the mid-1960s, North Korea has been sending weapons as well as military personnel to a number of Third World countries. According to American and South Korean sources, more than 40 countries, primarily in Africa and Latin America, received military experts, and some 30 countries imported weapons from North Korea in the period 1966–82.[18] For a country with a GNP per capita of far less than $1,000, such military industrialization is almost unthinkable without the ideological rationale of building a self-reliant defence at the expense of other sectors of the economy, especially light industry.

*Politicization of the Military and the Militarization of Politics*   The practice of extensive ideological and political

*Table 5.1* **North Korea's Military Expenditures (in 10,000 North Korean won)**[a]

| Year | Local Government Expenditures (A) | Military Expenditures (B) | Bas % of A (C) |
|------|------|------|------|
| 1960 | 196 787 | 6 100 | 3.1 |
| 1961 | 233 800 | 5 917 | 2.5 |
| 1962 | 272 876 | 6 163 | 2.2 |
| 1963 | 302 821 | 6 359 | 2.1 |
| 1964 | 341 824 | 25 637 | 7.5 |
| 1965 | 347 613 | 35 109 | 10.1 |
| 1966 | 357 140 | 44 643 | 12.5 |
| 1967 | 394 823 | 120 026 | 30.4 |
| 1968 | 481 289 | 155 938 | 32.4 |
| 1969 | 504 857 | 156 506 | 31.0 |
| 1970 | 508 200 | 149 412 | 29.4 |
| 1971 | 630 168 | 195 982 | 31.1 |
| 1972 | 738 861 | 125 606 | 17.0 |
| 1973 | 831 391 | 128 034 | 15.4 |
| 1974 | 967 219 | 155 722 | 16.1 |
| 1975 | 1 136 748 | 186 426 | 16.4 |
| 1976 | 1 232 550 | 205 835 | 16.7 |
| 1977 | 1 334 920 | 209 582 | 15.7 |
| 1978 | 1 474 360 | 234 423 | 15.9 |
| 1979 | 1 697 260 | (256 287)[b] | 15.1 |
| 1980 | 1 883 691 | (275 019)[b] | 14.6 |
| 1981 | 2 033 300 | (300 928)[b] | 14.8 |
| 1982 | 2 254 600[a] | (326 917)[b] | 14.3* |

*Sources:*
*Tong'a yŏn'gam*, 1975, (Seoul: Tong'a Ubo-sa, 1975), p. 508: *Kita Chôsen Kenkyâ*, April 1975, pp. 23, 26; May 1976, p. 7; May 1977, pp. 8–9; May 1978, pp. 47–8; June 1979, pp. 24–5; May 1980, pp. 5–6: *Vantage Point*, May 1981, p. 14; April 1982, p. 15. All of these sources use North Korea's official budget reports.
[a] The exchange rate for the North Korean currency in 1972 was estimated by Koye S. Lee to be between 2.26 and 2.57 won to US$1.00 in terms of purchasing power parity. See his article 'An Estimate of South Korea's National Income', *Asian Survey* 12 (June 1972), pp. 521–5. In August 1981 the official exchange rate quoted in Pyongyang was 2 won to US$1.00.
[b] Since North Korea stopped publishing absolute figures for defence spending in 1979, the numbers in the parentheses were derived from percentages projected*, not actual expenditures.

training in the military curriculum was commonplace in Mao's China and has been so in North Korea. The Soviet Party-army models were expanded by the Chinese. The necessity of politically reliable troops in conducting a guerrilla war has meant that in China even more emphasis was placed on the political education of soldiers. Mao succeeded in developing the concept of a 'people's army' and the 'people's war' strategy in part because both elevated political commitment over military hardware as the key to victory. On this basis, the ability to match the technological sophistication of the enemy was downplayed, and therefore the need to buy foreign weapons systems or weapons technology was minimized, reinforcing the military dimension of self-reliance. The impact of these developments has been stated by Jane Price: 'The Chinese Communists . . . have made the military a major instrument for transforming Chinese institutions and society. In this capacity, the Red Army became the backbone of the Chinese Communist movement and the organizational model for other aspects of Communist political and social life'.[19] The increased emphasis on the political aspects of military training projected the Chinese Communist system well beyond the Soviet model. The Chinese system provided for political education of the officer and the soldier, ensured Party representatives in the military, and limited the commanders' authority strictly to military matters.

The role of the military in politics and, conversely, the politicization of the military can be seen in the extensive involvement of military personnel in politics. As shown in Table 5.2, there were 127 active military members present at the 9th Congress (1969) of the Central Committee of the Chinese Communist Party, representing 45.5 per cent of the 279 present, a massive increase from only 48 of the 193 members (24.9 per cent) at the 8th Congress (1956). Similarly extensive military involvement is observed in all areas of the Chinese power structure, as illustrated in Table 5.3. The evidence provided here indicates that the militarization of politics was most pervasive during the Cultural Revolution.

The fact that the involvement of the military in politics

*Table 5.2* **Active military Membership of the Central Committee of the Chinese Communist Party**

| Party Congress | Total | Regular | Alternate |
|---|---|---|---|
| 11th | 104 (31.2%) | 62 (30.8%) | 42 (31.9%) |
| 10th | 86 (27.0%) | 57 (29.2%) | 29 (23.4%) |
| 9th | 127 (45.5%) | 77 (45.3%) | 50 (45.9%) |
| 8th | 48 (28.2%) | 26 (26.8%) | 22 (30.1%) |

*Sources:*
Warren Kuo, 'The Political Power Structure in Mainland China', *Issues & Studies*, vol. 14 (June 1978), pp. 24–5; *China News Analysis*, 1093–94 (16 September, 1977); Galen Fox, 'Campaigning for Power in China During the Cultural Revolution Era 1967–76', (PhD dissertation, Princeton University, 1978) pp. 237–40

*Table 5.3* **Military representation in the Chinese power structure, 1969–71**

| Position | Total membership | Military men Number | (%) |
|---|---|---|---|
| Politburo | 25 | 10 | 44 |
| CC members* | 170 | 77 | 45 |
| Alternates | 109 | 50 | 46 |
| RC Chairman | 29 | 22 | 76 |
| First Secretaries of Prov. Committees | 29 | 22 | 76 |
| Secretaries & Deputy Secretaries of Prov. Committees | 158 | 95 | 60 |
| Ministers of the State Council | 29 | 20 | 69 |

*Sources:*
Donald Klein and Lois Hager, 'The Ninth Central Committee', *CQ*, 45 (Jan.–Mar. 1971), pp. 37–56; William Whitson, ed., *The Military and Political Power in China in the 1970s*, pp. 62, 118.

Various sources give somewhat different figures owing to differing interpretations of just what constitutes a 'military man', but the same trend is clear, e.g., Elegant calculates 56% representation, and Powell 47% for the military. See Robert Elegant, *Mao's Great Revolution*, p. 456, and Ralph Powell, 'The Party, the Government and the Gun', *Asian Survey*, 10 (June 1970), p. 45.

coincides with the emphasis on self-reliance has also been observed in North Korea. It was in the mid-1960s that a huge increase in military representation on the Politburo of the Korean Workers' Party occurred, and the trend has been sustained to the present (Table 5.4). This indicates that North Korea has adhered to the principle of self-reliance since the manifestation of Sino-Soviet tensions in the 1960s.

The politicization of the military has also been evident in its structure and management in both countries. In China, the role of commissars in the operation of the military was extensive and usually superior to that of military commanders. Military commissars are the political representatives dispatched by the Party. In order to ensure central Party control over the military, the Party encouraged a division of labour in the People's Liberation Army (PLA) between commander and commissar. The commissar system itself fell under the control of General Political Department, initially headed by Mao himself. With his doctrine of 'Learn from the PLA', Mao formalized support for the commissar that set the stage for the rest of the decade. The commissars generally overwhelmed the commanders. By the mid-1960s, the commissars and political cadres were setting up PLA-style political departments in the communes, schools, and factories, as well as government and party offices to help guide society in 'learning from the PLA'.[20]

North Korea has been explicit about the politicization of the military as a means of self-defense:

For implementing the principle of self-reliant defence, it is important to give full play to the politico-ideological superiority of the people's armed forces. The decisive factor for victory in war does not consist of weapons or techniques, but in the high political and ideological principles of the popular masses who are aware of the justice of their causes.[21]

In this way, the Pyongyang leadership has constantly emphasized the necessity of arming the masses as a matter of military strategy. By instilling in the mass belief systems the notion that the people's militia is an indispensable force of national defence, North Korea has provided military training to the entire people:

*Table 5.4* **Military representation in the Politburo of the Korean Workers' Party**

| Party Congress | 1st (1946) | 2nd (1948) | 3rd (1956) | 4th (1961) | 2nd Conf (1966) | 5th (1970) | 6th (1980) |
|---|---|---|---|---|---|---|---|
| Civilian | 11 | 13 | 13 | 15 | 14 | 12 | 24 |
| Military | 2 | 2 | 2 | 1 | 6 | 4 | 10 |
| Total | 13 | 15 | 15 | 16 | 20 | 16 | 34 |
| % = M/T | 15 | 13 | 13 | 6 | 30 | 25 | 29 |

*Source:*
Lee Suck-ho, 'Party–Military Relations in North Korea: A Comparative Analysis' (PhD dissertation, George Washington University, 1983), p. 283.

Modern warfare is three-dimensional . . . In fact, no demarcation line can be drawn between front and rear. Hence, in order to repel imperialist aggression successfully, all the people should be ready to fight with arms in hand, and the whole country be turned into a strong fortress.[22]

At every level of education and in all walks of life, the North Korean leadership has provided programmes designed to militarize the entire society. Combat training combined with political indoctrination constitutes a central element of the school curriculum. In all cases, the focal theme is national self-defence. In this sense, North Korea today resembles China during the height of the Cultural Revolution.

The idea of citizens' militias is not unique to China and North Korea. In fact, the militarization of the masses is important in all Third World countries pursuing a national strategy of self-reliance because it encourages local self-defence and and also increases mass participation. More importantly, as Biersteker observes, 'citizens' militias enhance national security by decentralizing national defence and making it virtually impossible to control the country by occupation of its capital city'.[23]

## Economic Self-Reliance

In order to promote economic self-reliance, the two countries have been adopting similar strategies, although post-Mao China has shown remarkable flexibility in economic policies. The self-reliance principle has been reflected in their domestic and international economic policies with varying degrees of success. Policy measures intended to promote self-reliance include the development of balanced economic growth, avoidance of trade deficits, indigenization of science and technology, preservation of raw material and fuel bases, and, most of all, the injection of the 'right spirit' into the mass belief systems.

By insisting on the necessity of spiritual preparedness to overcome the hardships and difficulties of building a self-reliant economy, Kim Il Sung has maintained that: 'As economic construction . . . is a revolutionary struggle, without the spirit of self-reliance one cannot understand the arduous and complex task facing the construction of an independent national economy. He who lacks the idea of self-reliance can do nothing'.[24]

At a time when most Third World countries experienced trade deficits, China generally enjoyed trade surpluses until 1978 when concerted efforts were made to accelerate industrialization (Table 5.5). North Korea has been less successful in controlling trade deficits as she has had to import large quantities of machinery and transport equipment as well as relying totally on foreign crude oil (Tables 5.6 and 5.7).

The economic policies of both countries have been geared to the construction of a balanced economy, although the heavy industrial sector has been given a primary concern, for as discussed earlier, this sector is directly linked to the military industry. This pattern is especially the case with North Korea where both agriculture and heavy industry have gained significant growth throughout the various economic plans. It is particularly noteworthy that North Korea has been agriculturally self-sufficient in spite of the fact that the northern half of the peninsula has traditionally been ill-suited for agriculture.

China opened her door to promote a more pragmatic form of development in the late 1970s, and this has led to mounting trade deficits as well as increasing volumes of trade with the West. In this decade, Chinese trade with non-Communist countries has reached nearly ten times that with Communist countries (Table 5.5). But the stability of the leadership of North Korea has made her unable and unwilling to change economic policies overnight. Unlike post-Mao China, North Korea has not opened her doors to the West despite an apparent new policy orientation toward pragmatism. As evidenced in Table 5.8, most of North Korea's trade has been with Communist systems.

Following the Chinese experience, North Korea adopted a joint venture law in 1984 for the purpose of inducing foreign investment. However, North Korea has been unable to attract foreign economic participation in any significant way. In fact, since the adoption of the law, only Koreans living in Japan have increased their economic activity in North Korea: there were 15 new joint ventures signed as of March

Table 5.5 China's foreign trade*

| Year | Total foreign trade (millions of dollars) | | | | Foreign trade with communist countries (millions of dollars) | Foreign trade with non-communist countries (millions of dollars) |
| | Turnover | Imports | Exports | Balance surplus (+) on deficit (−) | | |
| --- | --- | --- | --- | --- | --- | --- |
| | 89 | 90 | 91 | 92 | 93 | 94 |
| 1949 | | | | | | |
| 1950 | 1210 | 590 | 620 | 30 | 350 | 860 |
| 1951 | 1900 | 1120 | 780 | −340 | 975 | 920 |
| 1952 | 1890 | 1015 | 875 | −140 | 1315 | 575 |
| 1953 | 2295 | 1255 | 1040 | −215 | 1555 | 740 |
| 1954 | 2350 | 1290 | 1060 | −230 | 1735 | 615 |
| 1955 | 3035 | 1660 | 1375 | −285 | 2250 | 785 |
| 1956 | 3120 | 1485 | 1635 | 150 | 2055 | 1065 |
| 1957 | 3055 | 1440 | 1615 | 175 | 1965 | 1090 |
| 1958 | 3765 | 1825 | 1940 | 115 | 2380 | 1385 |
| 1959 | 4290 | 2060 | 2230 | 170 | 2980 | 1310 |
| 1960 | 3990 | 2030 | 1960 | −70 | 2620 | 1370 |
| 1961 | 3015 | 1490 | 1525 | 35 | 1685 | 1335 |
| 1962 | 2670 | 1150 | 1520 | 370 | 1410 | 1265 |
| 1963 | 2775 | 1200 | 1575 | 375 | 1250 | 1525 |
| 1964 | 3220 | 1470 | 1750 | 280 | 1100 | 2120 |
| 1965 | 3880 | 1845 | 2035 | 190 | 1165 | 2715 |

| Year | | | | | | |
|---|---|---|---|---|---|---|
| 1966 | 4245 | 2035 | 2210 | 175 | 1090 | 3155 |
| 1967 | 3915 | 1955 | 1960 | 5 | 830 | 3085 |
| 1968 | 3785 | 1825 | 1960 | 135 | 840 | 2945 |
| 1969 | 3895 | 1835 | 2060 | 225 | 785 | 3110 |
| 1970 | 4340 | 2245 | 2095 | 150 | 860 | 3480 |
| 1971 | 4810 | 2310 | 2500 | 190 | 1085 | 3725 |
| 1972 | 6000 | 2850 | 3150 | 300 | 1275 | 4725 |
| 1973 | 10 300 | 5225 | 5075 | −150 | 1710 | 8590 |
| 1974 | 14 080 | 7420 | 6660 | −760 | 2440 | 11 640 |
| 1975 | 14 575 | 7395 | 7180 | −215 | 2390 | 12 185 |
| 1976 | 13 275 | 6010 | 7265 | 1255 | 2345 | 10 930 |
| 1977 | 15 055 | 7109 | 7955 | 855 | 2520 | 12 535 |
| 1978 | 21 165 | 11 170 | 9995 | −1175 | 3145 | 15 020 |
| 1979 | 29 265 | 15 630 | 13 635 | −1995 | 3665 | 25 600 |
| 1980 | 38 140 | 19 940 | 18 100 | −1840 | 3970 | 34 070 |
| 1981 | 43 125 | 21 565 | 21 560 | −5 | 4570 | 38 555 |

* Figures rounded to the nearest 5.

Sources:
1950–1966: Nai-Ruenn Chen, *China's Foreign Trade, 1950–74* (1975), p. 145.
1966–1977: *Handbook of Economic Statistics* (1979), p. 102.
1978–1981: According to data from Deutsches Institut fur Wirtschaftsforschung, Berlin. Table adapted from Willy Kraus, *Economic Development and Social Change in the People's Republic of China* (New York: Springer–Verlag Inc., 1982), p. 341.

*Table 5.6* **Commodity composition of exports and imports (per cent)**

|  | Exports | | Imports | |
|---|---|---|---|---|
|  | 1968 | 1970 | 1968 | 1970 |
| Food | 11.4 | 10.8 | 10.4 | 9.0 |
| Beverages and tobacco | 3.8 | 3.8 | 0.0 | 0.0 |
| Crude materials, inedible | 16.1 | 20.9 | 9.5 | 6.2 |
| Mineral fuels | 0.8 | 0.6 | 19.5 | 16.1 |
| Animal and vegetable oils, fats | 0.0 | 0.0 | 1.6 | 1.1 |
| Chemicals | 3.3 | 1.1 | 4.7 | 2.9 |
| Manufactured goods | 54.0 | 41.4 | 11.0 | 7.7 |
| Machinery and transport equipment | 2.2 | 3.7 | 30.2 | 45.0 |
| Miscellaneous articles | 7.0 | 9.8 | 1.9 | 2.9 |
| Unclassified | 1.4 | 7.9 | 11.3 | 9.1 |
| Total (US$ million) | 181 | 228 | 221 | 281 |

*Source:*
Far East Research Centre of Yŏngnam University, *Pukhan Muyŏkron* (International trade of North Korea), pp. 347–48.

*Table 5.7* **Balance of trade 1970–9 (US$ million)**

| Year | Export (A) | Import (B) | Trade balance (A) — (B) | Ratio (%) (A)/(B) |
|---|---|---|---|---|
| 1970 | 366 | 439 | − 73 | 83 |
| 1971 | 310 | 690 | −380 | 45 |
| 1972 | 360 | 630 | −270 | 57 |
| 1973 | 510 | 750 | −240 | 68 |
| 1974 | 770 | 1,200 | −430 | 64 |
| 1975 | 690 | 930 | −240 | 74 |
| 1976 | 620 | 800 | −180 | 78 |
| 1977 | 690 | 770 | − 80 | 89 |
| 1978 | 950 | 960 | − 10 | 99 |
| 1979 | 1,150 | 1,160 | − 10 | 99 |

*Source:*
National Unification Board *Nambukhan Kyongje Hyonyhwang Pigye* (An economic comparison of North and South Korea), (Seoul, 1980), p. 67.

Table 5.8 **North Korea's foreign trade by major trading groups, 1970–9 (millions of dollars)**

| | 1970 | Percent of total | 1974 | Percent of total | 1978 | Percent of total | 1979 | Percent of total |
|---|---|---|---|---|---|---|---|---|
| North Korean imports ......... | 391 | 100.0 | 1,244 | 100.0 | 959 | 100.0 | 1,300 | 100.0 |
| of which: | | | | | | | | |
| Developed countries ......... | 47 | 12.0 | 638 | 51.3 | 285 | 29.7 | 390 | 30.0 |
| Less developed countries | 8 | 2.0 | 87 | 7.0 | 131 | 13.7 | 180 | 13.8 |
| Communist countries ...... | 336 | 85.9 | 519 | 41.7 | 543 | 56.6 | 730 | 56.2 |
| North Korean exports ......... | 332 | 100.0 | 727 | 100.0 | 1,027 | 100.0 | 1,320 | 100.0 |
| of which: | | | | | | | | |
| Developed countries ......... | 64 | 19.3 | 190 | 26.1 | 196 | 19.1 | 290 | 22.0 |
| Less developed countries | 11 | 3.3 | 98 | 13.5 | 200 | 19.5 | 270 | 20.5 |
| Communist countries ...... | 257 | 77.4 | 439 | 60.4 | 631 | 61.4 | 760 | 57.6 |

Source:
East–West Trade: The Prospects to 1985 (US Congress: Joint Economic Committee, 1982), p. 193.

1984, and 11 of them were with the Korean Japanese.[25] The North Korean inability to succeed with pragmatic economic measures such as the joint venture effort seems to suggest that the principle of self-reliance might inhibit open-door economic policies.[26] In fact, even in China the pragmatic measures by the present leadership have recently been under attack because of the 'spiritual pollution' they are said to cause. In memory of the tenth anniversary of the death of Mao Zedong, *Beijing Review* (8 September 1986) reminded readers of the importance of the doctrine of self-reliance, advocated originally by Mao and further promoted by Zhou Enlai. The magazine cites Mao as saying: 'China must be independent ... Chinese affairs must be decided by the Chinese people themselves, and no further interference, not even the slightest, will be tolerated from any imperialist country'. Zhou echoed this when he said: 'With respect to foreign relations, we have a basic stand: we uphold China's national independence and the principle of . . . self reliance'. The seemingly renewed emphasis on self-reliance in China has resulted in the adoption of a resolution on 'the Guiding Principles for Building a Socialist Society with an Advanced Culture and Ideology' at the Sixth Plenary Session of the 12th Central Committee of the Chinese Communist Party on 28 September 1986. This resolution harshly criticizes the recent social and economic consequences of the open-door policies and private incentives. It further confirms that: 'We resolutely reject the capitalist ideological and social systems that defend oppression and exploitation, and we reject all the ugly and decadent aspects of capitalism'. In this regard, the Chinese define the ethics desirable for 'socialism with Chinese characteristics' as meaning 'love of the motherland, and the people'.[27] In this way, the belief system of self-reliance solidly established under the Mao's leadership shows signs of revival.

North Korea, with a continuously stable regime under the charismatic leadership of Kim Il Sung, has seldom deviated from the principle of self-reliance. Given the widespread fear of an imminent threat from the American-backed South Korea, Pyongyang may have been forced to rely on military assistance from the Soviet Union and China; but it has achieved a credible degree of military independence to enhance national self-defence. Furthermore, the doctrine of self-reliance as the backbone of *Juche* has been the dominant policy guideline in the economic and political spheres of one of the most autarchical political systems in history.

## CONCLUSION

At a time when the national security of any given nation is intricately related to the security of other nations, it is imperative to establish a common understanding of the conditions and requirements that are believed to be essential for national security in different political systems. Considering the fact that threats to national security may be diverse throughout the global community, it is important to explore the property of the very concept of national security in a variety of situations.

It is for this reason that we have examined the concept of self-reliance as an integral element of national security in some Third World countries. More specifically, we have observed some policies and political orientations of China and North Korea, as the two systems seem to represent model cases in which national self-reliance is considered a requisite component of their security. The two cases clearly indicate that a nation may not be considered secure unless it is politically sovereign, economically self-sufficient, and militarily capable of self-defence. Furthermore, we have learned that the doctrine of self-reliance can be most effective when incorporated into the mass belief system. China and North Korea have demonstrated that self-reliance is not merely a political slogan. It has been a principle that has guided the policies in economic, political, military, and cultural arenas in both countries for a long period of time.

In view of the growing sentiment for national self-reliance throughout the world, China and North Korea do not seem to be isolated cases at all. Indeed, many Third World countries share the political, economic, and social characteristics similar to the two Asian countries indicating that self-reliance can be a relevant factor to their national security. However, in a world of mutual interdependence, especially in the economic area, nations today will find it difficult to maintain self-reliance policies in isolation from other countries. None the less, nations such as China and North Korea will continue to make self-reliant security measures as feasible as possible. To the extent that this is the case, a realistic understanding of national security cannot be made without considering the ideological aspect of self-reliance, particularly in the context of the Third World.

NOTES

[1] An earlier version of this paper was presented at the annual conference of the International Studies Association, South, in Atlanta, Georgia on 6–9 November 1986.

[2] Edward Azar and Chung-In Moon, 'Third World National Security: Toward a New Conceptual Framework', *International Interactions*, vol. 11, no. 2, p. 103.

[3] Ibid., p. 109.

[4] The theme that politicization of the people will be increasingly less effective as the society undergoes industrialization is discussed more fully in Han S. Park, *Human Needs and Political Development* (Cambridge, MA: Schenkman, 1984), especially in Chapter 6.

[5] A comparison of China and North Korea in terms of their strategies for development is comprehensively discussed in Kyung A. Park, 'Regime Legitimacy in China and North Korea' (unpublished doctoral dissertation, University of Georgia, 1984).

[6] From 'Reform in Learning, the Party, and Literature', a speech delivered at the opening of the Party school in Yenan on 1 February 1942, cited in *Chieh-fang jih pao*, 27 April 1942.

[7] Han S. Park, 'Changes in Chinese Ideology' in Gary K. Bertsch and Thomas W. Ganschow (eds), *Comparative Communism* (San Francisco: W.H. Freeman and Co., 1976), pp. 144–50.

[8] *Kim Il Sung: Selected Works* (Pyongyang: FLPH, 1976), Vol. 1, p. 591.

[9] On the subjective and objective conditions of *Juche*, see Han S. Park, 'Chuch'e: North Korean Ideology' in Eugene Kim and B.C. Koh (eds), *A Journey to North Korea* (Berkeley, CA: Institute of East Asian Studies, 1982), pp. 84–98.

[10] Chang-ha Kim, *The Immortal Juche Idea* (Pyongyang: FLPH, 1984), p. 42.

[11] For an account of North Korean education, see Sung Chul Yang, 'Socialist Education in North Korea' in Kim and Koh, *A Journey to North Korea*, pp. 63–83.

[12] The trend of North Korean foreign policy is concisely yet comprehensively discussed in Young C. Kim, 'North Korean Foreign Policy', *Problems of Communism*, January–February 1985, pp. 1–17; for an excellent collection of articles on North Korean foreign policy, see Jai–Kyu Park (ed.), *Bukhan ui Dae Woe Jung Chek* (Seoul: Kyungnam University Press, 1986).

[13] Kim, *The Immortal Juche Idea*, p. 324.

[14] Ibid., p. 325.

[15] Edward A. Olsen, 'North Korea' in James E. Katz (ed.), *Arms Production In Developing Countries* (Lexington, MA: Lexington Books, 1984), pp. 235–245.

[16] *World Military Expenditures and Arms Transfers* (Washington, DC: US Arms Control and Disarmament Agency), 1971 and 1985.

[17] For a further discussion on this point, see Joseph S. Chung, *The North Korean Economy, Structure, and Development* (Stanford, CA: Hoover Institution Press, 1974).

[18] Jong Chun Paik, 'Bukhan ui Kunsa Ryuk' in Park, *Bukhan ui Dae Woe Jung Chek*.

[19] Jane Price, *Cadres, Commanders, Commissars: The Training of Chinese Communist Leadership, 1920–1945* (Boulder, CO: Westview Press, 1976), p. 66.

[20] William W. Watson, *The Chinese High Command* (New York: Praeger, 1973).

[21] Kim, *The Immortal Juche Idea*, p. 328.

[22] Ibid., p. 327.

[23] Thomas J. Biersteker, 'Self-Reliance in Theory and Practice in Tanzanian Trade Relations', *International Organization*, vol. 34, no. 2 (Spring 1980), p. 234.

[24] Kim, *The Immortal Juche Idea*, p. 317.

[25] *Pukhan Chongram* (Seoul: Pukhan Yunkuso, 1985), p. 69.

[26] For an elaboration on this theme, see Han S. Park, *'Juche* as a Foreign Policy Constraint in the Democratic People's Republic of Korea', paper presented at the 27th annual meeting of the International Studies Association, Anaheim, CA, 25–29 March 1986.

[27] *Beijing Review*, 6 October 1986.

# 6. Economic Development and National Security

ETHAN B. KAPSTEIN

---

## ECONOMIC DEVELOPMENT AND NATIONAL SECURITY

According to the pure theory of international trade, states maximise social welfare by specializing in the production of goods in which they hold comparative advantage. Given that countries possess different combinations of land, labour and capital, such goods are those made with factors that the state has in relative abundance. Thus, the theory predicts that states which have abundant capital will exchange capital-intensive goods for the labour-intensive goods produced elsewhere.

Economists have noted for some time that the empirical data on trade provides only partial support for pure theory.[1] For a number of reasons, states have diverged from the dictates of comparative advantage, and have pursued the production of a wide range of goods. Many producers of primary goods, for example, have accepted the structuralist argument that they inevitably face declining terms of trade, and in response have sought economic diversification. Most industrial states continue to subsidise a substantial agricultural sector, owing to such diverse reasons as the political power of the farm constituency and the desire to maintain 'traditional rural values'.

This chapter examines the national security factor in economic development policy. Surprisingly, few post-war works on economic development explicitly address national security issues.[2] The academic literature tends to reflect a 'liberal' bias, in which the economic and politico-military spheres of state action are viewed as separate. As Robert Gilpin has written, 'for the liberal, the goal of economic activity is the optimum or efficient use of the world's scarce resources and the maximization of world welfare'.[3] National security is simply not perceived as a major goal of economic policy. The result is that economic development has been treated in the literature as if it were formulated without regard to the internal and/or external threats facing Third World regimes.

Unfortunately, this narrow 'economistic' view is also found in much of the contemporary writing on international political economy. David Mares, for example, suggests that 'national economic strategy may be outward- or inward-oriented; it may respond quite directly to international market forces, or it may insulate the domestic economy to a greater or lesser degree from them'.[4] Nowhere does Mares acknowledge that international forces other than *market* ones may be crucial to development policy.

Students of comparative politics have also adopted the economistic perspective. Thus, in a recent article, Stephan Haggard notes that many students of South Korean economic policy, focus on the 'economic ideologies prevailing among political elites and their technocratic allies'. Less attention has been paid to national security as a critical component of South Korean economic planning.[5]

This chapter discusses the link between economic and national security policies in Third World countries. Specifically, it will argue that national security concerns have influenced the scope, timing, and trajectory of economic development. National security has also played a role in determining the geographical location and ownership of those capital-intensive projects which are important to the military, and the choice of technology employed in the project.

In certain cases, such as South Korea and authoritarian

Latin America, 'national security' has even been used as an ideology of economic development, supplanting economic nationalism and other contending philosophies. This ideology identified Communism as the greatest threat to national economic progress, and it called for the creation of 'statist' regimes in which a combination of public enterprise, multinational direct investment, and local private economic activity provided for sustained growth and an indigenous military-industrial complex. By placing national security concerns along an East–West axis, Third World countries have also been able to solicit superpower economic support for their development programmes, thus making more resources available for investment or government spending.

II

One hypothesis stated at the outset of this chapter was that Third World states have allocated scarce resources to meet national security threats, and in so doing have influenced the timing and/or trajectory of economic development. In this section we will probe that hypothesis, drawing heavily on the developing world experience during the first half of this century, with special emphasis on Brazil.

Until the mid-twentieth century, little in the way of industrialization had taken place in the 'South'. Third World countries largely reflected comparative advantage by exporting primary products and importing capital goods. In many countries, economic life had barely changed since the early years of colonization.[6]

The outbreak of World War I caused a sea-change in these traditional trade patterns. Owing to domestic demand in the belligerent countries, and to wartime disruption of trade routes, the Third World suddenly lost access to imported capital goods, as well as to export markets. In the case of Brazil, along with much of Latin America, the war led to the development of light industry, and indeed industrial production tripled during the conflict.[7]

The experience of World War I contained many economic lessons for officials in the First and Third Worlds alike.

Above all, the war had been an industrial conflict which called for near-total economic mobilization. Steel and oil emerged as especially crucial commodities, in the absence of which a nation was militarily doomed. State support for the steel and fuel industries became a component of national security policy throughout Europe.[8]

Less well known is Third World attention to these economic lessons. In Brazil, the army came to play an increasing role in economic policy during the 1920s and 1930s, and it focused its concerns on the development of the steel and oil industries. The Constitution of 1891 was amended to read that 'mines and mineral deposits necessary for national security and the land in which they are found cannot be transferred to foreigners'.[9] The belief that an independent state must control its military inputs grew stronger during the 1930s, as Europe again headed toward conflict. As historian John Wirth has argued, it was clear to the Brazilian Army that it must build an industrial base 'in the event of war or blockade'.[10]

World War II provided another major spur to Brazilian industrial development. The Army's economic programme continued to focus on steel and oil, but now its efforts were aided by Brazil's alliance with the USA (Brazil was the only Latin American nation to send troops to Europe). In 1942, the Cooke Mission arrived from the USA with the objective of determining Brazil's potential economic contribution to the war. According to economist Werner Baer, the Mission called for 'a basic reexamination of the structure of the economy, with a view toward influencing the direction of its growth'.[11] Owing to common security concerns, the US assisted in the development of a Brazilian economy that could provide war material, with only partial consideration for the laws of comparative advantage. Most notably, the war resulted in the development of Volta Redonda, the great modern steel complex that was the crowning achievement of Getulio Vargas's *Estado Novo*.[12]

The crucial point to make regarding the above history is that external politico-military factors acted as the impetus to Brazil's economic development. The steel plant at Volta Redonda was built during the war because of its potential military contribution. It was a Brazilian Army project owing to the fact that the military was the first organization to recognize the need to overcome comparative advantage in order to meet national security requirements.

Volta Redonda reflected the impact of national security considerations on economic planning in other ways as well. First, and rarely mentioned in the development or political economy literature, was the *location* factor. The steel plant was located 50 miles inland, 'well beyond the range of naval gunfire'.[13] While it would have been more economic to locate the plant near the coast, security considerations overwhelmed economic ones. By placing the plant inland, Brazilian economic development shifted westward, breaking the economic hegemony of the coastal cities.

Second was the question of *ownership*. During the 1930s, Brazil had many opportunities to accept private, foreign direct investment in the creation of a steel industry. Given Brazil's limited domestic capital, and its lack of technology, the 'economic' choice would have been to accept one of these offers. Brazilian army officers, however, had visited many of the state-sponsored steel works in Europe, and were also aware that the Japanese, Soviet, and Turkish militaries were active in national steel programmes. This experience led them to 'oppose . . . turning over control of a key industry like steel to foreign interests'.[14] The choice of ownership, then, also reflected national security, in contrast to economic considerations.

Finally, we may note that *technological choice* mirrored security rather than economic factors. In the case of Volta Redonda, the Brazilians were determined to build a plant that could use low-quality and inefficient, but readily available, indigenous coal. Many foreign experts had told the government that the technology did not exist which could burn Brazilian coal. Undaunted, the military worked with German (until the war) and American engineers to find a solution. The development of a technology that used local coal was a victory of national security over economics: 'thus, in the event of war, continuous steel production, though expensive, would be assured; the primary military goal of self-sufficiency was attainable'.[15]

To summarize, the experience of war has significantly shaped Brazil's economic development. Although not a participant in World War I, the scope of state activity in the economy expanded during the conflict with the cut-off of trade, and afterwards owing to the economic lessons drawn by the military. World War II, in which Brazilian troops fought, provided a further stimulant to industrial development, with the USA now supporting Brazil's divergence from the trajectory determined by comparative advantage. These 'macro-political' factors aside, national security considerations played a role regarding the location, ownership, and technology of the steel industry. Clearly, external threats have played a key role in Brazilian economic history.

We must also emphasize that the story of Volta Redonda is not simply 'anecdotal' with regard to the impact of national security on economic development in Latin America. The world wars reverberated throughout the continent, forcing economic policy to cope with the loss of trade and with the demands of the armed forces.[16] The conclusion that must be drawn from this history is that economic development policy has responded to more than 'market' forces; it also responded to systemic politico-military crises.


III


The end of World War II saw the emergence of a bipolar international system in which the capitalist West and Communist East contended for hegemony. While the immediate post-war decade is often called a period of 'cold war', hot war erupted in Korea, and revolutionary activity engulfed many parts of the world, including such states as Cuba in which Communism ultimately prevailed. In the Third World, economic development policy accounted for internal and external security threats by allocating resources to the military-industrial sector, and by formulating growth policies that would hopefully satisfy the rising expectations of nascent middle classes.

South Korea provides an obvious example where

economic policy specifically addressed the state's security needs. Faced with the failure of United Nations troops to win a unified Korea during four years of warfare, President Syngman Rhee sought to create a military-industrial complex. In economic aid discussions with the USA, Rhee argued that South Korea's greatest needs were for 'an army and the heavy industry to support a large defence establishment'.[17] This theme was carried by President Park, whose major economic objective was to develop 'a military industrial capability sufficient to produce endogenous weapons systems'. During the latter part of the Park regime, more than 75 per cent of available investment funds went to 'the heavy industrial sector with linkages to the military industrial sector'.[18]

American economic assistance has been of vital importance to South Korea. During the period 1951–65, Korea received $6.8 billion in aid, or over 1.5 times its defence expenditures! According to economist Emile Benoit, 'such aid was clearly intended to make it possible for Korea to maintain a large military effort, and at the same time to achieve rapid economic progress which would strengthen the political support it could obtain from its own people'.[19]

Statistics reveal the continuing importance of the military in the South Korean economy. During the period 1970–82, defence expenditures rose from 23 per cent of the central government budget to 35 per cent. This increase has occurred, however, at a time of American troop withdrawals from Korea, and in 1975 the regime levied a 'special defence tax' to help finance the military-industrial sector. As this is being written, South Korea is engaged in a 'second plan of military modernization'.[20]

For South Korea, the primary 'cold war' threat has been external, and economic policy has attempted to respond to that threat by subsidizing the defence sector in non-inflationary fashion (i.e. through taxation and curbing of domestic consumption). In Latin America, the cold war presented a different set of challenges. The Communist threat was viewed as internal, though it often appeared that authoritarian regimes simply labeled every 'enemy' a Communist. Given the 'internal' nature of the threat, a unique set of economic development policies were designed which simultaneously attempted to allocate resources to the military while providing sufficient growth in domestic consumption to legitimize authoritarian rule.

For the military rulers of Latin America, the traumatic event of the cold war was unquestionably the Cuban revolution of 1958 and Castro's defeat of a conventional army. According to Fernando Cardoso, the armed forces

> adopted and adapted the Franco-American doctrines of internal warfare and became increasingly preoccupied with internal repression. They also became preoccupied with the necessity of implementing policies that promoted accelerated economic growth in order to pass quickly through the initial phase of economic 'take off' in which ... there is a greater likelihood that social revolution will occur.[21]

Unlike the purely military threat posed by an external aggressor, the internal Communist threat was viewed by the regimes in such countries as Argentina, Brazil, Uruguay, and Peru as multi-faceted. To be sure, internal revolutionary activity involved a struggle of contending military forces. But military leaders believed that revolution was nurtured on economic discontent, particularly among the middle class; Cuba, these rulers knew, had not been the poorest country in Latin America, and many of Castro's supporters were drawn from the bourgeoisie. The appropriate political 'solution', therefore, involved a combination of military counterinsurgency against revolutionary forces with an economic development programme that satisfied the rising expectations of the middle class.[22]

The counterinsurgency operational techniques employed by the armed forces in many Latin American countries during the 1960s required the use of relatively sophisticated military hardware. In Peru, 'strategic doctrine took full cognizance of the importance of a modern economic, especially heavy industrial, base to the conduct of sustained military operations'.[23] Between 1965 and 1968, nearly 20 per cent of Peruvian manufacturing output was destined for the defence sector. In Brazil, the comparable figure was 28 per cent.[24]

It would seem safe to assume that military outlays like

those cited above would undercut economic policies bent on rapid growth and the production of consumer durables. In his pioneering study of defence and economic development, however, Emile Benoit discovered otherwise. Defence programmes, he argued, 'make some positive contribution to the civilian economies' for at least three major reasons.

First, and most important, military training has provided recruits with 'tools' that ultimately make them more productive workers when they enter the civilian labour force. Second, military infrastructure outlays, like airports and roads, often served civil functions as well. Finally, Third World militaries often provided many civic functions in the areas of education and health care. Military doctors, for example, are also used to meet the demands of citizens who work at or live near armed forces installations.[25] The end-result is that military spending has not necessarily detracted from economic growth in civilian sectors.

The linkage between economic development and national security was a key issue in the academic curricula of military schools in such countries as Brazil and Peru. In Brazil's Escola Superior de Guerra (ESG), military officers and selected civilians were taught that the problem of internal security embraced 'all aspects of social, economic and political life'.[26] There was no question regarding the identity of the 'enemy'. According to historian Bradford Burns, the ESG propagated 'an almost pathological brand of anti-Communism'. Revolutionary activity in Brazil was viewed as part of the international 'struggle between east and west in which there could be no neutral position'.[27] ESG students learned that they were waging a major battle in the cold war, a battle that must be fought with political and economic weapons, as well as military ones.

Common to authoritarian rule in Brazil, Peru and South Korea was the formulation of economic development policies that had 'national security' — as opposed to nationalism — as their ideological theme. The regimes set themselves up as the legitimate defenders of national core values that were threatened by Communism. In employing this ideology, these states tied themselves to the cold war, and they identified with America's struggle against the Soviet bloc. It was hoped that increased American economic and military aid would be one by-product of this anti-Communist alliance.

This ideology, it should be noted, did not arise full-blown from Third World origins. Rather, it passed along a transmission belt that was rooted in Washington. In the next section, a brief sketch of post-war American policies *vis-à-vis* Third World development will be provided. This will help us to understand the anti-Communist linkage forged between First and Third Worlds during the 1950s and 1960s.

## IV

Prior to World War II, the USA had shown little interest in the problem of economic development. By the war's end, the emerging countries had assumed major importance in the strategic calculus of policy-makers. This shift coincided with increasing fears that, from a raw materials perspective, America had become a 'have not' nation, dependent upon foreign suppliers for petroleum and strategic minerals (see Table 6.1). As David Baldwin reminds us, 'even before the advent of the Korean War, United States policy viewed economic development as related to broad national security

*Table 6.1* **US imports of selected raw materials (as a percentage of consumption)**

| Raw material | 1950 | 1955 | 1960 | 1965 | 1970 | 1975 |
|---|---|---|---|---|---|---|
| Iron ore | 11 | 18 | 18 | 32 | 30 | 30 |
| Lead | 40 | 39 | 33 | 31 | 22 | 11 |
| Manganese | 77 | 79 | 89 | 94 | 95 | 98 |
| Nickel | 90 | 84 | 72 | 73 | 71 | 72 |
| Petroleum | 8 | 10 | 16 | 19 | 21 | 35 |
| Zinc | 41 | 51 | 46 | 53 | 54 | 61 |

*Source*: Alfred Eckes, *The United States and the Global Struggle for Minerals* (Austin, University of Texas Press, 1979), p. 274.

considerations'.[28] Secure access to such materials required co-operative political relations with newly independent nations, and American officials regarded economic aid as the most effective instrument for winning the hearts and minds of Third World peoples (see Table 6.2).

The first post-war American policy to address the specific problems of Third World development was the 'Point Four' Programme, so called because it was introduced as the fourth point in President Harry Truman's 1949 inaugural address. The programme, which passed into law in 1950 as the Act for International Development, was 'a security measure' according to Secretary of State Dean Acheson. Acheson explained that 'as a security measure, it is an essential arm of our foreign policy, for our military and economic security is vitally dependent on the economic security of other peoples'.[29]

The Point Four Program was founded on the belief that the most favourable conditions for Communist revolution existed in countries characterized by widespread poverty and social unrest (e.g. China). With the virtue of hindsight, this belief may appear naive. But at that time, Eugene Staley reminds us, policy-makers assumed that if living conditions were improved in the developing world, 'other good things will come automatically, such as progress in democracy, more peaceful international attitudes, and rejection of Communism'.[30] The issues of economic and political development, therefore, were inseparable.

*Table 6.2* **US foreign aid to developing regions, 1951–3 ($ millions)**

| Area | Net foreign aid |
| --- | --- |
| Near East and Africa | 372 |
| Asia and Pacific | 2,886 |
| American Republics | 456 |
| International Organizations | 309 |

*Source*: Commission on Foreign Economic Policy, *Staff Papers* (Washington, DC, February 1954), p. 40.

Indeed, the United States tied economic and political development together in the anti-Communist ideology of national security. The first principle of this ideology was that the Soviet Union and its Communist agents represented the greatest threat to world peace and economic recovery. Economic development policy had to satisfy a critical mass of consumer needs; at the same time, the armed forces in Third World countries must be capable of handling internal, if not external, security problems.

The successful implementation of this ideology would mean not only political stability and economic growth in the developing world, but also secure American access to minerals and raw materials. David Baldwin has neatly summed up American post-war attitudes toward the problem of Third World development:

During the 1949–53 period American policy statements reflect concern for the national security aspects of economic development in terms of vague concepts of the economic causes of war, less vague concepts of the relationship between communism and poverty, and relatively concrete concepts of the relationship between the underdeveloped areas and strategic raw materials for use in rearmament.[31]

For the purpose of this chapter it is important to note that the ideology of national security was not indigenous to most Third World countries, but rather imported from the USA. By adopting an anti-Communist ideology, authoritarian regimes strengthened their economic and military ties to the USA, with the USA becoming a partner in achieving the dual objective of defeating revolutionary opponents in the field while creating economic conditions that satisfied rising consumer expectations.[32]

For a while, it appeared that, in Brazil at any rate, the ideology of national security would provide a durable path to political stability and economic growth. But the flip side of the national security ideology was a harsh authoritarianism, and repression and inflation lay beneath the political-economic surface. Over time, the middle class grew dissatisfied with its trade of political representation for economic security.[33] Faced with a loss of legitimacy, the military in Brazil (as in Argentina) stepped aside for civilian rule and redemocratization.

V

What happens to the national security–economic development link in countries that are experiencing redemocratization? We have seen that, historically, national security
considerations have shaped the scope, timing and trajectory
of economic development policy. Owing to the positive
externalities associated with military spending (e.g.
education that ultimately makes recruits more productive
civilian workers), regimes have also been able to allocate
relatively large amounts to the military while pursuing
development policies based on rapid economic growth. In
this section, which is of necessity tentative, we offer some
comments regarding the development–security linkage in
the light of the nascent redemocratization trend in Latin
America.[34]

Perhaps the first point to make is that, despite the
replacement of military with civilian regimes in such
countries as Argentina and Brazil, the military remains an
important political and economic force. In Brazil, for
example, a large number of military officers remain in
prominent positions in state-run industries. Further, military officers retain a strong voice regarding the development
of such industries as 'electronics, communications and
informatics, where they do not want to see foreign investment'.[35] In industries with close ties to the military, therefore, we would not expect to see a radical shift in policy
away from those pursued by previous regimes.

During the years of authoritarian reign, military leaders
also established close ties with local entrepreneurs who
executed autarkic industrial policies. Support for such
policies thus goes beyond the military to other sets of elites.
These industrial elites enjoy political prominence in the
current civilian regimes, making it even more unlikely that
sectoral policies with military links will be dismantled.[36] It is
of interest that the ESG in Brazil continues to serve as a central point of contact between officers and industrialists.

That said, we may still expect important changes in
economic development policy. To begin with, the ideology
of national security would appear inappropriate for new,

civilian regimes. Indeed, democratization itself has become a theme of economic policy. In announcing its new economic stabilization measures in February 1986, for example, the Brazilian government stated that its anti-inflationary policies represented 'a commitment to democracy'.[37] Economic policies would address the social welfare demands of the 'poorest of the poor', as opposed to the consumption demands of the middle class. This, of course, is rhetoric; the jury is still out on whether redemocratization will lead to flatter income distribution in Brazil and Argentina.

Second, we may expect new, democratic regimes to become increasingly independent in their foreign economic policies. President Alfonsín of Argentina, for example, has travelled to Moscow on a trade mission, and Brazil has extended diplomatic recognition to Cuba. This suggests that the East–West, cold war axis on which foreign economic policy was largely based is now in the process of being altered. Despite the importance of the government of the United States to debt restructuring, Washington will find it difficult to prevent growing Latin American trade with the Communist bloc.

Finally, we would predict, if anything, secular increases in spending on military weaponry. This is not, however, because of a need to 'pay off' the military. Rather, it is the result of growing independence in economic and military policies. By delinking the state from the cold war, regimes must demonstrate their political resolve by providing military forces that can meet a range of external threats and maintain national sovereignty.

In conclusion, then, the national security–economic development link is of more than historical interest. Even in the absence of a national security ideology, direct military spending and state support of industries with military ties will remain an important component of economic policy. Far from treating Third World economic policies as if they were formulated without regard to internal and/or external threats, students of international politics must recognize the role of security considerations in the allocation of scarce resources.

## NOTES

[1] Richard Caves and Ronald Jones, *World Trade and Payments* (Boston: Little, Brown, 1981), pp. 144–51.

[2] See, for example, Richard T. Gill, *Economic Development: Past and Present* (Englewood Cliffs, NJ: Prentice-Hall, 1967); and Jan Tinbergen, *The Design of Development* (Baltimore, MD: Johns Hopkins University Press, 1958). But for a notable exception that explicitly links defence and development, see Emile Benoit, *Defence and Economic Growth in Developing Countries* (Lexington, MA, Lexington Books, 1973).

[3] Robert Gilpin, *US Power and the Multinational Corporation* (New York: Basic Books, 1975), p. 25.

[4] David R. Mares, 'Explaining Choice of Development Strategies: Suggestions from Mexico, 1970–82', *International Organization*, vol. 39 (Autumn 1985), p. 667.

[5] Stephan Haggard, 'The Newly Industrializing Countries in the International System', *World Politics*, vol. 38 (January 1986): pp. 343–70.

[6] For the classic if disputed account of economic development, see W.W. Rostow, *The Stages of Economic Growth* (Cambridge: Cambridge University Press, 1960).

[7] Werner D. Baer, *Industrialization and Economic Development in Brazil* (Homewood, IL: Richard D. Irwin, 1965), p. 16.

[8] See Martin Van Creveld, 'The Origins and Development of Mobilization Warfare' in Richard Bissell and Gordon McCormick (eds), *Strategic Dimensions of Economic Behavior* (New York: Praeger, 1984).

[9] Quoted in E. Bradford Burns, *Nationalization in Brazil* (New York: Praeger, 1968), p. 81.

[10] John D. Wirth, *The Politics of Brazilian Development, 1930–1954* (Stanford, CA: Stanford University Press, 1970), p. 84.

[11] Baer, *Industrialization*, p. 31.

[12] For a detailed history of Volta Redonda, see Wirth, *Brazilian Development*.

[13] Ibid., p. 118.

[14] Ibid., p. 93.

[15] Ibid., p. 109.

[16] David Green, 'The Cold War Comes to Latin America' in Barton Bernstein (ed.), *Politics and Policies of the Truman Administration* (Chicago: Quadrangle Books, 1972).

[17] Gene Lyons, *Military Policy and Economic Aid* (Columbus: Ohio State University Press, 1961), p. 174.

[18] Edward Azar and Chung-in Moon, 'Third World National Security: Toward a Conceptual Framework', *International Interactions*, vol. 11 (1984), p. 122.

[19] Benoit, *Defence and Economic Growth*, p. 249.

[20] Walter Galenson and David Galenson, 'Japan and South Korea' in David Denoon (ed.), *Constraints on Strategy* (McLean, VA, Pergamon-Brassey's, 1986).

[21] Fernando Henrique Cardoso, 'On the Characterization of Authoritarian Regimes in Latin America' in David Collier (ed.), *The New Authoritarianism in Latin America* (Princeton, NJ: Princeton University Press, 1979), p. 44.

[22] See Fernando Henrique Cardoso, 'Associated Dependent Development: Theoretical and Practical Implications' in Alfred Stepan, (ed.), *Authoritarian Brazil* (New Haven, CT: Yale University Press, 1973).

[23] David Becker, *The New Bourgeoisie and the Limits of Dependency* (Princeton, NJ: Princeton University Press, 1983), p. 56.

[24] Gavin Kennedy, *The Military in the Third World* (New York: Charles Scribner's Sons, 1974), p. 298.

[25] Benoit, *Defence and Economic Growth*, p. 17.

[26] Alfred Stepan, 'The New Professionalism of Internal Warfare and Military Role Expansion' in Stepan, *Authoritarian Brazil*, p. 51.

[27] Burns, *Nationalism in Brazil*, p. 121.

[28] David Baldwin, *Economic Development and American Foreign Policy: 1943–1962* (Chicago: University of Chicago Press, 1966), p. 74.

[29] Ibid., p. 75.

[30] Eugene Staley, *The Future of Underdeveloped Countries* (New York: Praeger, 1961), p. 4.

[31] Baldwin, *Economic Development*, p. 75.

[32] See Green, 'The Cold War Comes to Latin America'.

[33] On this trade-off, see Philippe C. Schmitter, 'The Portugalization of Brazil?' in Stepan, *Authoritarian Brazil*.

[34] This section is largely based on interviews with Brazilian officials conducted in November 1986.

[35] Economist Intelligence Unit, *Quarterly Economic Review of Brazil*, 1985 Annual Supplement, p. 7.

[36] See Emanuel Adler, 'Ideological Guerillas and the Quest for Technological Autonomy: Brazil's Domestic Computer Industry', *International Organization*, vol. 40 (Summer 1986), pp. 673–705.

[37] Ministero João Sayad, *Economic Stabilization Program* (Brasilia, Secretariat of Planning, n.d.).

# 7. Arms Acquisition and National Security: The Irony of Military Strength

ANDREW L. ROSS

There are multiple dimensions to the national security problematic in the Third World. National security, to borrow Arnold Wolfer's phrase, is an 'ambiguous symbol' in the South as well as the North.[1] Not only the externally orientated, political-military dimension of security traditionally emphasized by American and Western European defence analysts is of concern in the Third World.[2] The internal, military and non-military dimensions of security are of equal or even greater concern. The threats posed to the state and regime, territorial integrity, the larger political and socioeconomic order, and domestic peace and tranquility emanating from indigenous sources are often of more immediate concern than those threats emanating from external sources.[3] The non-military dimensions of security, such as economic vulnerability, ecological scarcity, ethnic/communal fragmentation, protracted social conflict, and the inadequacy of social coping mechanisms have rightly received more attention in recent literature.[4]

Yet military power remains central to national security in

the South as well as the North. Military power, in some form, is perceived by policy-makers and analysts alike to be a vital instrument of security. National military power is viewed as essential in defending against not only external threats but also a wide range of internal threats. The military in the Third World is frequently called upon to utilize its power of coercion in the domestic arena, to ward off or eliminate indigenous threats to the survival of the polity and/or the longevity of a regime, and to attempt forcefully to resolve ethnic and communal conflicts.

*3RD world military used internally as well*

While military power is typically acquired to enhance security against internal and external threats, the acquisition of military power may itself erode rather than enhance security. The dilemmas resulting from a military buildup go well beyond the familiar problems recognized by John Herz[5] and Robert Jervis[6] in their insightful elucidations of the 'security dilemma' and by Barry Buzan[7] in his description of the 'defence dilemma'. The fact that the means by which the implements of modern, industrialized warfare are acquired impacts directly upon security has, thus far, escaped the notice of most defence analysts.

The utility of military power, whether it is to be exercised in the international or domestic arena, is dependent upon secure and reliable sources of weaponry. Yet many Third World countries must cope with threats to their national security in the face of insecure and often unreliable sources of arms. Even though the most dependable and invulnerable sources of arms are those that are found within one's own country, the vast majority of developing countries must still import most, if not all, of their military hardware. Only 51 out of some 120 developing countries produce conventional weapons of some kind. Thirty-four of those 51 produce at least one of the four major types of conventional weapon systems: aircraft, armoured vehicles, missiles, or naval vessels. Production in the other 17 countries is limited to small arms and ammunition. Only seven Third World countries — Argentina, Brazil, Egypt, India, Israel, South Africa, and Taiwan — have developed an across-the-board production capability.[8] Even those developing countries that have initiated defence manufacturing programmes must still rely on arms imports to acquire needed military equipment.

The various forms of the arms acquisition options available to Third World countries and the impact of alternative acquisition strategies upon national security will be examined in this chapter. Of special concern is the relationship between specific arms acquisition strategies and a country's political and military autonomy. The maintenance of policy and behavioural autonomy — the minimization of external constraints on policy and behaviour — is at the heart of national security. Yet policy and behavioural autonomy may be severely circumscribed if the optimal mix of acquisition strategies is not adopted. Particular acquisition options entail vulnerability to externally imposed restraints on state sovereignty, restraints which severely circumscribe the effective range of available policy options in both the domestic and foreign policy realms.

For both developed and developing countries, there are three analytically distinct options — two pure options and one mixed option. A country may seek to rely solely on either producing arms domestically or importing arms from abroad. Or it may choose to manufacture some weapons locally and to import others. Even though there are only three distinct options, however, there are numerous forms of each. The discussion here, following the Third World's experience, will proceed temporally, beginning with the arms import option and then continuing with a consideration of local production and the mixed strategy.


## THE ARMS IMPORT OPTION

Given the historical context of military relations between the advanced industrial countries of the Northern core and the developing countries of the Southern periphery, it should come as no surprise that developing countries initially had little choice but to acquire arms through the arms import 'option'. Prior to having acquired formal political independence, local military establishments of the then colonies were fully integrated into the command structures of the colonial powers. Indigenous military forces were commanded, trained, equipped, and financed by the European colonial powers. Since a modern manufacturing capability was virtually non-existent, procurement of military equipment within the colonial territories was either impossible or limited to small arms and ammunition and non-lethal supplies such as uniforms. Manpower alone was locally generated.

The new countries, consequently, were in a state of military as well as economic underdevelopment at the dawn of independence. The revenue collection systems needed to raise the resources to finance the armed forces and other state operations either were not yet in existence or were unreliable. Few experienced officers were available — colonial training, after all, had emphasized administrative skills and following orders over generalship and initiative. And, most importantly, there were no indigenous sources of military equipment.

The lack of a viable military infrastructure served to exacerbate the all too numerous security challenges confronting many of the newly independent countries. The artificiality of many Third World countries generated both domestic and international conflicts. All too often the new countries were a crazy patchwork of diverse national, ethnic, tribal, and religious groups that were typically at odds with one another. The lack of fit between state and nation made internal conflict inescapable. Groups previously united in a joint struggle to oust colonial rulers came to contend for state power and dominance. Contending ideological factions, which had subordinated their differences and collaborated in the overthrow of colonial rule, turned on one another in the attempt to seize control of the state apparatus. Priorities were assigned not to building a viable state and society, but to the more primordial groups that, despite the conflicting claims of modernization, still laid claim to the loyalty traditionally expected of their members.

The poor correspondence between state and 'nation', or society, contributed to conflict among as well as within the new countries. State boundaries established by the former colonial powers were often ill-defined and ill-conceived. Lands traditionally occupied by particular communal/ ethnic communities were in many cases split between two or more sovereign countries, thereby leaving such communities without a clear national homeland. Not surprisingly, these torn and displaced communities became the source of international conflict. Territorial disputes reinforced by territorially divided communal groupings have been a major cause of conflicts among developing countries.

To counter these long-term internal and external threats, the newly established countries had only poorly trained and equipped armed forces, forces that had been mere appendages of Europe's far-flung imperialist military establishments. Even after the withdrawal of direct political and military control, the new countries remained militarily dependent — initially upon their former colonizers and subsequently upon the two superpowers that have sought to build neo-colonial empires. Their dependence was most dramatically evidenced by their continued reliance upon external sources of military equipment. Confronted with external threats to their security and often even more threatening domestic conflict, possessing inadequately armed military forces, and lacking the industrial/technological base required to manufacture essential military equipment, developing countries had little alternative but to import massive amounts of foreign military hardware to equip their armed forces. Consequently, the Third World's dependence upon arms imports from the advanced industrial countries, the former colonial powers, became the defining characteristic of post-colonial North–South military relations.

## SINGLE/PREDOMINANT SOURCE ACQUISITION

It was during the immediate post-independence period that single/predominant source acquisition, the first of the two forms of the arms import option, was most in evidence. Though there were exceptions (such as the Algerian–French non-relationship), developing countries tended to acquire arms from their former colonizers during the immediate post-colonial period. Having served with and been trained by core militaries, many Third World militaries were quite reluctant to sever the close ties established between the armed forces of the core and the periphery under colonialism. Militaries accustomed to being commanded by a foreign military elite, and the equipment, training, and standard operating procedures of that elite, were typically inclined to turn to their former rulers for arms. Former British colonies, for instance, imported military hardware from the United Kingdom, while the former French colonies turned to France. In Africa, France remained the near exclusive supplier to former colonies such as Benin, Burkina Faso, the Central African Republic, Chad, Gabon, the Ivory Coast, the Malagasy Republic, Mauritania, Niger, Senegal and Togo. France was also Morocco's exclusive source of military supplies in the 1950s and remained a major source of armored vehicles through the 1960s. Kenya after independence acquired its arms primarily from Britain. Britain was also the dominant supplier of Ghana and Nigeria, providing virtually all of the armoured vehicles and naval vessels acquired by the two countries. And Britain was South Africa's primary supplier through the 1950s. In other areas, Britain was the dominant source of military equipment for Jordan, Kuwait, Oman, Brunei, Sri Lanka, and even India until the 1960s.[9] During the late 1950s and the decade of the 1960s, of course, the USA and the Soviet Union, in their cold war scramble for post-colonial empires, displaced the former European colonial powers as the major arms suppliers to the developing world. Thereafter, one of the two superpowers tended to play the role of single or predominant supplier.

The arms transfer policies of the advanced industrial countries fostered the Third World's dependence upon Northern arsenals. Though commercial transfers have become increasingly important since the early 1970s, during the 1950s and 1960s developing countries were often able to acquire arms from what had become the two dominant suppliers, the USA and the Soviet Union, through grant aid or other financially attractive means. American arms transfers to the Third World during the 1950s and 1960s were primarily in the form of grant aid. And the Soviet Union provided arms on extremely generous terms, offering 40 per cent discounts, eight- to ten-year loans at the far below market interest rate of merely 2½ per cent, and accepting payment in soft currencies and even commodities.[10]

Even though American grant aid declined dramatically during the 1970s and the Soviet Union has toughened the terms of its arms sales — reducing the number and size of grants and often requiring payment in hard currencies[11] — by having provided arms through grants or at bargain basement prices, the two leading suppliers had, purposely or not, discouraged the pursuit of alternative arms acquisition strategies. Providing military equipment at low or no cost had reduced the incentive to initiate costly military import substitution programmes. The great cost disparity between importing arms and producing arms locally made it difficult to justify the more costly option, especially in the face of widespread economic difficulties. Its low economic cost made military dependence appear relatively benign. And once addicted to foreign arms, developing countries found it difficult to terminate their dependence upon Northern suppliers.

Most Third World leaders, however, soon came to a full realization of the vulnerabilities and limitations inherent in dependence upon foreign arms suppliers, especially dependence upon a single or predominant external source of arms. Singapore's former foreign minister, S. Rajaratnam, vividly portrayed the dangers of military dependence in an address before the General Assembly of the United Nations:

The most dangerous consequences are political. The flow of arms carries with it a measure of dependency on the part of the client on the seller of arms not unlike that prevailing under the old imperial system. . . . The massive flow of arms to the third world confronts it with a new danger. It is, first of all, a drain on the economies of third world countries; but even more important is the fact that it creates a new form of dependence on the great Powers, which can exploit the third world's dependence on them to manipulate them, to engineer conflicts between them, and to use them as proxies in their competition for influence and dominance.[12]

The greatest danger to the security and autonomy of Third World countries posed by military dependence is the threat of arms embargoes. The flow of arms can be cut off at the whim of capricious suppliers. Embargoes, especially during ongoing hostilities, severely restrict military autonomy and represent a direct threat to a country's security. The vulnerability of developing countries to arms embargoes has been demonstrated on a number of occasions. In September 1965, the USA and UK both imposed embargoes following the outbreak of the Indo-Pakistani conflict of that year. Pakistan at the time was almost entirely dependent on American equipment and Britain was India's most important suppler. During the 1971 Indo-Pakistani war, the USA again exercised its power to cut off supplies. Despite the American 'tilt' towards Pakistan, both Pakistan and India were subjected to an arms embargo. Export licences for more than $3 million worth of military equipment bound for Pakistan were cancelled and $11.3 million worth of military and other 'sensitive equipment' earmarked for India remained undelivered.[13] In 1967, France terminated Israeli arms supplies following the Six Day War. France had been Israel's single most important source of arms prior to the war. The United Nations in 1963 imposed a voluntary arms embargo on South Africa and followed the voluntary embargo with the mandatory embargo of 1977. And in April 1982, when Argentina invaded the Falkland Islands, the European Community voted to cut off the flow of arms to Argentina.

Militarily dependent developing countries have had to contend with interruptions in the flow of spare parts, upon which the continued operation of foreign equipment depends, as well as interruptions in the supply of complete weapons systems. The British in 1973 refused to supply spare parts for Israel's Centurion tanks. Subsequent to Sadat's expulsion of Soviet advisers in 1972, the Soviet Union refused to provide needed spare parts for Egypt's Soviet weaponry, prompting Sadat to characterize much of his military equipment as 'nothing but scrap'.[14] And the USA refused to supply Khomeini's Iran with spare parts for its American military equipment after the Iranian

Revolution and the taking of the American embassy hostages.

Foreign arms purchases bring not only arms but also the foreign technicians and advisers required to train local militaries in the maintenance, repair, and operation of sophisticated military systems, thereby injecting an irksome and sometimes insidious external presence into the core of the national security apparatus. Rajaratnam and Robin Luckham have both pointed out the dilemmas inherent in introducing foreign weapons and the following train of advisers and technicians. According to Rajaratnam:

The weapons now being imported are not only highly sophisticated but also packaged as parts of a very complex, very comprehensive and very expensive weapons system. When a country buys a weapons system it imports not only weapons but a whole array of experts and advisers. Arms contracts today include provisions for training, technical support and the establishment of facilities to maintain and repair equipment. Often these contracts include provisions for foreign experts to build roads, communication networks and other facilities which come under the term 'infrastructure'.[15]

Luckham's analysis echoes Rajaratnam's evaluation:

The implications of military training and assistance programs for external dependence are easy to see. They train soldiers in the use of the technologies of the donor countries. They give sustenance to the social relations of force around which the professional armies of both metropolis and periphery are organised. They create networks of professional contacts both with the metropolitan military institutions and among course-mates in different peripheral countries. And they are often explicitly intended . . . to promote the political philosophy and interests of the country which provides the training.[16]

The USA and the Soviet Union have been quite adept at following up their arms deliveries to Third World countries with an infusion of logistical support and training teams. In 1975, for instance, the USA had 9,535 people serving in 132 technical assistance and training teams in 34 countries, with the largest contingencies in South Vietnam, Saudi Arabia, and Iran.[17] Almost 40,000 Americans were involved in military activities in Iran before the Shah was ousted.[18] In Saudi Arabia, the US Army Corps of Engineers has been kept busy since 1953 supervising the construction of a military infrastructure consisting of airfields, ports, and communications systems, and training Saudi military personnel.[19] During the period 1950–85, 33,396 military personnel from the Near East and South Asia, 268,101 from East Asia and the Pacific (excluding Japan), 9,562 from Africa, and 99,296 from Latin America were trained under the USA's military assistance programme.[20]

The Soviet Union and its Warsaw Pact allies, according to a CIA report, had 15,865 military technicians stationed in the Third World in 1979 — 6,825 in Africa, 110 in Latin America, 4,780 in the Middle East, and 4,150 in South Asia.[21] The largest concentrations of Warsaw Pact military technicians were in Algeria (1,015), Libya (1,820), Angola (1,400), Ethiopia (1,250), Iraq (1,065), South Yemen (1,100), Syria (2,480), and Afghanistan (4,000).[22] During the period 1955–79, the Soviet Union trained a total of 45,585 Third World military personnel — 14,420 from Africa, 7,590 from East Asia, 780 from Latin America, 16,370 from the Middle East, and 6,425 from South Asia.[23]

These data indicate the nature of the continuing military relationship that can accompany arms imports. The military assistance (i.e. training) programmes that follow in the wake of arms imports can provide suppliers with a direct military presence on the territory of recipients and tend to reinforce military dependence by institutionalizing corporate and personal ties between the armed forces of the core and periphery. This military assistance relationship is, like the central relationship itself — the arms supply relationship — an instrument that can be wielded by the supplier to exert influence upon the domestic and foreign policies of recipients.

In addition to suspending deliveries of weapons and spare parts and complementing arms transfers with military assistance programmes, arms suppliers have typically imposed restrictions on the end-use of military equipment. The USA, for instance, has traditionally provided military equipment on the condition that it be used solely for defensive purposes. Consequently, Turkey's use of American arms in the 1974 invasion of Cyprus resulted in the cancellation of American military aid and assistance in 1975. And before Portugal had divested itself of its last African colonial holdings, both West Germany and Italy had prohibited Portuguese use of their arms in Africa.[24]

Suppliers have also imposed restrictions on the resale of military equipment. Prior approval of retransfers, on a case-by-case basis, has long been a part of American arms transfer policy. When Saudi Arabia expressed interest in acquiring American F-14s from Iran after the overthrow of the Shah and the seizure of the American embassy in Teheran, the USA halted the deal.[25] Even the sale of foreign military equipment containing American components is subject to American approval, as Israel discovered when it first attempted to sell its American-engined Kfir fighter to Ecuador and Taiwan. In order to avoid unknowing participation in triangular deals, France, West Germany and Switzerland have also prohibited retransfers in the absence of their formal consent.[26]

Developing countries that are dependent upon arms imports must also contend with the attempts of suppliers to use the supply relationship to exert influence on their foreign and domestic policies. The prospect of acquiring leverage over recipients is one of the major forces driving Northern arms transfers in the first place. Northern suppliers have long used arms transfers as a means of gaining access to foreign political and military leaders, shoring up alliance commitments, and instituting friendlier relations, all in the hope of obtaining influence, whether it be explicit or implicit. Barry Blechman and his former ACDA colleagues correctly noted that

The recipient's dependency on the donor for maintenance, spare parts, and replacement of major items of military equipment is seen to provide leverage in difficult situations. The arms donor need not actually threaten to curtail supplies because the two superpowers know that this dependency will influence recipient's decisions long before the donor would need to contemplate such threats.[27]

Arms transfers have played a central role in the post-World War II American–Soviet competition for influence in the Third World. Both superpowers have provided military hardware with the expectation, and often the explicit requirement, that recipients would align themselves politically and militarily with the supplying country and would adopt policies that furthered the interests of their supplier. The USA, for instance, has seldom hesitated to draw upon the influence derived from its security relationship with the Philippines. Leaders of the Philippines, both civilian and military, have relied heavily on the advice of the Joint US Military Advisory Group (JUSMAG). In 1950, JUSMAG reorganised the Filipino intelligence apparatus and the military campaign against the Huk insurgency, and managed to assure the selection of Ramón Magsaysay as Secretary of National Defence.[28] In 1953, American officials in the Philippines engineered Magsaysay's election to the presidency.[29] And the Philippines loyally supported the USA during both the Korean and the Vietnam wars, going so far as to contribute a combat battalion to the cause in Korea and a civic action unit in Vietnam.[30]

American attempts to exploit its security relationships with Third World countries are not, of course, limited to the Philippines. The USA has often manipulated the flow of arms to the Middle East in its efforts to prevent peace negotiations from collapsing. Israel was provided with F-15s and other weapons in return for its approval of the 1975 Sinai accords, and F-5s were sold to Egypt in 1978 to keep Sadat from breaking off talks with Israel.[31] The USA has on occasion terminated the flow of arms to countries judged to be violators of basic human rights. In 1974 the US Congress adopted legislation terminating arms sales and military assistance to Chile in an effort to curtail the severe repression being perpetrated by the military junta that had overthrown Salvadore Allende. Concern for human rights played an even more central role in the Carter administration's arms sales policy. During its first year in office, the Carter administration reduced the flow of arms to countries such as Argentina, Uruguay, and Ethiopia, all of which had been cited as human rights violators in the administration's first report on the subject. Latin American countries appear to have been special targets of Carter's effort to utilize the leverage thought to be derived from the military supply relationship in the administration's crusade to safeguard human rights and eliminate state violence and repression.[32]

## MULTIPLE SOURCE ACQUISITION

Not surprisingly, developing countries have sought to counter the constraints inherent in dependence upon a single or primary source of arms. The first of two counter-dependence strategies, and typically the first to be adopted, is to import arms from multiple sources. This first counter-dependence strategy is a short-run, relatively low-cost option, and has as its objective the distribution of dependence across a large number of suppliers so that no one supplier could effectively limit recipient political and military autonomy. The multiplication of suppliers has as its primary goal not so much the elimination of military dependence as the reduction of the relative significance of any particular supplier. The aim is to reduce not the fact but the impact of arms import dependence by spreading it around and distributing it over a larger number of suppliers. It is assumed, not unreasonably, that a large number of suppliers will find it much more difficult to manipulate and exploit a country's dependence upon imported arms than would only one or two suppliers.

Numerous developing countries have turned to multiple source acquisition. Nigeria, after gaining its independence from the UK in 1960, quickly turned to a variety of sources for its military equipment. Although most of its naval vessels have been obtained from the UK, Nigeria has acquired its other military equipment from a large number of countries. Aircraft have been obtained from Austria, Belgium, Canada, Czechoslovakia, Italy, the Netherlands, the Soviet Union, the UK, USA and West Germany. Exocet ship-to-ship missiles have been acquired from France; Aspide, Albatros, and OTOMAT missiles from Italy; and Seacat missiles from the UK. Though most of the armoured vehicles acquired during the 1960s came from the UK, Nigeria also acquired Panhard AML-60/90 armored cars from France in the late 1960s and T-55 main battle tanks from the Soviet Union in the late 1970s.[33]

While Nigeria imported arms from a large number of countries soon after independence, most developing countries maintained close military ties to one of the four major suppliers — the United States, the Soviet Union, France, and the UK — and turned to multiple source acquisition only in the 1970s. Egypt, for instance, though it initially relied on the UK for its military hardware, in the mid- to late-1950s turned to the Soviet Union. Since disassociating itself from the Soviet Union in 1972, when it ordered the withdrawal of 21,000 Soviet military technicians from its territory,[34] Egypt has acquired arms not only from the United States, its new patron, but from the UK, France, Italy and China. Peru, which was dependent upon American arms supplies during the 1950s and 1960s, turned to Australia, France, Italy, the Netherlands, the Soviet Union and West Germany in the 1970s.

The trend is clearly in the direction of multiple source acquisition for those countries that still rely on imported weaponry. In Africa, for instance, where few countries are able to produce a significant proportion of their arms, 25 countries were dependent upon a sole or predominant supplier during the years 1961–71. Only nine (26 per cent) had turned to multiple source acquisition during this period. During the years 1967–1976, however, 17 countries (41 per cent) turned to multiple suppliers (though 24 still relied upon a sole or predominant supplier). Sixteen of 37 (or 43 per cent) sub-Saharan African countries during the years 1974–8 acquired arms from multiple sources. Twenty-one still depended upon a sole or predominant supplier.[35]

Yet despite the increasing popularity of multiple source acquisition, there are major drawbacks to reliance on multiple suppliers as a counter-dependence strategy. Apart from the fact that dependence on imported military equipment is not actually reduced but merely made to appear somewhat benign, multiple source acquisition often results in a polyglot assemblage of military equipment that poses significant training and maintenance problems. Technicians and operators must learn to maintain, repair, and operate the aircraft, armoured vehicles, missiles, and naval vessels of several foreign countries. The operational and technical capacity of Third World military establishments can be strained to the limit. Egypt, for instance, with its vast, heterogeneous array of American, Chinese, French, and Soviet aircraft, must cope with an extremely complicated logistical system.[36] Multiple source acquisition clearly means that the traditional goal of military standardisation must be discarded.

Even though multiple source acquisition provides a degree of insulation from the effects of military dependence, any one supplier might still possess the ability to hinder military operations by withholding spare parts or withdrawing support and maintenance units for vital equipment, such as aircraft, that requires frequent or near-continuous service. The operation of essential systems could be seriously curtailed, or even terminated, by such tactics. Multiple source acquisition, therefore, is not a viable long-term counter-dependence strategy.

## MILITARY IMPORT SUBSTITUTION

The innate inability of multiple source acquisition to ensure military and political autonomy has prompted developing countries to turn to a second counter-dependence strategy: military import substitution (MIS). Substituting indigenously produced for imported weapons offers the prospect, albeit long-term, of achieving a high degree of military self-reliance. By acquiring the capability to manufacture domestically a large proportion of the military equipment it requires, a developing country can begin to reduce, and in the long-term perhaps eliminate altogether, the vulnerabilities inherent in dependence upon arms imports, whether from single or multiple sources. Domestic production removes the constraints imposed by import dependence. When military equipment is acquired at home rather than from abroad, military planning and operations are no longer hampered by the possibility of arms embargoes, the withholding of spare parts, supplier efforts to use the supply relationship as leverage to exert influence, and the other circumscriptions of military dependence.

MIS is a process that takes on different forms as it evolves through five distinct stages. The first stage involves simply the assembly of imported arms. Weaponry is still acquired from foreign suppliers, but is imported in the form of prefabricated components and assembled on delivery. The foreign supplier provides technical training and assists in erecting the facilities necessary for weapons assembly. Technical training includes not only assembly skills, but also the use of equipment needed to inspect, evaluate and test the weapons being assembled. In the second stage, components are produced under licence agreements with foreign suppliers. The complete weapon itself is still only assembled, but an increasing number of components are fabricated locally. It is in the third stage that MIS results in the actual production of complete weapons — foreign military equipment is manufactured under licence. In the fourth stage, developing countries engaged in MIS utilize the technological skills and capabilities acquired in earlier stages to modify, redesign or reproduce (through reverse engineering) foreign weapons systems. This is the first stage in which some element of indigenous research and development appears — in the form of either system redesign or reverse engineering. In the fifth stage MIS finally results in the production of indigenously designed arms. Fifth-stage production can take two forms: based on local research and development but still incorporating foreign-produced or designed components; or based entirely on indigenous, independent research and development.[37]

Large-scale MIS in the Third World is a relatively recent phenomenon. Only four developing countries (Argentina, Brazil, Colombia, and India) were producing any of the four types of major conventional weapon — aircraft, armoured vehicles, missiles, and naval vessels — in 1950.[38] By 1980, however, 26 developing countries were producing one or more of the major weapons system.[39] Of these 26 countries, 15 were producing aircraft, six were manufacturing armoured vehicles, nine were producing missiles, and 24 were building naval vessels. Six countries — Argentina, Brazil, India, Israel, South Korea, and South Africa — were producing each of the four types of weapon. A total of 18 developing countries had demonstrated, by 1980, the ability to manufacture either aircraft, armoured vehicles, missiles, or naval vessels that were the products of domestic research and development programmes. The tremendous increases in the number of Third World arms producers, the range of weapons produced, and the level of indigenous input are all the result of defence manufacturing and research and development programmes initiated during the late 1960s and the 1970s.[40]

That an increasing number of Third World countries have turned to domestic arms acquisition in an attempt to wean themselves from their dependence upon external suppliers is beyond dispute. The success of MIS programmes in actually reducing the level of external dependence and promoting military self-reliance and political-military autonomy has, however, triggered an as yet unresolved debate.

The growth of military manufacturing activities in the developing world has relied heavily upon imported military technology — technology acquired from the same sources that Third World countries have traditionally been dependent upon for imported arms. The Third World's defence industries were constructed upon a base of imported Northern military technology and many of its products continue to incorporate imported technology in the form of either foreign components or components manufactured locally under licensing arrangements with Northern suppliers. Consequently, dispensers of the conventional wisdom argue that little has changed with the expansion of the Third World's defence production capabilities. According to this line of argument, MIS has not even led to the reduction, much less elimination, of dependence upon imported arms. The declared goal of military self-reliance has not been, and will not be, attained. Instead, there has merely been a change in the form of dependence as countries have substituted locally produced for imported military equipment.

A number of observers are adherents of what has been identified here as the conventional wisdom. Anne Cahn *et al.* have asserted: 'Instead of creating independence, indigenous production usually creates a new set of dependencies'.[41] Stephanie Neuman has claimed that 'self-sufficiency in weapons production is beyond the reach of less developed countries. Domestic production creates other dependencies'.[42] According to the highly regarded International Institute for Strategic Studies, 'the dependence normally associated with arms transfers does not disappear with the establishment of domestic defence industries'.[43] Another analyst, Michael Moodie, has argued that 'Third World dependence associated with arms imports from industrial countries does not disappear . . . with the creation of local defence industries; the form of the dependence is changed'.[44] Elsewhere, he said: 'The nature of dependence is transformed from one of reliance on industrial producers for arms to dependence on them for inputs to make arms'.[45] Later, again: 'Third World arms producers have traded one form of dependence for another. They have shifted the nature of their requirements from the need for finished weapons systems to the need for the technologies to manufacture those systems'.[46] Peter Lock and Herbert Wulf have gone so far as to argue that 'The import of sophisticated capital-intensive technology and especially the establishment of complex arms production programmes *increases* the dependence on suppliers from industrialised countries'.[47] And Wulf has concluded that 'for the time being there is no short-term or even medium-term fulfilment of the desire of developing countries to reach a high degree of self-sufficiency in arms production'.[48] According to the received wisdom, therefore, as developing countries substitute locally manufactured weapons for imported weapons, technological dependence is simply being substituted for import dependence. Instead of achieving the proclaimed goal of military self-reliance, Third World defence producers are merely exchanging dependence upon imported arms for dependence upon imported military technology.

As I have argued elsewhere, however, it may well be that as MIS programmes develop and mature, far more takes place than a mere change in the form of military dependence.[49] The nature of military dependence undergoes a subtle but potentially profound transformation as developinging countries turn from arms imports to arms production. Instead of importing only a finished product, developing countries have begun to import and assimilate the technological capability necessary to manufacture, and eventually develop, weapons domestically. The Third World's arms manufacturers have consequently been acquiring the means to alter the traditional North–South dependency relationship.

A static dependence relationship is inevitable when a country relies upon foreign arms suppliers. But when arms production programmes are initiated, and military production technology rather than arms are imported, a more dynamic relationship is established, one that has an inherent potential for the reduction, if not elimination, of military dependence. Promulgators of the conventional wisdom have failed to recognize the crucial difference between dependence on arms imports and dependence on technology imports: the former engenders a static dependency relationship while the latter results in a dynamic relationship. The import of military technology has enabled a growing number of developing countries to build arms industries that may eventually provide the bulk of required military hardware, thereby greatly reducing the need for foreign hardware. As experience accumulates in the development and production of weapons, the world's newest defence manufacturers will also become increasingly less dependent upon foreign military technology. J. Fred Bucy, of Texas Instruments, was right on the mark when he wrote in a 1976 Defence Science Report that 'The release of technology is an irreversible decision. Once released, it can neither be taken back nor controlled. The receiver of know-how gains a competence which serves as a base for many subsequent gains'.[50]

Dependence on foreign military technology can be overcome in the long term just as technological dependence in other industrial sectors can be superseded.[51] The transfer of military technology from the advanced industrial countries of the North to the developing countries of the South has set in motion a process that may well eventuate in a dramatic reduction of the developing world's military dependence on the North. As Steven Spiegel has written on the subject of North–South military technology transfers:

This kind of assistance has the greatest effect of any kind of military aid on a consumer's power in the long run, both in terms of military capability and in terms of economic spin-off on domestic industries and the ability to produce arms for export. The political implications of helping a nation to produce its own arms are also far reaching. Once a country has gained this capacity, an increased level of political independence and increased freedom to pursue its own foreign policy goals is implied.[52]

The manner in which Third World arms manufacturers have gone about MIS has insured the national autonomy of their defence industries. Even though foreign defence technology has played a major role in building up the Third World's defence industries, foreign defence firms have not. The emergence and growth of defence production in the Third World is not the result of Northern defence manufacturers shifting production operations to the South. Whether defence production is concentrated in the public sector, as in India, the private sector, as in South Korea, or is spread across both sectors, as in Brazil, foreign defence firms have not been permitted to invest heavily in Third World arms industries. Foreign direct investment (FDI) in the defence sector has been strictly limited. Brazil, for instance, has sought to assure national control by restricting FDI in any given defence firm to 49 per cent. Unlike many other industrial sectors in developing countries, therefore, the defence sector has not been penetrated.

This challenge to the conventional wisdom is more than a mere argument based solely on logic. There is an empirical as well as an analytical basis for the challenge. The most advanced of the Third World's defence producers, producers such as Brazil, India, Israel, South Africa, and South Korea, have already been able to reduce the degree of their dependence upon both foreign arms and foreign technology. Brazil, in particular, has made tremendous strides. In 1970, just a year after Embraer, Brazil's leading aircraft manufacturer, had been founded by the state, only about 40 per cent of the Brazilian Air Force's fleet was of local origin.[53] The situation was quite different by the mid-1980s. In 1984, approximately 77 per cent of the Brazilian Air Force's total inventory of 740 planes and helicopters were of local origin. The tactical, maritime, transport, and training commands were all dominated by Brazilian-built aircraft. Furthermore, all 280 aircraft on order in 1984 were to be procured from Brazilian firms.[54] And, most importantly, the Bandeirante transport/maritime patrol aircraft, the Xingu transport/trainer, the Brasilia transport/reconnaissance aircraft, and the internationally acclaimed Tucano trainer being acquired from Embraer are all not only built but designed by Embraer.[55] Embraer's aviation design expertise received international recognition in 1980 when Embraer entered into a partnership with two Italian aerospace firms, Aeritalia and Aeronautica Macchi, to develop the AMX, a fighter/bomber and ground attack aircraft scheduled for introduction in late 1987 or early 1988.[56]

Brazil's programmes to substitute domestically produced for imported armoured vehicles, missiles, and naval vessels are also at an advanced stage. The army has been acquiring Engesa's Cascavel and Urutu wheeled armoured vehicles since the early 1970s and will soon have Engesa's Osorio main battle tank. Avibras Aerospacial has been providing the military with Piranna air-to-air missiles, Carcara air-to-surface missiles, 70mm air-to-surface rockets, 127mm surface-to-surface rockets, and the Astros II 16-tube rocket system. Although somewhat less progress has been made in nationalizing the procurement of naval vessels, the navy has been able to acquire locally built and designed patrol craft and corvettes. These armoured vehicles, missiles, rockets, and naval vessels, like Embraer's aircraft, were all designed by Brazilian firms.[57]

As a result of the success of its military import substitution programmes, Brazil during the first half of the 1980s no longer had to import light military aircraft such as trainers, transports, and COIN aircraft, armoured cars, armoured personnel carriers, wheeled armoured fighting vehicles, light tanks, rockets and missiles, small naval vessels, or small arms and ammunition.[58] The success of its nationalization effort is indicated by the fact that Brazil's arms imports fell from a high of $304 million in 1979 to only $38 million by 1983. At the same time Brazil's arms exports rose from $49 million in 1975 to a high of $300 million in 1982.[59]

Although few other developing countries have been as dramatically successful as Brazil in their attempts to nationalize arms procurement, countries such as South Africa, Israel, India, and South Korea have experienced varying degrees of success in their efforts to reduce dependence upon imported arms. South Africa has become virtually self-sufficient and arms are no longer imported in significant quantities.[60] Israel has invested heavily in a technologically sophisticated and internationally competitive defence industry that provides for an ever increasing proportion of the country's needs.[61]

Military self-reliance has been a major preoccupation of India's political leaders since the country gained its independence in 1947. The fact that some 63 per cent of the Indian Air Force's inventory of over 1500 aircraft in 1984 had been built by Hindustan Aeronautics Limited, India's state-owned aircraft manufacturer, is indicative of the success, even though limited, of India's MIS programmes.[62] And although India has acquired several hundred Soviet T-54 and T-55 tanks, the domestically produced Vijayanta comprised 65 per cent of the Army's tank force in 1984.[63] In addition, India was in the process of acquiring domestically built destroyers, frigates, corvettes, jet fighters, and helicopters in the mid-1980s.[64] India's defence industry, unlike Brazil's, however, has relied heavily on licensed production of foreign equipment, such as Soviet MiG-23s, which comprise the core of the Air Force's fighting force.[65]

Despite its special relationship with the USA and its reliance upon American weaponry and the presence of American troops, South Korea, too, has had success in nationalizing its arms procurement. South Korea, like Brazil, invested heavily in a defence industrial complex during the 1970s. As a result, according to a US Congressional Budget Office Study, 50 per cent of all required military equipment was being produced domestically by 1978.[66] By the early 1980s, 70 per cent of the weaponry needed by the Korean armed forces was being manufactured locally.[67] Again like Brazil, South Korea's arms imports have been declining and its arms exports rising. Arms imports fell from $722 million in 1978 to $278 million in 1983 while arms exports rose from a mere $8 million in 1975 to $950 million in 1982.[68]

Due to the rapid economic growth of the 1970s, South Korea has also assumed the financial burden of its own defence. In fiscal year 1966 the USA provided the funds for 85 per cent of Korean defence expenditures. By fiscal 1976 the USA was providing only 12 per cent of the country's military expenditures — and two-thirds of the funds provided by the USA in fiscal 1976 were in the form of foreign military sales credits that would be repaid.[69] By fiscal 1977 South Korea was 'funding essentially all of its defence costs'.[70] Even though American troops remain in South Korea (though in declining numbers since the late 1960s), South Korea has clearly demonstrated its ability to reduce its dependence upon the USA.

Despite the success of countries such as Brazil, South Africa, Israel, India, and South Korea, not all of the Third World countries that have turned to MIS have eliminated, or even will eliminate, the need for imported weapons and become self-sufficient. The need for external inputs remains. Argentina, for instance, even though it has long had an across-the-board production capability, still employed imported as well as locally manufactured weapons against the British in its attempt to annex the Falklands in 1982.[71] Egypt, with its more recently acquired across-the-board production capability, still relies heavily on arms supplied by the USA and various Western European suppliers. Other, less capable, producers, such as Chile, Indonesia, Mexico, Nigeria, Pakistan, Peru, the Philippines, Taiwan, and Thailand, are even further from the goal of military self-reliance. Even the most advanced producers have not yet completely eliminated the need for imported weapons. Israel still requires American supplies. The most technologically sophisticated weapons in the Indian arsenal are still imported. And even though South Korea produces some 70 per cent of the military equipment its armed forces have acquired in recent years, it still purchases American weapons and American troops have not yet departed.

Those Third World arms manufacturers that exist in a high-threat, technologically sophisticated military environment have found it extremely difficult to throw off the shackles of military dependence — even when, as in the cases of Israel, India, and South Korea, the resources devoted to military import substitution programmes have been far from insubstantial. While Brazil, situated in a relatively benign security environment, greatly reduced the level of its dependence upon imported arms in a short period of time, and South Africa, confronted only by militarily weak adversaries, has become essentially self-reliant, Israel, India, and South Korea have found the process of reducing military dependence to be somewhat more arduous. Israel is located in what is arguably the most volatile region of the world and is confronted with adversaries that have been able to acquire some of the most advanced conventional weaponry available. The threat to Israel's security is immediate, constant, and non-receding. India is confronted by two troublesome adversaries. One, China, has the world's largest military establishment. The other, Pakistan, has been armed with advanced American weaponry. And South Korea is confronted by an implacable foe: a North Korea that maintains a military establishment that is larger than South Korea's and that is supplied and supported by two major powers — the Soviet Union and China.

While Israel, India, and South Korea have been able to reduce the level of their dependence upon imported arms, it is inherently more difficult for them to become militarily self-reliant in the same sense that Brazil and South Africa have become self-reliant. Both South Africa and Brazil were able to utilize middle-level military technology in their quest for self-sufficiency. Given the nature of the threats they confront, however, Israel, India, and South Korea are compelled to acquire weaponry at the cutting edge of technology. In other words, the products of these three countries must be able to compete directly with those of the major arms suppliers — the two superpowers and the countries of Western Europe.

Yet despite the numerous obstacles confronted by

countries attempting to nationalize arms procurement and reduce the level of their dependence on arms imports, the manner in which Third World defence producers acquire arms increasingly resembles the manner in which many of the advanced industrial countries procure military equipment. Thirty per cent, for instance, of the defence contracts entered into by Italy in 1980 were for foreign military equipment. Over one-third of the military equipment purchased by Sweden during the 1970s was imported.[72] The UK, West Germany, Italy, and other Western European members of NATO, like Third World arms producers, continue to import some of the arms their military forces require. Many advanced industrial countries, again like Third World arms producers, also manufacture military equipment under licence. Britain, for instance, produces French Milan anti-tank missiles and American AIM-9 surface-to-air missiles, TOW anti-tank missiles, and Harpoon submarine-to-ship missiles, while Italy builds French Roland-2 surface-to-air missiles, Milan anti-tank missiles and a whole array of American missiles, helicopters, and armoured personnel carriers.[73] The sources of military equipment for the Third World's arms producers and the advanced industrial countries, therefore, are not terribly dissimilar.

## LOCAL PRODUCTION/IMPORT ACQUISITION

As has become evident, those Third World countries that have attempted to nationalize arms procurement have, in effect, adopted a 'mixed' local production/import acquisition (LP/IA) posture. The inability of even the most advanced Third World defence manufacturers to produce 100 per cent of the equipment their military establishments desire compels them to continue acquiring some of their requirements from foreign suppliers. Third World arms producers, therefore, like the Northern advanced industrial countries, manufacture what they can and import the rest. No Third World military establishment relies exclusively on the products of local industry. The pure form of domestic production does not yet exist in the Third World (nor, of course, does it exist in the North — even the USA and the Soviet Union import arms).

The 51 developing countries that had, by the mid-1980s, initiated MIS programmes, whether limited to the production of small arms and ammunition or committed to the development of an across-the-board production capability, had, *de facto*, adopted a LP/IA strategy. A LP/IA posture can take a number of forms, ranging from limited production capabilities and extensive arms imports at one end of the continuum to extensive production capabilities and limited arms imports at the other end. Arms imports may be from a single/predominant source or multiple sources — although countries that have made the effort to reduce military dependency by initiating MIS programmes are more likely to import arms from multiple sources than from a single/predominant source.

All things being equal, a country's political and military autonomy is to a large degree a function of where it is located on the LP/IA continuum. Countries such as the Philippines and Pakistan that have only limited production capabilities and a high import–production ratio are vulnerable and may well experience serious constraints on their political-military autonomy, especially if they depend on a single or predominant external supplier. Countries such as Brazil and South Africa that have built up extensive indigenous production capabilities and have a low import–production ratio will find that while they may be somewhat sensitive to disruptions in the supply of foreign arms, they are no longer vulnerable and they in fact possess considerable policy and behavioral autonomy. Although a handful of developing countries, including Brazil, South Africa, Israel, and South Korea, will be arrayed towards what they would certainly view as the positive end of the continuum (extensive production capabilities and a relatively low import–production ratio), the distribution of countries along the LP/IA continuum, given the limited capabilities of the majority of the Third World's arms producers, is skewed toward the 'negative' end of the continuum (limited production capabilities and a relatively high import–production ratio).

Of course, all things are not equal. As noted earlier, a high threat, sophisticated military environment complicates counter-dependence efforts. The level of indigenous content of locally manufactured equipment must also be taken into account. The further a country has advanced through the five stages of production, and the greater, therefore, the level of local input, the more likely it is that import dependence will have been reduced and autonomy enhanced. It is, however, quite possible for a country to have developed an across-the-board production capability but still be located closer to the negative end of the LP/IA continuum than expected — either because production is stalled at stage three with no local research and design input (Egypt), or the security problems confronting a country are of such magnitude that, even though stage four and/or five production of aircraft, armoured vehicles, missiles, and naval vessels is taking place, military supplies must still be acquired from abroad, especially during crises (Israel).

A major determinant of the level of local content (or value added) is a country's technological and industrial capabilities. Only when industrialization has spawned a corps of skilled workers, an industrial managerial elite, trained scientific and technical manpower, and when other industrial sectors, such as, for instance, the steel, chemical, electronics, and transportation sectors, are able to support the development of a local content-intensive defence industry is there any prospect for military self-reliance and policy and behavioural autonomy. Third World countries, such as Brazil and Israel, with relatively technologically advanced, diversified industrial economies have been more successful not only in building a defence industrial sector, and thereby reducing the range of weapons that must be imported, but also in turning out defence products that have a high degree of local content than have less technologically and industrially capable countries such as Pakistan.

## CONCLUSION

The countries of the Third World have available to them the same set of arms acquisition options available to the advanced industrial countries. In the South as well as the North, the choice of acquisition strategies impacts directly upon security. The countries of the Third World, however, given their subordinate position in the world military and economic order[74] and their limited (even though expanding[75]) technological and industrial capabilities, are confronted with *de facto* constraints on their choice of acquisition options. Existential reality, therefore, on both the international and the domestic level, has imposed structural constraints on the effective range of available acquisition options so that for the developing countries of the South more than for the advanced industrial countries of the North, arms acquired to promote national security may well erode rather than enhance security.

Of the three possible acquisition strategies, the arms import option, whether in the form of single/predominant source acquisition or multiple source acquisition, has proved to be the most problematic. Single/predominant source external acquisition results in military dependency and the concomitant diminution of state sovereignty and loss of policy and behavioural autonomy. Multiple source external acquisition, even though it has been adopted as a counter-dependence strategy, only enables an importer to spread its dependence across several suppliers. It does not reduce the level of dependence and serves to complicate training, maintenance and logistical requirements.

MIS, the second counter-dependence strategy, has enabled Third World arms producers to reduce their dependence on arms imports by substituting locally designed and manufactured weaponry for imported weaponry. By reducing dependence on external suppliers, a successful MIS strategy enhances security, preserves state sovereignty, and fosters policy and behavioural autonomy. Yet despite the potential counter-dependence, security and autonomy enhancing impact of MIS, those Third World countries that have initiated arms production efforts, even those with relatively mature, large-scale programmes, must still, to a greater or lesser degree, depending on their technological and industrial capabilities, the magnitude of the threat confronting them, and the technological sophistication of their security environment, import arms.

Since even the most advanced of the Third World's arms manufacturers have not yet proved capable of relying solely on local production to meet the requirements of their military establishments, available arms acquisition options have been reduced, in effect, from three to two. Two analytically distinct options, the MIS option and the mixed LP/IA option, have been merged in practice. Those countries that produce arms also import varying quantities of arms. In the final analysis, therefore, the choice for Third World countries (and the advanced industrial countries as well) boils down to either acquisition from abroad, whether entirely or predominantly from a single source or from several sources variety, or local production/import acquisition. The latter option, even though it can not assure absolute autonomy, has proved to be more conducive to policy and behavioural autonomy than the former.

## NOTES

[1] Arnold Wolfers, *Discord and Collaboration: Essays on International Politics* (Baltimore, MD: Johns Hopkins University Press, 1962), pp. 147–65.

[2] For examples of the traditional conceptualization of security that stresses external, military threats, see Robert J. Art, 'The Role of Military Power in International Relations' in B. Thomas Trout and James E. Harf (eds), *National Security Affairs: Theoretical Perspectives and Contemporary Issues* (New Brunswick, NJ: Transaction Books, 1982, for the National Strategy Information Service), p. 14; Richard Smoke, *National Security and the Nuclear Dilemma: An Introduction to the American Experience* (Reading, MA: Addison-Wesley, 1984), pp. 251–6; and Frank N. Trager and Frank L. Simonie, 'An Introduction to the Study of National Security' in Frank N. Trager and Philip S. Kronenberg (eds), *National Security and American Society: Theory, Process, and Policy* (Lawrence, KS: University Press of Kansas, 1973, for the National Security Education Program), pp. 35–48.

[3] See Mohammed Ayoob, 'Security in the Third World: The Worm About to Turn?' *International Affairs*, vol. 60, no. 1 (Winter 1983–4), pp. 41–51.

[4] See the other chapters in this volume; Edward Azar and Chung-

in Moon, 'Third World National Security: Toward a New Conceptual Framework', *International Interactions*, vol. 11, no. 2 (1984), pp. 103–35; Edward E. Azar and Chung-in Moon, 'Managing Protracted Social Conflicts in the Third World: Facilitation and Development Diplomacy', *Millennium: Journal of International Studies*, vol. 15, no. 3 (Winter 1986), pp. 393–406. Another attempt to broaden the concept of security to include non-military factors was made by Richard Ullman, 'Redefining Security', *International Security*, vol. 8, no. 1 (Summer 1983), pp. 129–53.

[5] John Herz, *Political Realism and Political Idealism* (Chicago: University of Chicago Press), 1951; *idem*, 'Idealist Internationalism and the Security Dilemma', *World Politics*, vol. 2 (January 1950), pp. 157–80; and *idem*, *International Politics in the Atomic Age*, (New York: Columbia University Press, 1959), pp. 231–43.

[6] Robert Jervis, *Perception and Misperception in International Politics* (Princeton, NJ: Princeton University Press, 1976); and Robert Jervis, 'Cooperation under the Security Dilemma', *World Politics*, vol. 30, no. 2 (January 1978), pp. 167–214.

[7] Barry Buzan, *People, States, and Fear: The National Security Problem in International Relations* (Brighton: Wheatsheaf, and Chapel Hill: The University of North Carolina Press, 1983), pp. 156–72.

[8] These data on the extent of arms production in the Third World are from M. Brzoska and T. Ohlson, 'Arms Production in the Third World: An Overview' in Michael Brzoska and Thomas Ohlson (eds), *Arms Production in the Third World* (London and Philadelphia: Taylor and Francis, for SIPRI, 1986), pp. 7–34.

[9] See SIPRI, *Arms Trade Registers: The Arms Trade with the Third World* (Stockholm: Almqvist and Wiksell International, and Cambridge, MA: MIT Press, 1975).

[10] Andrew J. Pierre, *The Global Politics of Arms Sales* (Princeton, NJ: Princeton University Press, 1982), p. 78.

[11] Ibid., pp. 46 and 79.

[12] *Official Records of the United Nations General Assembly*, Tenth Plenary Meeting, 29 September 1976, pp. 149–50.

[13] W. Norman Brown, *The United States and India, Pakistan, Bangladesh* (Cambridge, MA: Harvard University Press, 1972), p. 224.

[14] Andrew J. Pierre, *The Global Politics of Arms Sales* (Princeton, NJ: Princeton University Press, 1982), p. 164.

[15] *Official Records of the UN General Assembly*, Tenth Plenary Meeting, p. 149.

[16] Robin Luckham, 'Militarism: Force, Class and International Conflict' in Mary Kaldor and Asbjorn Eide (eds), *The World Military Order: The Impact of Military Technology on the Third World* (London: Macmillan, 1979). p. 241.

[17] Philip J. Farley, Stephen S. Kaplan and William H. Lewis, *Arms Across the Sea* (Washington, DC: The Brookings Institution, 1978), p. 30.

[18] Andrew J. Pierre, *The Global Politics of Arms Sales*, (Princeton: Princeton University Press, 1982), p. 152.

[19] Ibid., p. 180.

[20] Figures derived from Data Management Division, Comptroller, Defence Security Assistance Agency, *Foreign Military Sales, Foreign Military Construction Sales and Military Assistance Facts As of September 30, 1985*, pp. 85, 87, and 89. For an examination of the role of the US military assistance programme in the political socialisation of Third World military officers, see the following two works by Miles D. Wolpin: *Military Aid and Counterrevolution in the Third World* (Lexington, MA: D.C. Heath, 1972), and *Militarism and Social Revolution in the Third World*, (Totowa, NJ: Allanheld, Osmun & Co., 1981), pp. 27–42.

[21] See National Foreign Assessment Center, Central Intelligence Agency, *Communist Aid Activities in Non-Communist Less Developed Countries, 1979 and 1954–1979: A Research Paper*, ER-80-10318U, October 1980, pp. 6 and 15.

[22] Ibid., p. 15.

[23] Ibid., p. 16. For an overview of the Soviet military assistance programme, see Roger E. Kanet, 'Soviet Military Assistance to the Third World' in John F. Copper and Daniel S. Papp (eds), *Communist Nations' Military Assistance* (Boulder, CO: Westview Press, 1983), pp. 39–71.

[24] SIPRI, *The Arms Trade with the Third World*, (Stockholm: Almqvist & Wiksell, and New York: Humanities Press, 1971), p. 39.

[25] Pierre, *Global Politics*, p. 153.

[26] SIPRI, *The Arms Trade with the Third World*, pp. 37–9.

[27] Barry M. Blechman, Janne E. Nolan and Alan Platt, 'Pushing Arms', *Foreign Policy*, no. 46 (Spring 1982), p. 139.

[28] Stephen Rosskamm Shalom, *The United States and the Philippines: A Study of Neocolonialism* (Philadelphia: Institute for the Study of Human Issues, 1981), pp. 75–6.

[29] Ibid., pp. 86–93.

[30] Ibid., pp. 75–109.

[31] Ibid., p. 16; and Geoffrey Kemp with Steven Miller, 'The Arms Transfer Phenomenon' in Andrew J. Pierre (ed.), *Arms Transfers and American Foreign Policy*, (New York: New York University Press, 1979), p. 49.

[32] See Lars Schoultz, *Human Rights and United States Policy Toward Latin America* (Princeton, NJ: Princeton University Press, 1981), especially pp. 211–66.

[33] SIPRI, *The Arms Trade Registers: The Arms Trade with the Third World* (Cambridge, MA, and London: MIT Press, 1975), pp. 81–83.

[34] For an account of Soviet attempts to influence Egyptian policy during the period of Egypt's military dependence upon the Soviet Union, see Alvin Z. Rubinstein, *Red Star on the Nile: The Soviet–Egyptian Relationship since the June War* (Princeton, NJ: Princeton University Press, 1977).

[35] Data derived from Tables 3–3, 3–4, and 3–5 in Edward J. Laurance, 'Soviet Arms Transfers in the 1980s: Declining Influence in Sub-Saharan Africa' in Bruce E. Arlinghaus (ed.), *Arms for Africa: Military Assistance and Foreign Policy in the Developing World* (Lexington, MA: D.C. Heath, 1983),pp. 43–5.

[36] See Clarence A. Robinson, Jr., 'Egypt Plans Review of Military Needs', *Aviation Week and Space Technology*, (16 November 1981), p. 50.

[37] In actuality, of course, there is a continuum between these two forms of the fifth production stage.

[38] See Stephanie G. Neuman, 'International Stratification and Third World Military Industries', *International Organization*, vol. 38, no. 1 (Winter 1984), p. 172.

[39] It should be noted that the data presented here differ from the data provided in the introduction. The data here are for 1980, while the data presented earlier are for the mid-1980s. The earlier data have been utilised here because the manner in which the 1980 data were presented provides greater detail about the range of weapons produced and the extent of local input.

[40] For details concerning the growth of the Third World's arms production programmes, see Andrew L. Ross, 'Security and Self-Reliance: Military Dependence and Concentional Arms Production in the Third World' (PhD dissertation, Cornell University, August 1984), pp. 122–64.

[41] Anne Hessing Cahn, *et al.*, *Controlling Future Arms Trade*, (New York: McGraw-Hill Book Co., 1977), p. 78.

[42] Stephanie G. Neuman, 'Arms Transfers, Indigenous Defence Production and Dependency: The Case of Iran' in Hossein

Amirsadeghi (ed.), *The Security of the Persian Gulf* (London: Croom Helm, 1980), p. 145.

[43] International Institute for Strategic Studies, *Strategic Survey 1976* (London: IISS, 1977), p. 23.

[44] Michael Moodie, 'Defence Industries in the Third World' in Stephanie G. Neuman and Robert E. Harkavy (eds.), *Arms Transfers in the Modern World* (New York: Praeger, 1979), p. 301.

[45] Michael Moodie, 'Sovereignty, Security, and Arms' *The Washington Papers*, vol. 7, no. 67 (Beverly Hills, CA, and London: Sage Publications, 1979), pp. 31–2.

[46] Michael Moodie, 'Vulcan's New Forge: Defence Production in Less Developed Countries', *Arms Control Today*, vol. 10, no. 3 (March 1980), p. 2.

[47] Peter Lock and Herbert Wulf, 'The Economic Consequences of the Transfer of Military-Oriented Technology' in Kaldor and Eide (eds.), *The World Military Order: The Impact of Military Technology on the Third World*, p. 226. See also IFSH-Study Group on Armaments and Underdevelopment, *Transnational Transfer of Arms Production Technology* (University of Hamburg: Institut fur Friedensforchung und Sicherheitspolitik, 1980), pp. 87–9.

[48] Herbert Wulf, 'Developing Countries' in Milton Leitenberg and Nicole Ball (eds.), *The Structure of the Defence Industry: An International Survey* (London: Croom Helm, 1983), p. 341.

[49] See Andrew L. Ross, 'World Order and Third World Arms Production' in James Everett Katz (ed.), *The Implications of Third World Military Industrialization: Sowing the Serpents' Teeth* (Lexington, MA: D.C. Heath, 1986), pp. 278–80. I have unabashedly drawn on this earlier piece in preparing this section of the chapter.

[50] Quoted in Michael T. Klare, *American Arms Supermarket* (Austin: University of Texas Press, 1984), p. 167.

[51] See Charles F. Dolan, George Modelski and Cal Clark (eds), *North–South Relations: Studies of Dependency Reversal* (New York: Praeger, 1983); Dieter Ernst (ed.), *The New International Division of Labour, Technology and Underdevelopment: Consequences for the Third World* (Frankfurt: Campus, 1980); Heraldo Munoz (ed.), *From Dependency to Development: Strategies to Overcome Underdevelopment and Inequality* (Boulder, CO: Westview Press, 1981); and James H. Street and Dilmus D. James (eds), *Technological Progress in Latin America: The Prospects for Overcoming Dependency* (Boulder, CO: Westview Press, 1979).

[52] Steven L. Spiegel, *Dominance and Diversity: The International Hierarchy*, (Boston: Little, Brown and Company, 1971), p. 135.

[53] Derived from data in *The Military Balance 1970–71*, (London: IISS, 1970), p. 74.

[54] Derived from data in *The Military Balance 1984–5*, (London: IISS, 1984), p. 117.

[55] Although the proportion of domestic content continues to increase, Embraer does still incorporate some foreign components in its aircraft.

[56] On the AMX programme see Andrea Natvi, 'AMX: A 'Dedicated Attack Aircraft' for the '90s', *Military Technology*, vol. 9, no. 7 (1985), pp. 14–24.

[57] A few, however, such as the Piranna AAM, appear to be copies of foreign designs and are the product not of original design work but of reverse engineering. Some of these armour, missile, and naval systems, like Embraer's aircraft, still contain imported components.

[58] For details about the expansion of Brazil's MIS programmes see Ross, *'Security and Self-Reliance'*, pp. 165–315. Alexandre de S. C. Barros, 'Brazil' in James Everett Katz (ed.), *Arms Production in Developing Countries: An Analysis of Decision Making* (Lexington, MA: D.C. Heath, 1984), pp. 73–87; William Perry and Juan Carlos Weiss, 'Brazil' in Katz, *The Implications of Third World Military Industrialization*, pp. 103–17; P. Lock, 'Brazil: Arms for Export' in Brzoska and Ohlson, *Arms Production*, pp. 79–104; and Klaus Wolff-Casado Revuelta, 'The Brazilian Defence Industry — Partner or Competitor to the Established Western Defence Industries?', *Military Technology*, vol. 9, no. 10 (November 1985), pp. 92–119.

[59] These figures are in constant 1982 US dollars. Brazil's arms imports actually fell to a low of $30 million in 1982 before increasing to $38 million in 1983, and arms exports decreased from $300 million in 1982 to $110 million in 1983. From US Arms Control and Disarmament Agency (ACDA), *World Military Expenditures and Arms Transfers 1985* (Washington, DC: ACDA, Publication 123, August 1985), p. 97.

[60] *World Military Expenditures and Arms Transfers 1985*, p. 86. On the development of the South African defence industry see Ewan W. Anderson, 'South Africa' in Katz, *Arms Production in Developing Countries*, pp. 321–38; and M. Brzoska, 'South Africa: Evading the Embargo' in Brzoska and Ohlson, *Arms Production*, pp. 193–214.

[61] On the development of the Israeli defence industry see W. Seth Carus, 'Israel: Some Economic and Social Considerations' in Katz,

*The Implications of Third World Military Industrialization,*
pp. 135–50; Robert E. Harkavy and Stephanie G. Neuman, 'Israel'
in Katz, *Arms Production in Developing Countries,* pp. 193–223;
Gerald Steinberg, 'Israel' In Nicole Ball and Milton Leitenberg
(eds), *The Structure of the Defence Industry: An International Survey*
(New York: St Martin's Press, 1983), pp. 278–309; G. M.
Steinberg, 'Israel: High-Technology Roulette' in Brzoska and
Ohlson, *Arms Production,* pp. 163–192; Gerald M. Steinberg,
'Technology, Weapons, and Industrial Development; The Case of
Israel', *Technology in Society,* vol. 7, no. 4 (1985), pp. 387–98; Alex
Mintz, 'Military-Industrial Linkages in Israel', *Armed Forces and
Society,* vol. 12, no. 1 (Autumn 1985), pp. 9–27; and Alex Mintz,
'The Military-Industrial Complex: American Concepts and Israeli
Realities', *Journal of Conflict Resolution,* vol. 29, no. 4 (December
1985), pp. 623–39.

[62] Derived from data in *The Military Balance 1984–5,* p. 99.

[63] Ibid. The Vijayanta MBT is an Indian-modified version of the
Vickers Chieftain, a British-designed tank.

[64] Ibid., pp. 99–100.

[65] On the development of the Indian defence industry see Ross,
*'Security and Self-Reliance',* pp. 316–455; Thomas W. Graham,
'India' in Katz, *Arms Production in Developing Countries,*
pp. 157–91; Raju G. C. Thomas, 'India: The Politics of Weapons
Procurement' in Katz, *The Implications of Third World Military
Industrialization,* pp. 151–63; and H. Wulf, 'India: The Unfulfilled
Quest for Self-Sufficiency' in Brzoska and Ohlson, *Arms Pro-
duction,* pp. 125–46.

[66] Congressional Budget Office, *Force Planning and Budgetary
Implications of U.S. Withdrawal from Korea* (Washington, DC: US
Government Printing Office, May 1978), p. 15.

[67] Shim Jae Hoon, 'South Korea: Standing on its Arms', *Far Eastern
Economic Review,* (23 October 1981), p. 26. For accounts of South
Korea's MIS programmes see Ross, *'Security and Self-Reliance',* pp.
456–537; Young-Sun Ha, 'South Korea' in Katz, *Arms Production
in Developing Countries,* pp. 225–33; Chung-in Moon, 'South
Korea: Between Security and Vulnerability' in Katz, *The Implications of Third World Military Industrialization,* pp. 241–66; Chung-
in Moon, 'South Korean Defence Industry', *Journal of Defence and
Diplomacy,* vol. 4, no. 6 (June 1986), pp. 2–27; Chung-in Moon
and Kwang-il Baek, 'Loyalty, Voice, or Exit? The US Third-
Country Arms Sales Regulation and R.O.K. Countervailing Strategies', *Journal of Northeast Asian Studies,* vol. 4, no. 1 (Spring 1985),

pp. 20–45; and J.E. Nolan, 'South Korea: An Ambitious Client of the United States' in Brzoska and Ohlson, *Arms Production*, pp. 215–32.

[68] South Korea's arms exports actually declined, however, to $355 million in 1983. Figures are in constant 1982 US dollars. Data are from *World Military Expenditures and Arms Transfers 1985*, p. 111.

[69] US Embassy, Seoul, *Report on Korea 1976*, p. 10.

[70] US Embassy, Seoul, *Report on Korea 1977*, p. 8.

[71] On the Argentine defence industry, see Edward S. Milenky, 'Arms Production and National Security in Argentina', *Journal of Interamerican Studies and World Affairs*, vol. 22, no. 3 (August 1980), pp. 267–88.

[72] See Sergio A. Rossi, 'Italy', in Ball and Leitenberg, *The Structure of the Defence Industry*, p. 220; and Per Holmstrom and Ulf Olsson, 'Sweden' in ibid., pp. 147–8.

[73] See SIPRI, *World Armaments and Disarmament SIPRI Yearbook 1983*, (New York: International Publications Service, Taylor & Francis Inc., 1983), pp. 338–44.

[74] See Mary Kaldor, *The Baroque Arsenal* (New York: Hill and Wang, 1981), pp. 131–68.

[75] See K. J. Holsti, 'The Horsemen of the Apocalypse: At the Gate, Detoured, or Retreating?' *International Studies Quarterly*, vol. 30, no. 4 (December 1986), pp. 357–68.

# 8. National Security Regimes and Human Rights Abuse: Argentina's Dirty Wars

CARLOS EGAN

---

During the day the soldiers walked through the torrents in the streets with their pant legs rolled up, playing with boats with the children. At night, after taps, they knocked doors down with their rifle butts, hauled suspects out of their beds, and took them off on trips from which there was no return.[1]

Scenes like these were common in Latin America during the 1970s. In one year alone between 5,000 and 30,000 disappeared in Chile; in seven years the same fate would befall at least 9,000 and possibly as many as 25,000 Argentinians; in Uruguay one person in 500 would be imprisoned for political reasons and many would never be seen again.[2] Targeted for systematic elimination by the state for alleged subversiveness, these *desaparecidos* became dramatic casualties in a unique kind of civil war.

Beginning in 1964, from Argentina to Ecuador, military leaders with similar visions seized power. Their aim was to end persistent stagnation, indebtedness and unrest.[3] As the post-war boom slowed down during the mid-1960s widespread social unrest had escalated into armed confrontation between the state and militant critics. To the military this was nothing less than war, a Dirty War inspired by Soviet sympathizers determined to capitalize on internal disarray for their own expansionist designs.[4] What was supposed to have become the Decade of Development under the Alliance for Progress became instead a period of shattered hopes, social revolution and harsh government repression.[5] Civilian regimes had foundered helplessly, unable to maintain social peace while their economies sunk to depths unknown since the 1930s. As instability mounted, technocratic 'modernizers' within the military began to envision a 'national security regime' which, by eliminating the subversive threat, would be able to guarantee effective economic development.[6]

As Argentina's generals were quick to point out, however, this was no conventional war. 'There were no clear battle lines,' argued General Viola in 1979, 'no large concentrations of arms and men, no final battle to signal victory'.[7] Waged across ideological frontiers this 'total' war threatened the most elemental spheres of daily life: the family, the school and the work place. As civil society itself was being threatened, the smallest private matter became an issue of urgent public concern. The armed forces, as the only truly 'national' institution, would have to assume the public responsibility of wresting control away from the 'terrorist delinquents' hiding in the interstices of the social fabric.[8] The modalities of a free and open society could have no place in this war against subversion. Parliaments would have to be dissolved and judiciaries disabled; political and union activity suppressed; the media censored; and universities purged. Civil guarantees, including the right to a fair trial, had to be suspended because of the cloak of secrecy needed to carry out essential anti-terrorist operations.[9] War could not abide by the paralysing mechanism of democratic society. What in peace would be considered a gross violation of internationally recognized human rights became imperative in the Dirty War against Western civilization. According to an Argentinian government official, it even became necessary for the government at times 'to use against the terrorists the drastic measures they themselves

had employed'.[10] Gross violations of human rights characterized these regimes as much as the *desaparecidos* became
emblematic of their style. They institutionalized state terrorism in the name of economic development and justified
abuse of fundamental human rights in the name of a cold
war doctrine of national security.

Yet García Márquez's account cited at the beginning of
this chapter refers to a historical period long before the cold
war, during the 1928 Colombian government's crackdown
on banana workers striking against the United Fruit
Company. One hundred died in the confrontation, many
were imprisoned, and Communist trade unions were
singled out for especially harsh persecution by the army.[11]
As in Colombia so elsewhere in the region, the regimes
which came to power in the 1920s bear striking similarities
to the Dirty War regimes of 50 years later. They too seized
power — on the eve of the 1929 crash — at a time when
world economic crisis seemed to threaten the very life of
capitalism. Challenged by a working class weaned on
European radical ideologies and willing, at a time of sharp
economic depression, to put the question of capitalism itself
up for discussion, elites responded with the full weight of
the state's repressive apparatus to protect the system which
ensured their privilege.[12] With total disregard for civil
guarantees and basic human rights, the state systematically
went about physically eliminating those groups and individuals pressing for structural change. According to the
'official history' of the 1920s labour was the tool through
which European Bolsheviks proposed to supplant the
traditions and institutions of Latin American society with
foreign ideologies. Labour became the principle target of the
repression and its most militant cadres the object of murder,
'disappearance' and deportation.

Historical retrospective suggests that Latin America's
recurring national security regimes weigh upon our history
like the traits inherited by generations of Buendías in *One
Hundred Years of Solitude*. The first task of this chapter is to
uncover those historical continuities. I will try to show that,
conceived in the womb of colonial Hispanic America, the
national security regime was first hatched 100 years ago at

the end of the protracted civil wars, reappearing transmuted as a regional phenomenon twice, first in the 1920s, later in the 1970s. By recognizing the similarities between these two historical conjunctures we will be in a better position to discern the logic which compelled ruling elites to engage in periodic Dirty Wars against their own domestic critics by arbitrarily depriving them of life and inflicting torture and other forms of degrading treatment on a scale unapproached during normal times. This historical excursion is more than academic. If the brutal regimes of the 1960s and 1970s were not merely an 'accident' but instead structurally rooted in our historical experience, then we might better guard against ever again repeating such unhappy chapters in the future.[13]

The second task of this chapter is more immediately bound to the topic of this volume. We need to re-examine the national security dimensions which surrounded the emergence of these regimes. In the 1920s no less than the 1970s the attacks levelled by the state on significant sectors of civil society were explained in the name of national security. But was the actual threat to *national* security or to the system of *class* privilege which dependent capitalism had created and reproduced? I will try to show in the analysis which follows that the regimes which came to power in Argentina in the 1920s and 1970s invoked the national security threat to launch their respective Dirty Wars as a cover for an armed attack by the dominant elites against a sector of the population whom they considered threatened the system of capitalism itself. What was supposed to be a Dirty War against a foreign threat was, in reality, a class war between capital and its domestic critics.

An excursus into the 1920s, then, is important not only to dispel the notion that the horror of the recent past was unique but also to understand the long-term context of national security doctrine as it has been invoked historically by Latin American elites during periods of profound social and economic crisis. Analytically, Argentina's two Dirty Wars this century bear a striking family resemblance. Both occurred at a time when continued 'modernization' along capitalist lines would require the kind of social engineering likely to produce loud protest from popular sectors adversely affected. The survival of capitalism seemed to require precisely that, or so the official story would claim. And so a compliant, prudent and moderate working class prepared to abandon or postpone any discussion of *structural social change* would have to be guaranteed even if it meant that the state needed to eliminate those domestic critics less willing to compromise.

Both Dirty Wars succeeded in silencing those critics for a while at a tremendously high cost to human life and civilized behaviour. And both succeeded in large measure by a war of words which managed to *redefine* the threat to parochial class interests as a global threat to the nation itself. That verbal war was embedded and routinized in the public discourse controlled from above a carefully crafted doctrine of 'national security' which availed itself of existing national and ethnic cleavages to fuel a wave of ultranationalism sufficiently intoxicating to sustain the officially created mystification that good Argentines simply did not criticize the government and those who did were tools (*idiotas útiles*) of some foreign interest or ideology. The account which follows is about Argentina's Dirty Wars, past and present.

## EXPLAINING HUMAN RIGHTS ABUSE IN LATIN AMERICA

Authoritarian regimes in Argentina have historically trampled on *political* rights. What set the national security regimes apart was their gross violation of *human* rights. As crucial as the distinction is, the two are often confused. In 1979 Jeane Kirkpatrick wrote that traditional authoritarian governments were less repressive than revolutionary autocracies.[14] By this example of 'ethical realism' — soon to be used by the Reagan administration to add the academic imprimatur to its evolving foreign policy — she meant to suggest that abuses committed by friendly nations could be excused on the grounds that even *such* friends were better than any Marxist alternative. Unwillingness by Congress to nominate Ernest Lefever for the State Department's human rights post and increasing impatience with Alexander Haig's determination to exorcise the Carter administration's human rights initiatives forced a shift in Reagan policy in late 1981. In an October confidential memo to Haig it was recommended that human rights be included in its agenda after all, but 'human rights' so redefined to reflect administration cold war priorities and not internationally recognized categories of jurisprudence. For the administration the East–West split represented the fundamental dichotomy of the age, the Soviet Union was still the primary target, and so it became necessry to put the USA squarely on the side of 'human' rights in spite of its friendliness to brutal regimes throughout the world. The memo urged the administration to wage a battle of words, appropriating for itself and its cause the broad concept of 'human' rights to narrowly denote those precise 'individual' liberties which only Western liberal thinking considered the privileged desideratum of democratic society (the right to vote, for example, or equality before the law).[15] To put the West on the side of 'human' rights in this Manichaean world necessarily placed the East, the evil Empire, against them.

So successful was the battle of words and so thoroughly did the rhetoric of deception infiltrate public discourse that leaders of Congress who had previously spoken eloquently against abuses were unable to distinguish political from human rights. Yet American and international law is quite clear about the difference between *human* rights, which can never be suspended (that is, they are 'non-derogable') and *political rights* such as freedom of speech and assembly, which can be suspended in time of emergency when the life of the nation is threatened.[16] Tom Farer, a scholar of international law, specifies which rights are non-derogable under various regional and global provisions:

Under the [United Nations] Covenant there are the right not to be arbitrarily deprived of life, . . . the right to security from physical torture and other cruel, inhuman and degrading treatment or punishment, the right not to be enslaved . . . . [U]nder the American Convention (which places additional sources of restraint on the countries of the Western Hemisphere), article 27 expressly preserves as well in times of emergency the judicial guarantees essential for the protection of the enumerated non-derogable rights.[17]

By requiring that various forms of American assistance should be withheld from governments which engage in a consistent practice of grossly human rights violation, American law clearly recognises the international standard.[18]

The effect of this battle of words resonated well beyond the political arena. Even scholars attempting to explain the violation of human rights by national security regimes were, and continue to be, profoundly confused about this fundamental difference.[19] Liberal political theory takes it as axiomatic that certain basic rights having to do with life and the physical integrity of the person cannot be abrogated under any circumstance even if national security is at stake. The regimes which concern us here are precisely those which have attempted to invoke national security to justify abrogation of these basic, human rights. These are a very special (limiting) case of generic authoritarian regimes which routinely trample on political rights. Both are objectionable, but the difference between them is qualitative. The 'disappearance' of 9,000 citizens bears greater moral weight and blame than censoring a newspaper.

That Latin American governments have committed a disproportionate share of human rights abuses has been widely acknowledged. Scholarship has grappled with this apparent historical quirk and spilled considerable ink to advance an explanation. Yet the link to 'national security' is relatively recent. Older accounts have emphasized other factors such as cultural heritage, the prominence of the military, and an American connection. In that literature at least four types of explanation can be discerned, all of which attempt to put this regional pathology in perspective. According to one substantial body of writing, a distinct Iberian tradition of hierarchy and deference has created in the former colonies social arrangements in which functional (interest) groups of civil society are subordinately linked to the state. Unlike liberal arrangements in which social groups are supposed to interact freely with the state, in this 'corporatist' social structure access to the state by private interests is controlled and mediated by a superordinate public sphere which filters, certifies and incorporates the articulation of private demands. The unequal distribution of power thus reified at the apex of the social system has lent itself, according to this literature, to all manner of abuse, free of accountability both in the routine functioning of the political process and, especially, during crises when the interests of the elite appear to have been threatened.[20]

A second group of explanations points to the weighty presence of the military in civilian affairs, especially politics. Specifically, the military's role as a key political actor coupled with its recognized function of maintaining internal order has facilitated the use of military and police measures (with ample room for abuses of all kinds) when it has seized control of the state machinery during a *coup d'état*. After the European missions (mostly German and French) had helped professionalize the armies by 1900, and once the fear of war subsided, instead of withering away the profession began to emerge as 'a political pressure group with its own mission: national integration, education, nationalization of indigenous and immigrant conscripts, and overseer of internal economic development'.[21] Not long after the civil wars in Argentina, President Sarmiento, looking to form a professional army to eliminate or control the *gaucho* militias belonging to *caudillos* who had stood in the way of national integration for 50 years since independence, established the National Military Academy. By the time Julio Roca assumed the presidency in 1880 the army had in effect become the tool of the executive, well equipped and mobile by virtue of a vast railroad network and capable of rendering powerless once autonomous provincial governors. The Argentinian army's function of maintaining internal order dates back to these early years of national consolidation. After 1880, in alliance with conservative civilian groups, and espousing a nationalist and anti-labour ideology, the Argentinian army became 'the praetorian guard of an all-powerful president representing the landed aristocracy'.[22] Increasingly uneasy during the turbulent 1920s with the conciliatory labour policies of post-war democratic administrations, between 1927 and 1937 military elites and their civilian allies seized power in Argentina, Bolivia, Brazil, Chile and Peru. Citing civilian ineptitude in economic matters, these regimes broke with traditional parties, suppressed leftist movements, and through force and fraud managed for the next decade or so to prevent other 'popular' governments from coming to power. Throughout the remainder of the century the military's abuse of the democratic process increased as its role became ever more pivotal in the national political game.

Inter-state warfare has been rare in the region and military expenditures have ranked with sub-Saharan Africa as the lowest in the world.[23] But classical geopolitical thinking has dominated politically significant elements within the Latin American military establishment. According to that military doctrine traditional military concerns with security and defence are inseparable from national development aspirations. According to a third perspective, this fact goes a long way to explain the abuse of human rights by *de facto* governments. Inspired by Karl Haushofer's German School of the 1930s, the doctrine sees the military as emblematic of the state in its task of struggling to survive and develop in ruthless competition with other states. As a 'living organism' which responds to all sorts of pressures, the state's vulnerability hinges on the military's unique capability of defending against armed attack from abroad.[24] Thus is born the possibility of an alliance which, if conditions warranted, would require extending the military's traditional concern over defence into the area of internal security. And so general geopolitical doctrine has allowed waging 'war' on domestic soil against 'nationals' loyal to 'foreign' interests or ideology. Only in the Argentinian writings is the connection explicitly made between the nation's geopolitical standing and the military's ability to maintain domestic order.[25] In all cases, however, alleging a 'state of war' necessarily involving armed attack 'against the physical integrity' of the citizen makes a legitimate tactic of war out of what in civil society would be considered an illegitimate derogation of human rights.

A fourth perspective places blame on the American postwar policy for encouraging state terrorism and exporting repression. Hammered out in the 1945 Rio Pact (a collective security arrangement explicitly orientated against Communist intervention) and given its ideological and legal clout by act of Congress, the USA, it is argued, systematically nurtured alliances with repressive military governments willing to participate in the crusade to contain communism and consolidate the economic vision of Bretton Woods in the Western hemisphere.[26] In general, American policy up to 1960 provided military assistance to defend the continent against external aggression. After the Cuban revolution, however, a shift in emphasis to a concern with internal security was reflected in arms sales useful only for counter-insurgency and internal repression (small arms and communications equipment, for example). Arms were channelled through military sales programmes: Public Safety (OPS), Military Assistance (MAP), and Foreign Military Sales (FMS); police weapons made their way through funds designated for narcotics control: International Narcotics Control (INC) and the Drug Enforcement Agency (DEA); tear-gas grenades and chemical 'Mace' were channelled through the Commercial Sales (CS) programme; and finally, transport planes, search radars, computers and 'crime control and detection equipment' were exported, like chewing gum, through conventional trade programmes of the Commerce Department.[27] Commerce Department channels have even been used by American corporations to circumvent embargoes on major violators of human rights like Chile.[28] Supplying a steady flow of arms for 'internal control', this perspective suggests, is the glue which holds together an American-dominated system of inter-American defence aimed at protecting its 'national security' by guaranteeing the friendliness of its hemispheric 'backyard'. Enforcing that hemispheric hegemony has been achieved at the expense of democracy and human rights for Latin America.

All four perspectives shed considerable light on the problematic of human rights abuse and, in fact, by suggesting systemic causes help discredit the official story that the Dirty War can be explained away as the result of 'individual excesses' by overzealous subordinates.[29] Yet the pattern of human rights abuse is by no means constant. Argentina, for example, has experienced periods of substantial social peace and governmental tolerance in addition to its seamier historical moments. But what accounts for these shifts? The answer for Latin America is by no means clear. What can be said about the case of Argentina, however, is that though *necessary* perhaps, the four explanations are not *sufficient* to explain the variations. Other factors must be at work during certain historical conjunctures which enable Argentina's potential for state-sponsored human rights abuse to surface. In the discussion which follows I will suggest a fifth perspective, complementary to the other four, which seeks to identify in the international political economy the factors which account for cycles of human rights abuse.

Close examination of key historical moments will be central to the argument. In particular, we will try to link the propensity to human rights violations during periods of exceptional social strain caused by major changes in the international division of labour. Specifically focusing on captialism's two major crises of the twentieth century as they play themselves out in Argentina (in the 1920s and again in the late 1960s and 1970s), it appears that the social convulsions generated by those crises, interpreted by the elite as a war against capitalism itself and redefined as a threat to the national rather than its own class interests, set in motion a two-step process which would attempt to perpetuate in the world economy undergoing reorganiz-ation the traditional bases of power and wealth. The first step takes place during severe economic downturn and involves outright military defeat of 'subversive' elements in order once again to put the question of capitalism safely beyond discussion. The Dirty Wars of the 1920s and 1970s refer to this first step. It is precisely in the course of this mili-tary phase of the 'class war' that wholesale elimination of individuals, actually radical or simply perceived as such, becomes official state policy. The remainder of the essay will focus on this step in which the naked brutality of Argentina's national security regimes can be seen most clearly. In the course of the subsequent political realignment that occurs after the crisis is over and the economy begins to rebound, an organized labour movement cleansed of its most militant members is co-opted by meliorative legislation, wage concessions and partial inclusion in the political game. During the second step the state is able to retract its claws in order to renegotiate, for a while, a social pact in which gross violation of human rights is simply unnecessary.

## ARGENTINA'S NATIONAL SECURITY REGIMES

Crises of capital accumulation on a world scale have occurred with remarkable consistency every 50 years or so.[30] The general retrenchment and sudden drop in world prices has tended to affect export economies in particular since their economic lifeblood depends so heavily upon attracting sufficient foreign exchange to purchase critical imports. In Argentina such crises have resulted in sudden drops in exports, general economic stagnation, governmental fiscal crisis, foreign indebtedness, and severe unemployment. The domestic crisis which ensues appears, at least in the case of Argentina, to have been the result of an exhausted economic model incapable of generating further internal growth. Only by abandoning those exhausted models for others more in tune with the structural incentives and opportunities of a world economy undergoing transmutation has it seemed possible to solve the crisis of accumulation on a national scale. The success of Argentina's long-term recovery has of course hinged upon the particular models chosen to insert itself at key points into the evolving global division of labour.

Three distinct economic models have been pursued in Argentina since political independence in the nineteenth century. Between 1860 and 1929 the country produced grain and meat which it exchanged on the world market for practically everything else. A propitious world market favoured Argentina during these initial 'golden years', but as the boom began to fade, and a few years before the crash of 1929, many began to question the wisdom of this agroexport model which so disarticulated the domestic economy, making it helplessly dependent on outside factors and vicissitudes. After the crash, the vague outline of a new model began to make itself evident. Depleted of foreign exchange reserves, and thus able no longer to purchase abroad the inputs and consumer goods it previously imported, an 'import-substitution' model of industrialization (ISI) began to produce — with considerable government protection — those light industrial goods which it previously had exchanged on the world market. Healed from the worst ravages of the depression, the economy began to rebound under the new industrializing economy, so that by 1936 industrial production had surpassed rural output in value. By the early 1960s, as the post-war boom began to fade, Argentina's economic health began to falter once again, this time under an exhausted ISI model which had already saturated the local market with domestically produced light industrial goods. As in the previous conjuncture at the end of the export boom, many began to look to new models. It was thought that the partial industrialization achieved under ISI would have to be completed by deepening. A model of 'integrated industrialization' able also to produce heavy (capital) goods might, by reducing dependence on expensive foreign imports, overcome the crippling stagnation. The national security regime which came to power in 1966 did so principally to install a deepening model of industrial development.[31]

The timing of these structural transitions was no accident. Each new economic model surfaced at the trough of the economic cycle when the system of world capitalism was in a state of transition. A thorough reorganization of world production would eventually solve the crisis of accumulation. Key in that reorganization was the divergence between profits obtainable in the 'core' and the 'periphery' and hence the altered structure of incentives and opportunities. The first transition began around World War I. By the 1920s three decades of prosperity under the export model had made possible the decentralization of consumer goods production away from the core industrial nations. The cost advantages for Europe and the USA to export heavy industrial products alone more than compensated for relinquishing part of the light industrial market to peripheral producers. The turning point was in 1929 when ISI began to insinuate itself on the agro-export model as a serious contender. Recovery and ISI industrialization advanced apace throughout World War II until the mid-1950s when ISI itself began to show some strains. Like 1929, 1970 was another major turning point in world capitalism. Two decades of economic growth in the core countries had reduced unemployment and strengthened the bargaining position of unions sufficiently to make feasible the relocation of production to areas of lower wages. The traditional cost advantages for the core (education, stability, and proximity to consumers) were no longer sufficient to compensate for other cost advantages encountered in the periphery (low wages, adequate labour productivity and government subsidies). The recession of 1973–4 provided the catalyst for rethinking the conventional wisdom of ISI and so the possibility of deepening began to insinuate itself among policy-makers. Each crisis, in the 1920s as well as the 1970s, marked the end of economic downturn under an exhausted model and the start of an upswing under a new one.

At the trough of the economic cycle the insufficiencies of the old order and the dislocations occasioned by the new one kindled acute social unrest. Class and industrial structure, employment patterns and opportunities, production conditions, social cleavages were all being profoundly transformed. So was the political game. The old social pact which for a while had guaranteed domestic peace was beginning to break down as those most affected by the downturn began to challenge existing relations of production and the legitimacy of the state which enforced them. Economic crisis quickly turned into a crisis of authority. Escalating social unrest and organized labour demands for structural change prompted economic and political elites to form a 'national emergency coalition' to face the radical challenge and to renegotiate the social pact. The national security regimes which emerged, citing the extraordinary circumstances, suspended the modalities of civil society and the democratic process in order to conduct a 'war' against unpatriotic elements bent on destroying the nation. Eliminating the radical threat to the system brought with it social peace and the conditions for economic recovery. As the economy rebounded informed by a promising new economic model it became possible once again under a social contract to forge a new political realignment.

The economic and social conditions which lead to the creation and eventual dismantlement of what we have been calling Argentina's national security regimes were described over a decade ago by O'Donnell in his pathbreaking work on 'bureaucratic-authoritarianism' (B-A).[32] His own recent work, and the growing literature which it engendered, eloquently traces the political economy of these regimes and the Archimidean logic they seem to obey. Yet O'Donnell's early work on Argentina in particular, but the comparative studies by others as well, concentrate exclusively on the very recent wave of regimes of the 1960s and 1970s. This literature is well known and will be quickly summarized. The B-A thesis holds that there is an 'elective affinity' between advanced industrialization and authoritarianism in Latin America. The literature suggests that the regimes which came to power within a few years of each other in Brazil (1964), Bolivia (1971), Argentina (1966 and 1976), Uruguay (1972), and Chile (1973) resemble one another in two important ways. They emerged during a crisis of capital accumulation to put in place a model of industrialization which, it was hoped, would solve the economic crisis; and they relied on horrific brutality and totalitarian control to silence any opposition to its stringent austerity measures. The logic traced by these B-A regimes should sound familiar by now.

That sequence described by that logic follows five distinct and discernible steps. By the late 1960s the high cost of importing intermediate and capital goods for the production of consumer (ISI) goods manifested itself in severe balance-of-payments deficits, foreign indebtedness and hyper-inflation. The severe: Economic downturn prompted elites to shift to 'orthodox' austerity measures de-emphasizing redistribution to the popular sector and heightening the deteriorating conditions for labour. Previously mobilized under a populist coalition, labour responded to the gap between demands and performance by; challenging government policies in the work-place and in the streets. Intensifying; class conflict then prompted military and civilian technocrats increasingly frustrated with the social disorder to form a 'coup coalition' to establish a regime able to; defeat labour's challenge. The attack by the state on sectors of society actually or potentially critical of the government programme, and the gross violation of human rights which it required, was justified in the name of preserving; national security and the national way of life. Industrial deepening raised the political cost of tolerance to a degree requiring the virtual dismantlement of civil society and the suspension of the political process.

The brutality upon which these regimes were predicated is well known. What is less well known, and what is the subject of this chapter, is that the same five-step logic traced out in the 1960s and 1970s had been encoded 50 years before when this century's first national security regime surfaced in order to enforce a solution to an earlier crisis of capital accumulation. In the remainder of this chapter I will trace the events leading up to this earlier national security regime and its attendant Dirty War, drawing comparisons with the more recent regime described in the B-A literature as space permits, in order to draw some conclusions about national security in Argentina which a narrower historical optic would not allow.

## ECONOMIC DOWNTURN AND RADICAL CHANGE

The outbreak of Word War I marked the end of Argentina's export boom and the beginning of a 20-year descent into economic stagnation.[33] The year 1913 marked the beginning of a decline in foreign capital flows and a declining capacity to import. Though the war did create demand for the nation's raw materials and local industries did thrive, the *general* prosperity between 1918 and 1929 was marred by sharp fluctuations and a level of capital flow which never exceeded that of 1914.[34] For labour *specifically*, however, conditions deteriorated sharply. Inefficient local industry and a shift to export crops raised the price of basic commodities and food. Trade fluctuations and an industrial sector incapable of absorbing an already bloated urban population saw sharp increases in unemployment.[35] Between 1913 and 1921 the cost of living increases outpaced wage increases, and, contrary to common belief that workers prospered in the 'world's granary', evidence shows that workers suffered a steady decline in wages between 1910 and 1918.[36] Working conditions involved long hours, few safety measures and arbitrary disciplinary rules; few employers recognised unions, child labour was unregulated, and general living conditions were appalling.[37]

A wave of strikes throughout the region as well as in Argentina coincided with this period of declining wages and cost-of-living increases. According to Spalding, the period between the beginning of the war and 1920 saw:

Explosions of labour activity and a quantitative and qualitative expansion of the movement ... a time of intense labour agitation.... The movement spread into new geographic areas.... [E]xisting ideologies changed, and Communism challenged established lines of thought among workers.[38]

A peak year for social unrest, 1919 saw general strikes in both Sao Paulo and Rio de Janeiro attracting vast numbers; a strike at Puerto Natales when the Chilean army was sent in; post, rail and construction workers' strikes in Cuba; a month-long general strike in metropolitan Lima to fight rising prices marred by widespread looting and army retaliation; a miners' and port workers' strike to demonstrate against cost-of-living increases in Ecuador; a waterfront workers' strike in Uruguay which paralyzed the port of Montevideo.[39] 1919 was also the year of Argentina's Tragic Week during which a small metalworkers' strike escalated into a general strike, paralyzing Buenos Aires and inviting harsh army retaliations which left 1,000 people dead and many more injured, jailed and deported. Because the factors leading up to Argentina's first Dirty War were crystallized in those seven days of January 1919 it will be useful to examine the *'Semana Trágica'* at closer range. It bears mentioning that 1919 was significant for yet another reason. Fifty years later, almost to the day, was the year of the

'Cordobazo' during which a bloody confrontation ensued between the army and a student–labour alliance protesting against General Onganía's regressive wage policies. Like the Tragic Week, the Cordobazo almost succeeded in bringing about a revolutionary collapse of the state.[40]

The militancy displayed during the days of 1919 demonstrated to the elites the power which labour could wield. Employers understood especially well the costliness of strikes: they temporarily weakened the economy, restricted the labour market, spilled over into looting and rioting, and above all raised the spectre of a 'Soviet Revolution'. A one-day strike alone by Argentina's Maritime Workers' Federation (FOM) supported by unions of cabinet-makers, shoemakers, railroad, naval construction and drivers totally paralyzed the port of Buenos Aires, causing a 30 per cent drop in the nation's commercial and industrial activity.[41]

That 1919 saw the most intense labour activity and social unrest to date is not coincidental. During labour's formative years the wealth being generated in the country was such that labour experienced relative prosperity. Wages were so much higher than in Europe, in fact, that in the 1880s it was profitable for *golondrinas*, as seasonal workers were called, to sail back and forth between the continents for the harvests. After the depression of 1890, and certainly by the general strike of 1902, as national income and economic opportunities for unskilled labour began to shrink, labour militancy grew. As the contradiction between the land-owning oligarchy and the working class intensified, so did the radicalism of labour's challenge.

As in the rest of Latin America, Argentina's labour movement up until the 1920s was anything but monolithic and was divided along three principle lines: Marxist 'maximalists' adhering to the class struggle and believing in the equalising power of social revolution; anarchists, prompting intensification of class struggle as a vehicle for bringing down the state; and 'revolutionary syndicalists' somewhere between the other two at first, but by the 1920s evolving a reformist position of accommodation with capital and promoting some sort of 'state socialism'.[42] Divisions notwithstanding, up until the Tragic Week in January 1919 within the organized labour movement anarchists were 'the tail that wagged the dog' and maximalists could mobilise as many as 30,000 to celebrate the October revolution.

As the events of January unfolded, however, an era was about to come to an end. As in other parts of the region, labour militancy was beginning to crumble. The reasons were several. Lack of unity and charges of sterile ideological debate alienated those who wanted concrete results. Constant government and employer opposition drained vital energy making those who had not been eliminated by repression or deportation more receptive to bargaining and accommodation. A general rise in salaries after 1924, and deliberate co-optation by established political parties, especially the Unión Cívica Radical (UCR) which needed working class votes, also served to tame the once revolutionary labour movement. News of two major massacres in Argentina's hinterland in which thousands of unarmed strikers were hunted down and killed probably served to daunt the spirits of their urban counterparts.[43] What is clear, however, is that when on 11 January the labour federation (FORA) and the Socialist Party (PS) called for an end to the general strike a new era of narrow unionism had taken firm hold of Argentina's labour movement.[44] The only radical threat to the established order had been eliminated during the massacre and purges of 1919. The willingness by the rest of organized labour to put the question of capitalism beyond discussion, on the other hand, made it a party to the social contract and thus guaranteed its protection.


## CLASS WAR AND EXCLUSION BY DEFEAT

Government reaction to the heightened social tensions of 1919 was swift and harsh throughout the region. Singling out Communists and anarchists as prime targets and passing laws sanctioning crackdowns, governments throughout the region began to target declared enemies of the system. Laws were passed which legalized police actions against workers; union meetings were closed at will; almost anyone could be arrested and foreign workers deported; the working-class press was closed; through paid informers and agitators workers could be more easily dismissed; meetings were harassed; permits were denied for public demonstrations; and internal co-operation in tracking down agitators made safe havens from persecution almost impossible.[45] In Argentina things were no different. A Buenos Aires policeman testified that he and his fellow officers had been given double orders to shoot to kill strikers without warning and, reminiscent of the Dirty Wars 50 years later, to remove all trace of their written orders so that no future blame could be affixed.[46] Labour unrest was looked upon by the state as a serious challenge to the survival of the landed oligarchy and to the social system through which it controlled its wealth. That in 1919 the state itself was openly prepared to use the weight of its repressive apparatus to eliminate that challenge strongly suggests the class interests to which it was responsive.

Private efforts against labour took on a variety of forms. In co-operation with police, and enforced by their hired spies and agents, employers exchanged 'blacklists' to deny work to suspected agitators. Private associations styling themselves as patriotic defenders of law and order were formed to promote and enforce a 'free labour market' and to discourage labour organization. In Argentina these organizations played an important role in trying to forestall the events which culminated in the Tragic Week. The 'Right to Work Association' was openly anti-labour and protected strike-breakers. The 'Argentine Patriotic League' (Liga), composed of youth from elite families and hired guns called *patoteros* and formed in the very early days of December when trouble began to brew, forcefully broke strikes, haunted subversives and supplied thugs to private armies hired by industrialists.[47] Of these 'White Guards' the Liga was by far the most influential. Hatched in the *Centro Naval*, meeting place for the naval officer corps, this paramilitary force attracted Buenos Aires' most aristocratic elements: Domecq García was its president, P. Christopherson its vice-president. In addition to members of the economic elite, naval and army officers made up the membership as well as prominent political figures (Arturo Goyeneche,

Delfor del Valle, Leopoldo Melo). The Liga collected vast sums of money donated by the most prominent land-owners, local and foreign businessmen, and newspaper owners. In his inaugural address, Rear Admiral Domecq García established the Liga's political agenda:

To stimulate above all the feelings of 'argentineness' in order to invigorate the personality of the nation; to co-operate with the authorities to maintain law and order, to guarantee the safety of the home at those moments when anarchic elements threaten to disturb the safety of the republic.[48]

Though the Liga's membership was made up of the sons of the oligarchy and the very upper middle class, there was also a sizeable representation of the petty bourgeoisie which, in time, would cause a significant split. In the years that followed, the Liga became organized labour's principal enemy, using its shock troops to break up strikes on demand. The government's attitude toward the organiz-ation was at first benevolent, allowing in fact government offices to advertise Liga propaganda. In time, however, embarrassed by the obscurantist, fascist-like tone of its rhetoric and principally afraid of its own political future, Yrigoyen's UCR government forbade Liga proselytizing in government offices. In August the Liga was prohibited from meeting in federal police stations and a general clean-up began. Only then did the extent of military participation become clear: 5 generals, 18 colonels, 32 lieutenant-colonels, 50 majors, 212 captains, 300 lieutenants, and 400 second lieutenants had been active members of the Liga.[49] The Liga was nothing less than the precursor of the Argentine Anti-Communist Alliance (AAA), the principle paramilitary organization which, in co-ordination with the Navy's Superior War College (ESMA) under the leadership of Admiral Emilio Massera, was responsible through its 'work groups' (*grupos de tarea*) for the torture and dis-appearance of many of the 9,000 'subversives' during the Dirty War of the 1970s.

Another private organization engaged in the campaign to cleanse the ranks of labour from radical elements was the

'National Labour Association' (ANT) formed in May of 1918 and composed of the most conspicuous representatives of landowning, industrial, commercial and transportation interests. To protect the 'freedom to work' and the rights of capital became its mandate. The ANT felt President Yrigoyen's labour policy was far too lenient toward strikers in particular since, in its view, immigrant labour was far better off than in its native land. It reasoned that worker discontent, therefore, had to be 'the work of *foreign* agitators who import[ed] their *strange* ideology to Argentine society with the view to subverting it' (my emphasis).[50] Their antiforeignism is noteworthy in light of the heavy British representation in its organization and the obvious veto power of the British ambassador in the Argentinian political game.[51]

By 16 January, 1919, Buenos Aires returned to normality. Workers went back to work and troops returned to barracks. It is impossible to ascertain the precise number of victims of this early Dirty War, but conservative estimates put the number at around 1,000 dead and 5,000 detained.[52] All in just one week.


## NATIONAL SECURITY AND THE IMAGINARY FOREIGN THREAT

As early as 1902 the growing social unrest was being characterized as a foreign threat to national security, and legislation was being drawn up to stop it. A Residency Act sanctioned that year authorized the executive to expel 'all foreigners whose behaviour placed in jeopardy the national security'.[53] In response to the cycle of disorder and emergency measures which punctuated the next eight years (culminating in the riots on the nation's centennial in 1910), Congress passed a Social Defence Act which broadened the offensive against foreigners and added considerable bite to the penalties: Entrance into the country was prohibited to 'anarchists and others' who professed violence against public officials or governments in general or against the nation's institutions; stiff penalties and mandatory jail sentences would be issued to those who, in bad faith, allowed such foreigners to enter the country; all meetings of persons for the purpose of committing acts prohibited by law were also prohibited; one to two years in jail for anyone who verbally or in writing excused in public any act deemed by law to be a crime; three to six years for anyone who fabricated, transported or had in his possession dynamite or any other explosive materials. And thus proportionate to the gravity of the offense the 34 chapters described escalating punishments up to the death penalty.'[54] The much-touted Electoral Reform Act (Roque Sáenz Peña Law) had already secured the electoral exclusion of foreigners by denying them the vote in 1912.

The hand of Bolshevik subversion was seen behind every act of political defiance. A November 1918 demonstration for higher wages was redefined by the elite as a 'maximalist' plot; a provincial strike by policemen the following month in pursuit of a demand for nine months' back pay was denounced in some papers as 'the beginning of a Soviet'. The ANT, the oligarchy's not-so-silent lobbyist, routinely explained away labour discontent as the work of 'foreign agitators' and their imported ideology.[55] The fearful climate of opinion evinced by high society was being certified by the Church which saw in 'anarchy, liberalism, nihilism, masonry and socialism' a frontal attack against the Catholic cause.[56] That fear turned into a real paranoia against Russians in particular. In December the British representative issued a formal protest concerning rumours of a daily influx of Russian agents into the country; the Argentinian consul in Brazil warned of a Bolshevik plot which was likely to affect his country; the Argentinian consul in The Hague warned that Soviet agents had sailed for Buenos Aires; throughout January the American consul in the Argentinian capital asked repeatedly that authorities investigate an alleged plan to assassinate President Wilson.[57] In the early morning of 11 January, Pedro Wald, the young editor of *Avantgard*, a Jewish paper friendly to union organisations of Russian emigres in Argentina (FORS), was arrested and his headquarters raided and sacked. Surrounding the events of his arrest is born the famous 'maximalist' plot. Wald was supposed to have become the 'President of the Argentine Soviet'.[58]

The case of the fabricated 'maximalist' plot, replayed almost exactly during the second Dirty War 50 years later, demonstrates the ability of the press and the government to turn a phantasm into a credible threat for its own ends.[59] In mid-January an anonymous letter from Buenos Aires signed 'a Russian' was received by Montevideo's Chief of Police warning of a coup to overthrow the government by 'maximalists' on either side of the River Plate. The letter gave as the plotter's address the headquarters of FORS! That the plot was an invention was made clear during the judicial proceedings following Wald's arrest. What is most significant, however, is the use to which this *fantasma ruso*, as an Italo-Argentine newspaper dubbed it, was put by police, press and government alike in order to justify the repression unleashed during the Tragic Week. Three of the four major Buenos Aires papers carried sustained coverage of the 'Russian Plot' for four days. Although denying any complicity with the fabricated plot, the government made implicit reference to it in its nationalist harangue against 'foreign elements' tending toward the dissolution of the Argentine nation. Congratulating his troops for their patriotic efforts in putting down the street violence, the Buenos Aires Chief of Police said that with a little more effort they would be giving a 'severe, unforgettable lesson to those elements destructive of Argentine nationalism'.[60]

That the foreign threat was Russian and Communist is clear enough. During the Tragic Week violence occurred predominantly in immigrant neighborhoods.[61] But it was also characterised as a Jewish threat and anti-Semitism in this early incarnation of the national security regime played as much a part as it did in the last Dirty War.[62] Apart from anarchists, Jews became the principal targets of repression, and a Jewish association helped to identify in an antinomial world Argentinians from non-Argentinians, the latter being Bolshevik, Jewish and delinquent. To be Jewish became synonymous with being *ruso* thus closing the hermeneutic circle which clearly established the lines of combat in this war in defence of national security. Unfocused anti-Semitism occasionally resulted in 'Jew-bashing'.[63] But several incidents — like the assassination of the Chief of Police by a Jew named Simón Radowitsky during the centennial Celebrations — helped to channel those anti-Semitic feelings into a proudly nationalistic movement which, with the assistance of the police, provided the oligarchy and the upper class with an ostensibly legitimate instrument with which to crush the labour revolt. By 1919 anti-labour reaction and violence against Jews became almost indistinguishable, making physical attacks against the strikers and Jews equally patriotic.[64] Press coverage could not conceal the racism which informed its ultra-nationalist appeal against the 'foreign threat'. Referring to the subversiveness of the strike, one paper supportive of Yrigoyen's UCR administration described its leaders as 'elements foreign to our nationality who repay our hospitality with this barbaric and despicable transgression'. Four days later the same publication made its anti-Semitic allusions much clearer. They were talking, it reported, about:

a minuscule minority which, under cover of darkness, planned and carried out the barbarities which, with tact and serenity, the government has put to a rest . . . . And we say that this is a minuscule minority because those responsible for recent events represent 1.18 per cent of the population of the republic and 1.79 per cent of the capital city.[65]

The figures cited by the newspaper correspond, according to the 1914 census, to the Russian population in the country.

The Manichaeanism which informed official rendering of political reality early in the century is not very different from that of the late 1960s and 1970s discussed earlier. In fact, the *content* of the antinomies which inform both Manichaean constructions of reality are so much alike that the other historical differences seem less important. The categories most often used by the military during the latest Dirty War to characterize the 'foreign threat' to national security were four. First, the enemy was leftist. Rear Admiral César A. Guzzetti put it this way:

My concept of subversion refers to terrorist organizations of the left. Subversion or terrorism of the right is not so. Contamination by a disease which attacks its viscera of the social organism produces its own antibodies. These antibodies must not be thought of in the same way that one does a microbe. Accordingly, as the government controls and destroys the guerrillas, the antibodies' function will become redundant. I am sure that in the next few months the right will become less active . . . What we are really talking about is the natural response of a diseased organism.[66]

Like the Liga and the private armies in the 1920s, the AAA was not described as a terrorist organization but rather as the antibody of a healthy nation driven to protect its intrinsic values against leftist values which pretended to attack it. Second, the enemy was also seen as foreign. According to *de facto* president General Jorge Rafael Videla, Argentine citizens were not victims of repression because the repression was aimed at a minority which the government did not consider Argentine.[67] Unlike a common criminal which could be rehabilitated the enemy had the third quality of being irretrievable. Such a characterization admitted no ambiguity about proper treatment. Like vermin, it would be found, and if any remained and turned himself in he or she would be turned over to the courts, and, if not, 'we would kill him'.[68] Finally, the enemy was non-Christian and a vile minority whose purpose it was to 'agitate the minds of the youth . . . inculcating them with ideas totally foreign to the national spirit'.[69] Terrorism was not just a matter of carrying guns or throwing bombs, *de facto* president Rafael Videla responded to a correspondent, but, even more insidiously, also 'about pushing one's cause with ideas contrary to our western and Christian civilization'.[70]

## CONTINUING THE WAR BY OTHER MEANS

The unrest and harsh repression which culminated in the Tragic Week inaugurated a new period of polarization in Argentine society. As helmsman of the middle class, UCR President Yrigoyen had attempted to play an arbitrating role between the two dominant social forces in the Argentine political scene: British capital and the local Conservative elite, on one hand, and the working class, on the other. Placed in check by these two forces, he was unable to bridge the social contradictions which exploded in early 1919. The absence of traditional political channels which might have permitted the immigrant population to articulate its demands provoked a violent social reaction to accumulating and worsening economic hardships. Forced to retreat in the face of Conservative and foreign pressure, Yrigoyen abandoned his democratizing agenda. His break-up of the meatpackers' strike inaugurated a flood of legislation aimed at severely repressing public demonstrations of working-class discontent and clearly designed to make the immigrants seem responsible for the upheaval and the backlash. The UCR government had become by 1919 what the conservatives had been seeking since 1912: a static and docile instrument whose only positive attribute resided in its capacity to enjoy a measure of popular prestige. Successful in isolating the more radical workers from the mainstream, the oligarchy's anti-foreign campaign was able once again to bring the labour movement under control. Decimated, detained or deported, the radicals were pushed out onto the fringes of the labour movement. Pigeon-holed as 'foreigners' and discredited as unpatriotic, non-Argentine for their opposition to participating in World War I, their marginality in any future political dialogue was virtually guaranteed. Labour's mainstream, on the other hand, organized in FORA, presenting itself as a tranquil and law-abiding working class, and backed by a Socialist Party which saw itself as 'the principal element of order and progress within the labour movement' re-established its credentials to participate in the national political game.

With peace, the government's policy of defeating labour shifted to a conscious policy of controlled incorporation. Even at the height of the repression Yrigoyen rarely deviated from his pro-labour posture. His ties to the FORA always intact, the administration defended the right to strike and publicly denounced conservatives who favoured a crackdown. It even went so far as to justify worker protest because, as an administration spokesman said, 'of the lack of legislation . . . appalling working conditions . . . and salaries all out of proportion to the wealth of the employers'.[71] But labour legislation was a sensitive issue, and clearly was not designed to go much beyond the alleviation of the most punishing social conditions in order to establish with clarity and precision the exact form in which the working class would be subordinated to the state. Though usually unenforced, the legislation which was passed in the 1920s tended to place labour under vigilant state control. During the parliamentary debate which began right after the Tragic Week and would continue throughout the year three positions emerged. Socialists believed that a 'healthy' unionism committed to 'parliamentarism, negotiation and arbitration' could only be achieved by strict regulation of syndicalist organizations. A second position, held by the UCR and some conservatives, held that a 'new type of unionism' could only come about by a strict subordination of working-class organizations to the state. A third position, held by staunch conservatives, believed in only partial unionization of skilled labour since they alone were capable of being prudent, reasonable and conservative'.[72] All three positions, however, were unanimous in the belief that labour needed to be controlled and subordinate in the political game. In time, a 'new unionism' which until then had been a minority tendency in the labour movement did in fact muscle its way on to centre stage realizing the wishes of the most conservative elements in the parliamentary debate. At the forefront was the railway worker's union (Confraternidad Ferroviaria) which had shown its 'prudence' during the Tragic Week, and which by 1920 had succeeded in imposing a general unification within the labour movement. This union — the first politically significant union committed to strict reformism and ideologically close to the Socialist Party — became the nucleus of a broadly-based labour movement inclined increasingly to more moderate positions. Subsequent events certified the agenda mapped out by the most recalcitrant conservatives. The legislative project failed to be approved, the increasingly mobilized Conservative opposition became the biggest winner in the 1920 elections, and Yrigoyen stepped down in 1922. Two years into Yrigoyen's second term the conservative offensive culminated in the September coup of 1930 when the military under Uriburu seized power which it would retain through electoral fraud until 1943.

The UCR party in Argentina, like its cousins in Uruguay and Chile, had exacted a share of power from the conservatives by: Building a close electoral relationship with reformists within the labour movement; effectively competing with the more 'progressive' Socialists; and reducing conservative and military criticism of their policies by successfully maintaining social peace.[73] As cracks in the armour of the export economy model appeared, the social pact which the UCR had forged with the voting working class began to strain under the pressure of the general strike and subsequent bloody repression. The party would itself have to take the heat for the repression, and in order to guarantee its continued share of power would need to redefine its position in a realignment which put unmistakable distance between itself and those in labour who still wished to put the question of capitalism up for discussion. The radical challenge to the system was for the moment dead and the book on the Tragic Week could be closed. Exclusion by co-optation had replaced exclusion by elimination.

## CONCLUSION

Argentine history has been punctuated by periodic Dirty Wars. Twice in this century, at key points when capitalism faced its severest accumulation crises, the social system seemed on the verge of disintegration. Responding to worsening conditions, labour's increased militancy in pressing for structural change was interpreted by elites as a threat to the system's survival. The Dirty Wars launched by the state in response aimed to salvage the system by eliminating the radical challenge. The most intransigent critics were physically eliminated and 'made to disappear in the night'; the others became part of the loyal opposition. In any case, the challenge to the dominant class was contained and social peace once again achieved. This chapter has tried to show not only that these so-called wars recur (that is, they are not unique events) but also that they obey a curious logic intricately linked to the structures of the world economy and Argentina's social system. That these 'wars' occur at key conjunctures in the development of capitalism when its survival is perceived to be at stake has allowed us to observe in its nakedness, as it were, certain features shielded from view during more normal times. How Argentine regimes have attempted to renegotiate, and eventually legitimate, the 'pact of domination' during exceptional crises is one of those features closely examined above. In the 1920s as well as the 1970s the regimes which waged the Dirty Wars did so by elaborating a spurious doctrine of 'national security' intended to exculpate the brutal measures taken to re-establish social peace.

The path of Latin America's political history is littered with familiar 'deformations' of all kinds: instability, domestic violence, corruption and militarism. This chapter has addressed the issue of 'state terrorism', another, if less common, political deformation. I have suggested that conscious, systematic and general policies of human rights violation by the state in Argentina occur in the trough of global economic cycles. This chapter would not attempt to claim that all such deformations have had economic causes, in Argentina or elsewhere. The evidence strongly suggests, however, that the severity of the dislocations caused during the downswing of these very unique 50-year cycles created conditions under which state terrorism insinuated itself to the ruling elites as a 'rational' policy option. Neither has this chapter attempted to suggest that the logic of state terrorism in Argentina is *necessarily* part of a larger, regional phenomenon. Further comparative research needs to be done. Yet the fact that state terrorism in Argentina has discernible, structural roots strongly suggests that the Dirty Wars may very well have their historical counterparts elsewhere in the periphery. If, as this essay has argued, the phenomenon discussed above is a deformation of the political process which dependent development imposes on Third World countries generally, then it is *likely* that comparable cases will be found. After the last round it is not clear that Argentina's fragile social fabric (or that of Latin America's southern cone for that matter) could withstand another Dirty War. For that reason alone including this issue in any future comparative research agenda becomes especially compelling.

## NOTES

[1] Gabriel García Márquez, *One Hundred Years of Solitude*, translated by Gregory Rabassa (New York: Avon, 1971), p. 287.

[2] Declarations by the US Department of State notwithstanding, independent human rights monitors such as the UN Human Rights Commission, the Human Rights Commission of the OAS, Amnesty International and Americas Watch have documented widespread abuses and corroborated their findings.

[3] General Roberto Viola, *de facto* president of Argentina for less than a year in 1981, described a vision shared by his counterparts in Brazil, Chile and Uruguay: '[T]o remove those factors which since 1930 have prevented us from achieving ... our genuine greatness' and which would enable their countries 'to be admitted into the phalanx of the planet's most advanced nations', *La Razón* (6 October 1981). (All newspapers not otherwise specified are Argentine. Translations are my own.)

[4] The term 'Dirty War' (*Guerra Sucia*), though coined by the leaders of Argentina's 1976 coup, denoted a reality of unrest and confrontation common throughout Latin America at the time. 'It is often forgotten,' said a retired general, Luciano Benjamín Menéndez, that in Argentina there were two camps vying for control, 'subversives on the one hand determined to transform the state into a satellite of the Soviet Union confronting, on the other, the legally constituted national forces' (*Clarín*, 29 December 1983). To General Ramón Camps subversion in Argentina was just one manifestation of the Soviet global offensive in the region whose purpose it was 'to annex ever more territory into its imperial domain by the use of Marxist ideology' (*La Prensa*, 28 December 1980).

[5] For a critical account of the Alliance, see Jerome Levinson and Juan de Onís, *The Alliance that Lost its Way: A Critical Report on the Alliance for Progress* (Chicago: Quadrangle Books, 1970).

[6] It is no secret that policy-makers in the Reagan administration share this Manichaean world view in which East is pitted against West and where internal and external subversion are indistinguishable from one another. The term 'World War III', however, was appropriated by a group of Republican advisors, calling itself the Committee of Santa Fe, whose blueprint for a 'non-interventionist policy of political and ethical realism' in the Americas became American policy when several of its members (Roger Fontaine, David Jordan, Lt General Gordon Sumner and Lewis Tambs) were given administrative posts. For a discussion, see Cynthia Brown (ed.), *With Friends like These: The Americas Watch Report on Human Rights and US Policy in Latin America* (New York: Pantheon Books, 1985), pp. 3–4 and *passim*. Self-designated 'national security regimes' came to power in Brazil in 1964; Bolivia in 1971 and again in 1980; Argentina in 1966 and again in 1976; in Chile in 1973; in Uruguay in 1972; and in Ecuador in 1976.

[7] General Roberto Viola, *La Razón*, (29 May 1979).

[8] The phrase is General José Antonio Vaquero's (*La Prensa*, 24 May 1979). For a critical analysis of the Argentine military's claim that the nation was actually at war, see Daniel Frontalini and Maria Cristina Caiati, *El Mito de la Guerra Sucia* (Buenos Aires: Centro de Estudios Legales y Sociales, 1984), p. 20 and *passim*.

[9] 'This type of secret warfare', argued General Tomás Sánchez de Bustamante, 'involving special operations prevents us from divulging who has been captured and who needs to be captured; there needs to be a 'cloud of secrecy' which is simply incompatible with freedom of the press' (*La Capital* (of Rosario), 14 June 1980).

[10] During a speech in Los Angeles by Economic Minister José Martínez de Hoz (*La Prensa*, 21 September 1978). Looking back on his role as Buenos Aires Chief of Police, General Ramón Camps discussed the difficulty of extracting information from suspected subversives. With the lives of innocent civilians hanging in the balance it was essential to act quickly (in less than 24 hours). Under the circumstances, he added, 'it is of course preferable to act without screams and torture, but that wasn't always possible' (*Clarín*, 1 January 1984).

[11] García Márquez's 'Macondo' is really Santa María, and the 3000 massacred were really only about 100. For a short account, see Hobart A. Spaulding Jr., *Organized Labour in Latin America: Historical Case Studies of Workers in Dependent Societies* (New York: New York University Press, 1977), pp. 66–67. For a more

detailed account, see Charles David Kepner and Jan Henry Soothill, *The Banana Empire* (New York, 1935), ch. 12.

[12] A note on the use of the terms 'state' and 'regime' is in order. Throughout, I shall be using the term 'state' to refer to 'the basic "pact of domination" that exists among social classes or fractions of dominant classes and the norms which guarantee their dominance over the subordinate strata'; see Fernando Henrique Cardoso, 'On the Characterization of Authoritarian Regimes in Latin America' in David Collier (ed.), *The New Authoritarianism in Latin America* (Princeton, NJ: Princeton University Press, 1979), p. 38. A less inclusive term, 'regime' will refer to the formal and informal structure of governmental roles and processes. Under the same 'pact of domination', Argentina has experienced two regime types (civilian and military) whose principal distinguishing feature or 'style' is the method of selection of government (election or coup). As will become evident in this chapter the 'degree of repressiveness' is *not* a distinguishing feature: Yrigoyen's civilian regime early in the century was capable of as much repression as the post-1976 military governments.

[13] On 15 December 1983, President Raúl Alfonsín of Argentina created a National Commission on Disappeared Persons (CONADEP) to investigate the events surrounding the Dirty War between 1976 and 1983. Ernesto Sábato, the writer, was chosen by the Commission's members to be its president. The findings, compiled from 50,000 pages of testimony and published 11 months later, served as the basis for the conviction of high-ranking junta leaders for their involvement in the disappearance of at least 9,000 people, 'the greatest tragedy in our history, and the most savage'; see Ernesto Sábato, *Nunca Más: Informe de la Comisión Nacional Sobre la Desaparición de Personas* (Buenos Aires: Editorial Universitaria de Buenos Aires, 1984), p. 7.

[14] Jeane Kirkpatrick, 'Dictatorship and Double Standards', *Commentary*, vol. 68, no. 5 (November 1979), pp. 34–45.

[15] Richard Kennedy, Under Secretary of State for Management, confidential 'Memorandum for the Secretary' (27 October 1981), cited in Brown, *With Friends Like These*, p. 5.

[16] Article 4 of the United Nations Covenant on Civil and Political Rights and the equivalent article in the American Convention authorize such derogation.

[17] Tom J. Farer, 'Human Rights during Internal Armed Conflicts: The Law Applicable to Western Hemisphere States' in Inter-American Commission on Human Rights, *Derechos Humanos*

(Washington, DC: The Organization of American States, 1984), p. 146. See also a good discussion in Brown, *With Friends Like These*, p. 34n. Lars Schoultz, *Human Rights and United States Policy Toward Latin America* (Princeton, NJ: Princeton University Press, 1981), p. 3, defines human rights as 'rights to life, liberty and the integrity of the person'.

[18] Such bans are to be found in laws denying abusive governments access to security assistance, economic assistance and multilateral development loans; see Brown, *With Friends Like These*, p. 247 notes 7–9.

[19] Margaret Crahan's overly general characterization of national security ideology as one 'that places national security above personal security, the needs of the state before individual rights, and the judgment of a governing elite over the rule of law' does not take us very far in distinguishing in any meaningful way a national security regime from any authoritarian regime, or, even, from a democratic regime in time of national emergency. See her 'National Security Ideology and Human Rights' in Crahan (ed.), *Human Rights and Basic Needs in the Americas* (Washington, DC: Georgetown Unversity Press, 1982), p. 101.

[20] The most important writings on the 'distinct tradition' are contained in two volumes, each with a useful bibliography: James M. Malloy (ed.), *Authoritarianism and Corporatism in Latin America* (Pittsburgh: University of Pittsburgh Press, 1977), and Howard J. Wiarda (ed.), *Politics and Social Change in Latin America: The Distinct Tradition* (Amherst: University of Massachusetts Press, 1974). This argument has served neo-conservatives, inside and out of government, well. See Howard J. Wiarda (ed.), *Human Rights and US Human Rights Policy: Theoretical Approaches and Some Perspectives on Latin America* (Washington, DC: American Enterprise Institute for Public Policy Research, 1982). It should be remembered that Kirkpatrick's tolerance of human rights abuses by 'friendly authoritarian' governments borrows heavily from the 'distinct tradition' arguments (see note 14).

[21] Fredrick M. Nunn, 'An Overview of the European Military Missions in Latin America', in Brian Loveman and Thomas M. Davies, Jr. (eds.), *The Politics of Antipolitics: The Military in Latin America* (Lincoln: University of Nebraska Press, 1978), p. 44.

[22] Martin Goldwert, 'The Rise of Modern Militarism in Argentina' in Loveman and Davies, *The Politics of Antipolitics*, p. 46.

[23] In the last 100 years there have been three major conflagrations: the War of the Pacific (1879–1933) between Chile against Peru

and Bolivia; the war of the Triple Alliance (1865–70); and the Chaco War (1932–5) between Paraguay and Bolivia. Two smaller wars have occurred more recently, between Peru and Ecuador in 1941, and between El Salvador and Honduras in 1969. On the issue of military expenditures, by the 1980s Latin America had the smallest military expenditure as a proportion of GNP, ranking below sub-Saharan Africa; see Henry A. Dietz and Karl Schmidt, 'Militarization in Latin America: For What? And Why?', *Inter-American Economic Affairs*, vol. 38, no. 1 (Summer 1984), pp. 44–64. For similar findings, see Phillipe Schmitter, 'Foreign Assistance, National Military Spending and Military Rule in Latin America' in Schmitter (ed.), *Military Rule in Latin America: Functions, Consequences and Perspectives* (Beverly Hills, CA: Sage, 1973). Gertrude Heare has found that, however low, the level of expenditures tends to increase in times of internal social tension, in *Trends in Latin American Military Expenditures, 1940–1970* (Washington, DC: US Department of State, 1971).

[24] For a good review of the literature, see John Child, 'Geopolitical Thinking in Latin America', *Latin American Research Review*, vol. 14, no. 2 (1979), pp. 89–111.

[25] See Miguel Angel Basail, 'Bosquejo de una apreciación geo-política argentina', *Estrategia*, vol. 36 (September-October 1975). The most developed, least bombastic geopolitical thinking has come from Chile, Argentina and Brazil. For a useful comparison of the three, see Child, 'Geopolitical Thinking'.

[26] For a sample of this literature, see Marcus G. Raskin, *The Politics of National Security* (New Brunswick, NJ: Transaction Books, 1971); James O'Connor, *The Fiscal Crisis of the State* (New York: St Martin's Press, 1973); Richard Barnet, *Intervention and the Revolution: The US in the Third World* (New York: World Publishing Company, 1968); Michael T. Klare and Cynthia Arnson, *Supplying Repression: US Support for Authoritarian Regimes Abroad* (Washington, DC: The Institute for Policy Studies, 1981). Walter LaFeber, *America, Russia and the Cold War, 1945–1980*, 4th edn (New York: Knopf, 1985).

[27] For a detailed account of all these programs, see Klare and Arnson, *Supplying Repression*, pp. 17–83.

[28] After Congress voted to ban all FMS and CS exports to the Pinochet regime the Carter administration approved the sale of four transport planes to Chile's police through Commerce Department channels. Using Brazil as a 'third country transfer', Chile's military planes have been equipped with American power plants

and surveillance equipment; see ibid., pp. 80–2.

[29] Seven months of testimony by defendents and witnesses alike in the Dirty War trials recently concluded in Argentina leaves no room for doubt that the excesses were the result of an ideologically informed, deliberate state policy often dependent on international co-operation for its successful implementation. See *El Diario Del Juicio* (Buenos Aires: Editorial Perfil), nos 1–26 (27 May 1985 to 19 November 1985).

[30] The literature on capital accumulation on a world scale is vast. For a classic treatment, see Samir Amin, *Accumulation on a World Scale: A Critique of the Theory of Underdevelopment*, translated by Brian Pearce (New York: Monthly Review Press, 1974). For a secondary account of the literature on 'long waves', see Folker Frobel, 'The Current Development of the World Economy: Reproduction of Labour and Accumulation of Capitalism on a World Scale', *Review*, vol. 5, no. 4 (Spring 1982), pp. 507–55.

[31] The 1976 regime reversed the 'deepening' strategy and, instead, returned to an agricultural export promotion strategy.

[32] Guillermo O'Donnell, *Modernization and Bureaucratic-Authoritarianism: Studies in South American Politics* (Berkeley: Institute of International Studies, University of California, 1973). For a sampling of writings on the B-A model and an extensive bibliography, see Collier, *The New Authoritarianism in Latin America*.

[33] Guido DiTella and M. Zymelman, *Las Etapas del Desarrollo Económico Argentino* (Buenos Aires: EUDEBA, 1967), p. 295. Adolfo Dorfman, *Historia de la Industria Argentina* (Buenos Aires: Solar/Hachette, 1970), p. 245 and *passim*.

[34] DiTella and Zymelman, *Las Etapas*, pp. 277–350.

[35] Edgardo J. Bilsky, *La Semana Trágica* (Buenos Aires: Centro Editor de América Latina, 1984), p. 32, cites sources which put the figure at 14 per cent.

[36] In a study by Alejandro E. Bunge, cited in ibid., p. 33.

[37] For a discussion of living conditions in the *conventillos* of Buenos Aires, see Carlos A. Egan, 'Peripheralization and Cultural Change: Argentina, 1880–1914', *PCCLAS Proceedings*, 10 (1981).

[38] Spalding, *Organized Labour*, p. 48.

[39] Spalding, Op. Cit. pp. 53–67 and *passim*.

[40] According to Juan Corradi's account of the May 1969 events, in *The Fitful Republic: Economy, Society and Politics in Argentina* (Boulder, CO and London: Westview Press, 1985), pp. 92–3: 'The exhaustion of conventional forms of political expression, the indefinite postponement of a solution to the political crisis that

had surfaced in 1966, the economic pinch, and the punitive arrogance of the military authorities led the people to experiment with new and violent forms of protest. Moderate ... labour leaders were rapidly losing power to more politicized cadres. Young workers seized their factories and took to the streets to fight the police and the troops .... Students joined workers at the barricades .... For the first time in Argentine history a classical popular uprising took place, linking the force of the urban proletariat with the middle sectors, the students, and significant sectors of the clergy. To regain the cities, the government had to send in armored columns with air support. Only the unity of the army and the ... spontaneity of the revolt prevented the episode from causing the revolutionary collapse of the state'.

[41] The day was 15 October 1918; see Bilsky, *La Semana Trágica*, p. 30.

[42] For a short account of Argentine labour history in these formative years, see Spalding, *Organized Labour*, pp. 1–93, 157–77. As organised labour grew in Latin America, cleavages proliferated among at least four different dimensions: in Colombia, Guatemala, Peru and the Dominican Republic between Communists and non-Communists; in Bolivia, Uruguay and Chile among Trotskyists, Communists, socialists, anarcho-syndicalists and even 'Wobblies'; in Chile and Argentina between party affiliates and independents; and within certain ideological camps between minority and majority factions, as among Argentina's anarchists.

[43] In Argentina's north-east workers at 'La Forestal' were locked out and strikers brutally hunted down by private armies three times between 1919 and 1921. In 1921 UCR president Yrigoyen sent the national army to Rio Gallegos, on the tip of Patagonia, to 'normalize' a stalemate between strikers and landowners. Thousands of unarmed persons were massacred, most after they had surrendered. Massacres were occuring elsewhere about this time. In Bolivia and Chile thousands of miners were killed; in Izalco, El Salvador, 10,000 peasants were gunned down in what is still recalled as *La Matanza*; in Ica, Peru, peasants were brutally repressed. See Spalding, *Organized Labour*, p. 90.

[44] Bilsky, *La Semana Trágica*, pp. 96ff.

[45] Spalding, *Organized Labour*, pp. 80–1, 91.

[46] Bilsky, *La Semana Trágica*, pp. 96ff.

[47] Spalding, *Organized Labour*, p. 44.

[48] Bilsky, *La Semana Trágica*, p. 131.

[49] Ibid., pp. 131–2.

[50] According to ibid., p. 131, the 'Liga Patriótica Argentina' espoused a 'rabidly nationalist ideology in everything except economic policy'. Its ties to British commercial interests, he adds, was strongly linked to its 'inflexible defence of the agro-export model'.

[51] In June 1917, the British ambassador threatened to cancel agreement to a sale of Argentine grain to the Allies if the government failed to put a stop to strikes against British companies. Two years later, at the height of the unrest surrounding the Tragic Week, the British ambassador once again threatened to boycott the port of Buenos Aires, forcing all maritime traffic from Europe to go elsewhere, in order to force President Yrigoyen to intervene against the maritime strike. See ibid., pp. 48, 60, 136.

[52] Police spokesmen claimed 130 gravely wounded, 150 with minor wounds; the major newspapers wrote about 200 dead in patently incomplete accounts; Communist sources spoke of 700 dead and more than 4,000 wounded; the press cited close to 5,000 detained just in the capital city. Aside from the bloated numbers offered by the anarchist press (45,000 detained) the next highest figures came from the United States' diplomatic archives, citing 1,356 dead and 5,000 wounded. See ibid., p. 135.

[53] 'Ley de Residencia', article 2, cited in José Panettieri, *Los Trabajadores* (Buenos Aires: Centro Editor de América Latina, 1982), p. 152. Article 4 gave the accused three days to leave the country and further empowered the executive to order their imprisonment until the moment of departure in order to 'ensure the public safety'.

[54] Cited in ibid., pp. 159–60.

[55] Bilsky, *La Semana Trágica*, p. 44, 51.

[56] Ibid., 123.

[57] Ibid., 124.

[58] Ibid.

[59] I refer to the Orletti Garage case, mentioned in Brown, *With Friends Like These*, pp. 76–7, and undergoing extensive investigation by Argentina's Centre for the Study of Legal and Social Issues (CELS).

[60] Bilsky, *La Semana Trágica*, p. 121.

[61] There was also a high participation rate of children and adolescents in acts of violence and destruction against public utilities and government establishments; see ibid., p. 83 and *passim*.

[62] For a personal testimony on anti-Semitism during the Dirty War, see Jacobo Timerman, *Preso sin Nombre, Celda sin Número* (New York: Random Editores, 1981).

[63] On 10 January the press reported one of the first pogroms during the parade: 'Many sported Argentine cockades and hailed the fatherland, the police and the army. Automobiles filled with army officers were loudly cheered as they drove by. All of a sudden ovations ceased, while at the yell of 'un ruso' groups began to pursue someone desperately trying to escape along the deserted street. The beating did not last long. Soon the escapee was turned over to the police . . . . No sooner was this over . . . [than] the hunt was on once again' (*La Nación*, 11 January 1919, cited in Bilsky, *La Semana Trágica*, p. 121).

[64] Jewish organizations and private homes became prime targets for arsonists during the early days of January, see ibid., p. 123.

[65] *La Epoca*, (19 January 1919), cited in ibid., 126.

[66] *La Opinión* (10 October 1976).

[67] *La Prensa* (18 December 1977).

[68] General Domingo Bussi, cited in *La Opinión*, (3 January 1976). Asked by foreign correspondents about the fight against subversion in his country, General Rafael Videla, who was soon to be-become *de facto* president, replied: 'If it is necessary for many people to die in Argentina in order to achieve the nation's security, then it will happen' (*Clarín*, 24 October 1975).

[69] The then director of ESMA, the notorious detention centre where many disappeared persons were 'processed', Rear Admiral Rubén Jacinto Chamorro, quoted in *La Nación* (4 May 1978).

[70] Cited in *Clarín* (18 December 1977).

[71] *La Epoca*, 18 January 1919, cited in Bilsky, *La Semana Trágica*, p. 135.

[72] Dr Estanislao Zeballos, cited in ibid., 136.

[73] The administrations of José Battle y Ordóñez in Uruguay (1911–15) and Arturo Alessandri in Chile (1920–4) played brokering roles compared to that of Yrigoyen.

# 9. Regime Legitimacy and National Security: The Case of Pahlavi Iran

MARK J. GASIOROWSKI

The Iranian revolution was a bewildering spectacle, taking most observers, both Iranian and non-Iranian, entirely by surprise. The Shah had used Iran's considerable oil wealth to build up a formidable military arsenal and to undertake a seemingly massive programme of social and economic development. In addition, the Shah had maintained a close and vital relationship with the USA, leading many observers to believe that American policy-makers would not permit his regime to fall. These measures were widely viewed in the 1960s and 1970s as more than adequate to protect Iran's national security for some time to come. Yet the Shah's regime had always led a precarious existence, being the object of simmering popular unrest that had threatened several times to depose the regime. And, of course, the Shah's regime *did* eventually fall, sending shock waves throughout the world and leaving Iran vulnerable to Soviet intimidation and to an eventual Iraqi invasion. One of the many lessons of the Iranian revolution, then, has been that traditional methods of pursuing national security in the Third World, such as building up security forces, promoting economic development, and maintaining close

*Why does he keep referring to Soviet intimidation?*

relations with a superpower, do not necessarily guarantee that security will, in fact, be preserved.

National security policies are those policies that governments undertake to protect or extend vital national values against threats from existing or potential adversaries.[1] Vital national values may include not only traditional national security concerns, such as the maintenance of national independence and territorial integrity, but also matters that have increased in importance with the emergence of 'mass politics', such as protecting the lives of citizens, improving the material welfare of the population, and perhaps even guaranteeing political freedoms and effective means of political participation. Most of the literature on national security policy has been written from the perspective of the developed countries. As a result, this literature has focused almost exclusively on threats to vital national values that originate abroad and on what Azar and Moon describe in the introduction to this volume as the 'hardware' side of security management: military and economic capabilities and a policy infrastructure encompassing matters such as strategic doctrine, force structure, intelligence policy, and so on.[2]

This perspective is inadequate, however, for understanding the national security concerns of many contemporary Third World countries. In much of the Third World today, domestic political instability poses a much greater threat to vital national values than threats originating abroad. As a result, national security policy in the Third World must focus not only on 'hardware' matters but also on policies that will reduce domestic unrest. This idea has led several writers focusing on Third World national security to advocate economic development and other measures designed to improve living standards as essential ingredients of national security policy for Third World countries.[3] Indeed, the development of appropriate 'hardware' and efforts to promote a high rate of economic development had been, together with a close relationship with the USA, the main cornerstones of Iran's national security policy under the Shah.[4] The case of Iran therefore indicates that a dual focus on 'hardware' and on economic development may not be sufficient to preserve national security in contemporary Third World countries. As emphasized by Azar and Moon, national security policy must also encompass 'software' matters such as an awareness of the political context and policy capacity within which vital national values are defined and pursued.[5]

This chapter helps to elucidate this latter notion by arguing that it was the failure of the Shah's regime to gain broad popular legitimacy that ultimately posed the greatest threat to Iran's national security. A regime is regarded as legitimate if wide agreement exists in society that it has a right to hold power. Regime legitimacy can derive from a variety of sources, including the claim of a divine mandate, revolutionary heritage, nationalism, charismatic authority, and democratic consensus.[6] The Shah's regime was widely regarded as illegitimate in Iran because its claim to sovereignty was controversial, having been installed by foreign powers and having once been reinstated in a foreign-backed *coup d'état*; it owed its subsequent existence largely to the USA, with which it was still closely and visibly associated; and its policies were not widely seen as serving the public interest. The failure of the Shah's regime to gain broad popular legitimacy produced simmering unrest in Iran that resulted in occasional mass demonstrations, frequent coup attempts, and the emergence of terrorist and guerrilla groups of various kinds throughout the Shah's reign. Domestic unrest also led eventually to the overthrow of the Shah's regime in a popular revolution, resulting in great political and economic turmoil and exposing Iran to Soviet intimidation and to an invasion by Iraq. Inasmuch as the Shah's failure to gain popular legitimacy was responsible for these threats to vital national values, it appears in retrospect to have been the greatest national security liability for Iran under the Shah's regime.

The first three sections of this chapter discuss the legitimacy of the regime of Mohammed Reza Shah Pahlavi in the three areas just mentioned: source of sovereignty, nationalism, and public policy. The implications of this discussion for Iran's national security are then examined. The conclusion summarizes the general argument and briefly attempts to draw some practical policy implications from it.


## SOURCE OF SOVEREIGNTY AS A LEGITIMIZING FORCE: THE ORIGINS OF THE PAHLAVI REGIME

Perhaps the most important potential source of legitimacy for a regime is the basis on which it claims the right to exercise state power. In the era before the idea of popular sovereignty swept the Western World, regimes typically claimed this right on the basis of either a divine mandate or monarchical tradition. In the modern era, many regimes claim power on the basis of a popular mandate. This may be embodied either in the tradition of a popular revolution, as in countries such as modern Mexico or Nasser's Egypt, or in the claim of democratic representation, as in the Western democracies. Popular legitimation in one of these forms can be quite effective in diffusing unrest that might otherwise be directed at the government.

The Pahlavi regime in Iran did not have a legitimate claim to sovereignty by any of these criteria. It was distinctly secular, and was often at odds with the Shi'a clergy. It had neither an established monarchical tradition nor a popular mandate, having come to power in a coup and making no pretence of adherence to democratic principles. Moreover, it was reinstated in a second coup in 1953, displacing a regime with a broad popular base that was widely regarded as legitimate in this sense.

Prior to 1906, Iran had been governed by a series of despotic monarchs who claimed legitimacy on the basis of both monarchical tradition and the tacit approval of the Shi'a clergy. Legitimation on this basis and the occasional use of force were sufficient to prevent a popular uprising in Iran until the last decade of the nineteenth century, when a coalition of bazaar merchants, clergymen, and Western-orientated intellectuals rose up in a series of protests that culminated in the establishment of a constitutional monarchy in 1906.[7]

The Constitutional Revolution of 1906 began the modern

era of Iranian history. Although the reigning Qajar dynasty was not overthrown in this revolution, a constitution and a parliament (known as the *Majles*) were imposed upon it. The new constitutional regime was accorded widespread legitimacy by the small segment of Iranian society that was politically active at this time. However, at the instigation of Britain and Russia, who were both deeply involved in Iranian politics in this period, the reigning Qajar shah closed the Majles in 1911. Although the Majles was reopened in 1914, it had been packed with pro-British candidates and could no longer claim popular legitimacy. In the following years, Iran was nominally a constitutional monarchy. The British, however, effectively controlled the Iranian state through their influence over the Majles and the weak shah.

During World War I and in its immediate aftermath, Iran was in a state of turmoil. Although the British controlled the central government, anarchy reigned in much of the country. Seeking a strong ruler who could re-establish control over the country, the British in 1921 encouraged an army officer named Reza Khan and a journalist named Sayyed Zia to undertake a coup. This coup succeeded, installing Sayyed Zia as prime minister and Reza Khan as commander of the army under the incumbent Qajar shah. Reza Khan soon ousted Sayyed Zia, was named prime minister in 1923, and ousted the shah in 1925, crowning himself Reza Shah.[8]

Reza Shah had a humble background and had come to power in a *coup d'état.* Although he sought to construct around himself the trappings of monarchical legitimacy, these basic shortcomings severely hindered his efforts. Because of his attempts to create a more secular society in Iran, Reza Shah was unable to gain the enthusiastic backing of the clergy and thus could not credibly claim a divine mandate. While he strove to reduce British influence in Iran, he was equally unwilling to permit manifestations of democratic rule, such as a free press, an independent Majles, or independent political parties. Reza Shah did not command broad popular legitimacy. His control over the state was based instead mainly on the use of repression.[9]

Reza Shah was ousted in 1941, when Britain and the

Soviet Union jointly invaded and then occupied Iran to secure a supply route for the Soviet war effort. Reza Shah's 21-year-old son, Mohammad Reza Pahlavi, was installed in his place. This initiated a 12-year period of intense political activity in Iran. The young Shah had no experience in politics and little interest in ruling the country. Censorship was lifted. An amnesty for political prisoners was declared. With the emergence of an open political environment, dozens of political parties emerged and the Majles soon became the focal point of political activity in Iran. By the end of World War II, monarchical despotism had been replaced by a vigorous constitutional monarchy that seemed well on its way toward bringing democracy to Iran.

Three main issues dominated Iranian politics in the postwar period. First, the Communist Tudeh party, which had become increasingly powerful during the war with help from the occupying Soviet forces, made an unsuccessful attempt in 1945 and 1946 to create a Soviet satellite state in the north-western province of Azerbaijan. Second, pressure began to mount in 1947 for a renegotiation of the 1933 agreement under which a concession for the production of Iranian oil had been granted to the British-owned Anglo-Iranian Oil Company (AIOC). Third, tensions gradually increased in this period between the Shah, who was attempting to consolidate power in his own hands, and a loose coalition of opposition figures, who were seeking to reduce the power of the royal court and increase that of the Majles. Moreover, the latter two issues had become closely intertwined: the British and their Iranian allies supported the Shah and benefited from his policies, while most Iranians who opposed the British oil concession also sought to reduce the power of the court.[10]

The oil dispute and the conflict between the Shah and his opposition reached the crisis point early in May 1951, when Mohammad Mosaddeq was named prime minister. Mosaddeq was the charismatic leader of the National Front, a broad coalition of political parties and prominent political figures that had been formed in 1949 to work for oil nationalization and for a reduction in the Shah's powers. Mosaddeq quickly nationalized the AIOC's assets, sparking a prolonged conflict between Britain and Iran. He also began a protracted effort to transfer political power from the royal court to the Majles and the cabinet. This included efforts to end the Shah's personal control over the military, to promote free and fair elections, and to mobilize popular participation in the political process. Mosaddeq remained in office until August 1953, when he was overthrown in a CIA-instigated coup.[11] This coup brought to power the first in a series of corrupt, repressive governments that were largely subservient to the Shah. In effect, the 1953 coup re-established dictatorship in Iran by removing state power from the cabinet and the Majles and concentrating it once again in the hands of the Shah.

The 1953 coup was a decisive turning point in Iran's history. The Mosaddeq regime had been extremely popular in Iran, both because of its quixotic struggle against the British and because it had been widely viewed as the vanguard of democracy in Iran. Having replaced such a regime in a coup instigated by foreign agents, the post-1953 regime of the Shah was widely regarded as having no legitimate claim to sovereignty. Moreover, the Mosaddeq regime had clearly followed in the tradition of the 1906 Constitutional Revolution, whereas the Shah's regime was regarded simply as a continuation of the dictatorship of Reza Shah. Therefore, not only had the post-1953 regime come to power in an illegitimate manner, but the monarchical tradition that it evoked was also widely regarded as illegitimate.

## NATIONALISM AS A LEGITIMIZING FORCE: BRITAIN AND THE USA IN PAHLAVI IRAN

Nationalism has long been recognized as a potent legitimizing force. A regime that manipulates nationalist sentiments can use these sentiments to increase its popularity or to deflect public attention from other issues, such as a dubious claim to sovereignty or public policy failures. The most obvious example of a regime claiming legitimacy on the basis of nationalism is Nazi Germany. However, nationalism need not entail dictatorship, war, or overt persecution to serve as a source of legitimation. Indeed, most regimes today rely at least partly on nationalistic appeals of some kind to maintain legitimacy. With the high levels of foreign economic, cultural, and political penetration in most contemporary Third World countries, nationalism is an especially potent legitimizing force for modern Third World regimes.

Because foreign powers have always coveted Iran for its strategic location and its oil reserves, nationalism has long been an important force in Iranian politics. Nationalism was, along with the desire for democracy, a major force behind the Constitutional Revolution of 1906. The destruction of the constitutional regime by Britain and Russia and the ensuing period of British domination further reinforced nationalist sentiments in Iran. Although Reza Shah had come to power with the complicity of outside forces, he was himself a nationalist, much like his Turkish contemporary, Mustafa Kemal Atatürk. He took steps to strengthen the military and reduce its dependence on outside advisers; he reduced Iran's economic dependence on Britain by broadening its trade base and strengthening its economy through import substitution and extensive investments in infrastructure; his efforts to improve education and modernize the bureaucracy were directed largely at strengthening Iran against outside forces; he even tried to create a sense of national pride in Iran through measures such as ending the system of foreign capitulations and purging Arabic words from the Farsi language.[12]

Although Reza Shah was able to claim a degree of legitimacy in this manner, his son, the late Shah, was not. Three main obstacles stood in his way. First, the Shah was installed on the throne during World War II in a joint Anglo-Soviet invasion. Throughout the war and until the end of 1946, foreign forces either occupied or indirectly controlled large portions of Iranian territory. As a result of these humiliating experiences, the Shah was widely regarded as a puppet of foreign powers, particularly of Britain. Second, the Shah actively courted Britain and the USA after 1946, in part to balance continuing Soviet pressure. As described above, this played a large role in the movement that culminated in Mosaddeq's accession to the premiership. The Shah, of course, paled in comparison to Mosaddeq as a nationalist. The overthrow of Mosaddeq was widely regarded not only as a blow to democracy in Iran but also as a victory for foreign powers and their puppet government.

The third major obstacle to nationalistic legitimation for the Shah's regime was its close relationship with the USA. The most important aspect of this relationship involved security matters. Roughly $1.2 billion in American military and economic aid was given to Iran in the decade after the 1953 coup, accounting for 21 per cent of government expenditures in this period. This aid was particularly important in the first year after the coup, when Iran's oil production was virtually nil. American military aid to Iran included training and the provision of sophisticated military equipment. Shortly after the coup, the USA also began to train the Iranian intelligence service, which later became known as SAVAK. This training covered the traditional tools of 'spycraft', such as surveillance and interrogation techniques, as well as instruction in the use of advanced equipment such as computers and eavesdropping devices. It played a major role in making SAVAK the pervasive, highly-effective intelligence organization that Iranians later came to dread. This security assistance was complemented by close liaison and interpersonal contact between the security forces of the two countries. Their security relationship closely identified the Shah's regime with the USA and linked the USA directly to the Shah's repressive policies.[13]

In addition to this security relationship, close economic and cultural ties emerged between the two countries. Trade increased from $27 million in 1951 to $2.4 billion in 1977, when the USA was Iran's second largest trade partner (after West Germany). American businesses became increasingly active in Iran in the 1970s, and Iranian shops were filled with American products. By mid-1976, about 24,000 Americans associated either with government agencies or with private contractors were living in Iran.[14] Tens of thousands of Iranian students were enrolled in American universities and colleges by the late 1970s.

American rock music blared in the streets of Iranian cities, and English was often spoken. These manifestations of foreign penetration were highly visible in Iran and were widely regarded as intrusions on Iran's rich traditions and culture; because of the close relationship between the two governments, they were widely viewed as inherent aspects of the Pahlavi regime.

In order to counter criticisms that he was a puppet of foreign powers and to claim legitimacy as an Iranian nationalist, the Shah presented himself as a 'positive nationalist', which he contrasted with the 'negative nationalism' of Mosaddeq and his followers. 'Positive nationalism' was defined as a nationalism based on improvement of the nation's well-being, whereas the nationalism of Mosaddeq, according to the Shah, had been negative in bringing only misery and turmoil to Iran.[15] Beginning in the early 1960s, the Shah attempted to fulfil his claim to positive nationalism by enacting a wide-ranging series of social and economic reforms. These reforms will be described below.

The Shah's credentials as a nationalist were never widely accepted in Iran. In the years after the 1953 coup, Mosaddeq's National Front continued to enjoy widespread support as the most prominent opposition group in the country. The programme of the National Front remained essentially unchanged: it continued to advocate democracy and criticized the Shah for compromising Iran's neutrality and independence.[16] Beginning in June 1963, a new challenge appeared that was ultimately to destroy the Shah's regime. In that month a series of large, violent demonstrations occurred in Tehran under the leadership of Ayatollah Ruhollah Khomeini. This new challenge combined appeals to nationalism (expressed in the metaphor of anti-imperialism) with radical interpretations of Shi'a Islam to mobilize Iran's impoverished lower classes. The lower and middle classes, under the leadership of the radical clergy and the National Front respectively, combined in 1978 and 1979 to topple the Shah's regime. As evidenced by the anti-American and anti-Western character of the revolution and its aftermath, nationalism clearly played a key role in this process.

## PUBLIC POLICY AS A LEGITIMIZING FORCE: UNDERDEVELOPMENT AND CORRUPTION IN PAHLAVI IRAN

In the absence of other sources of legitimation, a regime can often gain legitimacy by carrying out popular policies. Economic policies that improve the welfare of politically important sectors of society will make a regime more popular and thus enhance its legitimacy. Policies that affect society and culture, such as the promotion of education, sports, and the arts, can enhance a regime's legitimacy as well. Public policy can also affect the structure and evolution of society, especially in developing countries, by bringing about the emergence of new social groups, such as an industrial working class or a technocratic class. These groups are likely to feel indebted to the regime that created them, giving it a strong social base and thus enhancing its legitimacy. Regimes that have gained a measure of legitimacy through such policies include those in contemporary South Korea, authoritarian Brazil during its 'economic miracle', and the Soviet Union.

Reza Shah had been able to gain a certain degree of popular legitimacy in this manner. Although the peasants and tribal people that accounted for most of Iran's population saw little or no improvement in their lives under Reza Shah, most of the urban, politically active population was at least touched by the extensive social and economic changes that occurred. Reza Shah laid the foundations for a modern economy in Iran. He promoted industrialization through government subsidies and the development of economic infrastructure, including a national railway. He thoroughly reorganized the government bureaucracy and established a national bank and judicial system. Education at all levels was greatly expanded under Reza Shah and placed under secular control. Changes in social customs, such as dress and the role of the clergy, also occurred. These reforms helped to create a new, 'modern' middle class which was deeply beholden to Reza Shah, giving him a certain degree of popular legitimacy.[17]

Reza Shah's reforms were not, however, well received by traditional elements of society, such as landowners and the clergy. Moreover, he used his position to amass a great fortune, including, by one account, as much as 15 per cent of the arable land in Iran.[18] Raza Shah's legacy as a modernizer was therefore tarnished, limiting his ability to claim legitimacy on this basis.

In his first two decades on the throne, Reza Shah's successor, the late Shah, made no real effort to emulate his father's modernising policies. In the early years of his reign, the young Shah was relatively uninterested in affairs of state, preferring the comforts of court life and becoming preoccupied with the vast web of intrigue that surrounded him. During World War II and in its immediate aftermath, Iranian politics was, in any case, largely in the hands of the occupying powers. In the late 1940s and early 1950s, the Shah's struggle for pre-eminence with the progressive opposition made it impossible for him to embark on any major reform programmes. After the fall of Mosaddeq in August 1953 and the destruction of the Tudeh Party in September 1954,[19] and with the help provided by a large American aid programme, the need for social and economic reform became much less pressing.

Several changes in the late 1950s and early 1960s created a new urgency for reform, however. The conservative monarchy in neighbouring Iraq was overthrown in a bloody coup in July 1958, leading the Shah once again to begin pondering his destiny. The progressive opposition was becoming increasingly restless in Iran in this period, and several coup plots were reported.[20] By 1961, Iran had entered into a recession, adding to domestic unrest. Also in that year, the Kennedy administration came to power in the USA. With the liberal, activist views of the new administration, pressure for reforms inevitably appeared in Iran.

The Shah eventually responded to these various pressures with a wide-ranging programme of reforms. In May 1961, under pressure from the USA and from domestic forces, the Shah appointed the reformist Ali Amini the new prime minister. Amini quickly instituted a crackdown on corruption and unveiled a new development plan that called for large increases in spending on industrial projects and social services. An extensive land reform programme was begun in July 1961. In the next few years, plans to nationalize forests and water resources were announced, legislation was introduced to permit profit-sharing in private industry, and programmes to improve education and public health were introduced. Fearing that he was losing control over the reform programme, the Shah replaced Amini in July 1962. In early 1963, he announced a new series of reforms and sought popular backing for them in a nation-wide referendum, which was overwhelmingly approved. The most important element in this reform package was an expanded land reform programme, which ultimately benefited half of Iran's rural population. This new reform programme, which became known as the White Revolution, was, in effect, an attempt by the Shah to gain popular legitimacy by identifying his regime with the reform movement.[21]

The White Revolution was motivated largely by the Shah's fear that growing unrest in this period would get out of hand. It was therefore accompanied by a series of repressive measures designed to undermine the opposition, particularly the National Front. By mid-1963, this had largely been accomplished; the demonstrations that occurred in June 1963 were led not by the National Front but by a few clergymen. Although these demonstrations were large and many demonstrators were killed, the Shah was able to prevent further unrest from occurring simply by arresting and exiling the leaders of the demonstrations, notably Khomeini. Having checked the threat of further unrest by eliminating the opposition's leadership, the Shah had no further need to pursue reform. The efforts begun in the early 1960s soon ended.

By the early 1970s, steady economic growth, fuelled by growing oil revenues, had made Iran one of the wealthiest countries in the Third World. Iran was becoming increasingly industrialized, with large steel and automobile industries. Nuclear power plants were being built. The Iranian army was large and well equipped. Large numbers of Iranian students were enrolled at universities in Europe and the USA. The Shah travelled frequently to the major cities of the world. In 1971, he hosted a lavish, $100 million ceremony at the ruins of the ancient city of Persepolis to commemorate the 2500-year anniversary of the coronation of Emperor Cyrus the Great, founder of the Persian Empire.

Yet for all of Iran's new-found wealth and grandeur, life had changed very little for most Iranians. Although land reform had helped half of Iran's peasants, those who had not been helped were uprooted from the old feudal estates and forced either to work for subsistence wages as agricultural labourers or to migrate to the cities, where adequate employment was often not available. As a result, huge shanty towns sprang up in Tehran and other major cities, standing in bleak contrast to the opulence of more modern areas. Income inequality grew worse in the 1960s and 1970s. By the early 1970s, fully three quarters of the population was still illiterate. Basic health and sanitation facilities were not available to most Iranians.[22] Furthermore, gross oversights in planning and management during the oil boom of the early 1970s caused severe economic problems. By the mid-1970s, inflation had reached historically high levels and the Iranian government was forced to undertake austerity measures and borrow from foreign banks, further aggravating the problems of the poor.[23]

Although the Shah had sought legitimacy in the early 1960s through social and economic reform, his failure to address the problem of poverty ultimately made legitimation on this basis unattainable. Moreover, the Shah's policies caused widespread resentment, further eroding his claim to legitimacy. Corruption was endemic, especially among members of the royal family. One writer, referring to the problem of corruption, likened Iran to 'a haunch of meat thrown to an army of starving rats'.[24] The Shah's high military expenditures were widely viewed as unnecessary and exorbitant. His close relationship with the USA and the growing influence of Western culture were viewed as affronts to Iran's independence and rich traditions. The Shah's secularizing policies, such as the enfranchisement of women and rejection of the Islamic calendar, were regarded as heretical by much of Iran's religious community. Far from gaining it legitimacy, the public policies of the Shah's regime were perhaps its greatest liability.

# REGIME LEGITIMACY AND NATIONAL SECURITY IN PAHLAVI IRAN

The foregoing has argued that the Pahlavi regime's claim to legitimacy was very weak. Presumably because he recognized this, the Shah went to great lengths to construct around himself the trappings of legitimacy. His efforts to portray himself as a nationalist and a reformist have been described above. The Shah also took pains to identify his regime with the traditions of great Persian rulers such as Cyrus and Darius, as in the 1971 Persepolis ceremonies. He even sought legitimation on religious grounds, claiming divine guidance and to have had religious visions as a child.[25] Despite these efforts, the Shah's regime was never widely regarded as legitimate in Iran. In the absence of legitimacy, the Shah ruled through a combination of repression and co-optation.

The main instruments of repression under the Shah were the army and the secret police force known as SAVAK. The army was used extensively in the Shah's campaign to pacify the tribes and to put down urban unrest, most notably in the 1963 demonstrations. Even when it remained in the barracks, the army contributed substantially to the atmosphere of intimidation that prevailed in Iran under the Shah. SAVAK was notorious for its brutality and effectiveness.[26] Its tactics ranged from crude forms of torture to carefully orchestrated psychological operations designed to disrupt the opposition and promote loyalty to the Shah. SAVAK was effective not only in enabling the Shah to keep track of the opposition but also in creating an Orwellian climate of fear for many Iranians. Repression under the Shah was so severe that Amnesty International declared in 1975 that 'no country in the world has a worse record in human rights than Iran''.[27]

The Shah also used co-optation to maintain himself in power. The social and economic reforms of the early 1960s were directed in part at building support for the regime among disadvantaged groups such as the peasantry. Because the state played such a large role in the economy, a substantial percentage of skilled workers and professionals were employed directly or indirectly by the Shah, and thus were dependent on him for their livelihood. Access to foreign education and travel were controlled by the government and made available on a selective basis. Institutions such as the officially sanctioned political parties and labor unions also served as instruments of co-optation. Perhaps the most powerful such instrument was corruption, creating powerful vertical bonds of loyalty based on self-interest.

Repression and co-optation were not entirely successful in containing popular unrest in Iran and therefore in preserving Iran's national security. Because the Shah's regime was widely regarded as illegitimate, overt, often violent manifestations of popular unrest occurred frequently in Iran during the Shah's reign. In the late 1940s and early 1950s, popular unrest resulted in the emergence of a mass movement led by the National Front that nationalized the oil industry and almost stripped the Shah of his extensive powers. At the same time, a small, shadowy Islamic group known as the Fedayan-i-Islam began to use terrorist tactics in an effort to incite the faithful against the secular authorities, assassinating several prominent political figures and even trying to kill the Shah himself in February 1949. In the early 1960s, mass demonstrations again occurred on a regular basis, led by the National Front and by Khomeini. In early 1965, Prime Minister Hassan Mansur was assassinated by religious fanatics. Several leftist and Islamic-leftist guerrilla groups were formed in the late 1960s and early 1970s. These groups clashed frequently with the security forces and carried out a number of assassinations, including the killing of several American military officers and businessmen.[28]

These manifestations of popular unrest threatened certain of Iran's vital national values and therefore affected its national security. The nationalization of the British-controlled oil industry in 1951 prompted the AIOC and the British government to organize a blocade of Iranian oil exports that severely crippled the Iranian economy. The unrest of the early 1950s strengthened the pro-Soviet Tudeh Party, raising the possibility that Soviet influence in Iran might grow and eventually jeopardize Iran's independence.

Unrest in this period and in the early 1960s also plunged Iran into turmoil, resulting in many deaths and disrupting the lives of many Iranians. The guerrilla activity of the late 1960s and 1970s brought about an increase in government repression, heightening the climate of fear in which many Iranians lived.

The most dramatic consequence of the popular unrest that existed under the Shah was, of course, the revolution that culminated in early 1979. Several major interpretations of the origins of the Iranian revolution have by now appeared. The Shah himself bitterly accused the USA and Britain of fomenting the unrest that ultimately drove him from power.[29] Defenders of the Shah blame Communist subversion and the rapid pace of modernization that occurred under his regime.[30] Accounts by more objective observers have stressed the importance of underlying economic conditions, including the problems of poverty and inequality,[31] the class structure and political evolution of Iran under the Shah,[32] and the unique ability of the Shi'a clergy to mobilize the Iranian people.[33] Each of the latter factors is of obvious importance in understanding the origins of the Iranian revolution. Inextricably bound up with each, however, was the failure of the Shah's regime to gain popular legitimacy and thus to deny a popular base of support to the revolutionary leadership.

Indeed, in the absence of a clearly articulated ideology or an immediate political crisis, the legitimacy of the Shah's regime *was itself* the issue that united the opposition and mobilized popular support for the revolution. The secular opposition had long denounced the Shah as illegitimate because he had been installed in power by the USA and because his domestic policies were unjust and undemocratic. Beginning in the early 1960s, similar ideas were expressed in the metaphor of Shi'a Islam by clerics such as Ayatollahs Khomeini and Sayyed Mahmoud Taleqani and by lay writers such as Ali Shariati and Abol Hasan Bani-Sadr.[34] These men greatly influenced the main opposition groups of the 1960s and 1970s, including Mehdi Bazargan's Liberation Movement and the Mujahedin-i Khalq. These groups, together with the National Front and a loose network of unaffiliated clerics influenced by Khomeini, formed the main core of the revolutionary leadership. Many of the slogans advanced by these groups to mobilize the Iranian people focused on the legitimacy of the Shah's regime. This issue was, in fact, the only common bond uniting these disparate groups.

The implications of the revolution for Iran's national security are manifold and can only be mentioned briefly here. The most important immediate consequences of the revolution for Iran's national security were the rapid deterioration of the armed forces, the severing of Iran's close relationship with the USA, and the economic turmoil that ensued. These factors greatly undermined Iran's military capabilities, leaving it vulnerable to Soviet intimidation and to an eventual Iraqi invasion. The overthrow of the Shah initiated a complex power struggle among the diverse revolutionary groups that caused further turmoil and eventually triggered an extremely bloody confrontation between the fundamentalist Islamic clergy and its opponents, leaving tens of thousands dead. Beyond the human and material destruction, the revolution led many prominent Iranians to flee the country, producing shortages of highly educated and high skilled labour that will hinder the country's advancement perhaps for decades. Finally, the revolution brought to power a regime that held extremely intolerant views on matters such as secular culture and women's rights and cared little about economic development, political freedom, and Iran's standing in the international community. Short of invasion and occupation by foreign powers, it is difficult to imagine a scenario that could have brought more damage to Iran's vital national values.

## CONCLUSION

This chapter has argued that regime legitimacy is a fundamental requisite for national security in many contemporary Third World countries. This argument was illustrated with a case study of the late Shah's regime in Iran. The Shah's regime was widely regarded as illegitimate in Iran because its claim to sovereignty was not generally accepted; it was viewed as the instrument of a foreign power; and its policies were not generally seen as serving the public interest. The failure of the Shah's regime to gain broad, popular legitimacy produced recurrent unrest in Iran, culminating in the 1979 revolution. This unrest threatened certain of Iran's vital national values, and in this sense posed a major threat to Iran's national security.

The Shah was always acutely aware of the unrest that existed in Iran during his reign, and some of his actions suggest a realization that his regime lacked widespread legitimacy. As discussed above, the Shah made extensive efforts to contain popular unrest and even to enhance the legitimacy of his regime: he built up a formidable security apparatus; he maintained a very close security relationship with the United States, especially in the 1950s and early 1960s; he undertook wide-ranging development programmes and tolerated widespread corruption in order to coopt unrest; he even tried to legitimize his regime by identifying it with Iran's ancient traditions and with Islam. These efforts clearly failed to reduce popular unrest to manageable levels. Moreover, some of these efforts may well have exacerbated the threat to Iran's national security by reducing further the legitimacy of the Shah's regime: high levels of military spending, growing repression, widespread corruption, and a close relationship with the USA were among the most prominent criticisms of the Shah voiced by the opposition. In this sense, the Shah's lack of legitimacy may well have forced him into what Robert Rothstein describes elsewhere in this volume as a 'security trap':[35] efforts to reduce popular unrest through repression and co-optation may ultimately have exacerbated unrest by further undermining the legitimacy of the regime.

If the absence of legitimacy poses a threat to the national security of some contemporary Third World countries, what can be done to enhance the security of these countries? The obvious implication of the above analysis is that governments in such countries should undertake policies that enhance their legitimacy and thus reduce the threat of domestic unrest that might otherwise occur. Such policies might include attempts to establish a popular mandate through elections or appeals to popular symbols, such as a revolutionary tradition. For regimes with weak nationalist credentials, policies that visibly distance the regime from foreign powers or rhetoric that creates the appearance of greater distance may enhance legitimacy. Regimes that are not widely regarded as serving the public interest can undertake high-visibility policies to reverse this image, such as programmes to increase employment or improve social services.

Unfortunately, political realities and the limited resources available to most Third World governments may make it difficult or impossible to pursue these recommendations. If the case of Iran is any guide, domestic unrest and deteriorating national security may be the inevitable consequence for such governments.

## NOTES

[1] This definition is adopted from Frank N. Trager and Frank L. Simonie, 'An Introduction to the Study of National Security' in Frank N. Trager and Philip S. Kronenberg (eds), *National Security and American Society: Theory, Process, and Policy* (Lawrence, KS: University Press of Kansas, 1973), p. 36.

[2] Edward E. Azar and Chung-in Moon, 'Reassessing the Third World National Security: Legitimacy, Integration, and Policy Capacity', (seminar paper presented at CIDCM, July 1986).

[3] See, for example, Robert S. McNamara, *The Essence of Security* (New York: Harper & Row, 1968); and Abdul Monem M. Al-Mashat, *National Security in the Third World* (Boulder, CO: Westview, 1985).

[4] For an excellent analysis of the 'hardware' side of Iran's national security policy under the Shah, see Alvin J. Cottrell and James E. Dougherty, *Iran's Quest for Security: US Arms Transfers and the Nuclear Option* (Cambridge, MA: Institute for Foreign Policy Analysis, 1977).

[5] Azar and Moon, op. cit.

[6] This discussion is based in part on Dolf Sternberger, 'Legitimacy' in David L. Sills (ed), *International Encyclopedia of the Social Sciences*, vol. 9 (New York: Macmillan, 1968), pp. 244–8.

[7] On the Constitutional Revolution and the monarchical regimes that preceded it see Ervand Abrahamian, *Iran Between Two Revolutions* (Princeton, NJ: Princeton University Press, 1982), chs 1–2; Hamid Algar, *Religion and State in Iran, 1785–1906* (Berkeley: University of California Press, 1969); Peter Avery, *Modern Iran* (London: Benn, 1965), chs 8–9; and Nikki Keddie, *Religion and Rebellion in Iran: The Tobacco Protest of 1891–2* (London: Frank Cass, 1966).

[8] On Reza Shah's accession to power see Avery, *Modern Iran*, ch. 14; and Donald N. Wilber, *Riza Shah Pahlavi: The Resurrection and Reconstruction of Iran* (Hicksville, NY: Exposition Press, 1975), ch. 3.

[9] On Reza Shah's regime, see the references in note 9; also see Abrahamian, *Iran Between Two Revolutions*, ch. 3; and L.P. Elwell-Sutton, 'Reza Shah the Great: Founder of the Pahlavi Dynasty' in George Lenczowski (ed), *Iran Under the Pahlavis* (Stanford, CA: Hoover Institution Press, 1978), pp. 1–50.

[10] On the 1941–53 period see especially Abrahamian, *Iran Between Two Revolutions*, chs 4–5; Avery, *Modern Iran*, chs 17–26; Homa Katouzian, *The Political Economy of Modern Iran* (New York: New York University Press, 1981), chs 8–9; Richard W. Cottam, *Nationalism in Iran, Updated Through 1978* (Pittsburgh: University of Pittsburgh Press, 1979); and L.P. Elwell-Sutton, *Persian Oil* (London: Lawrence and Wishart, 1955).

[11] For an account of this coup by the CIA officer who led it, see Kermit Roosevelt, *Countercoup* (New York: McGraw-Hill, 1979). A more complete account is given in Mark J. Gasiorowski, 'The 1953 Coup d'Etat in Iran', *International Journal of Middle East Studies* (forthcoming).

[12] See Wilber, *Riza Shah Pahlavi*, chs 9–11; Rouhollah K. Ramazani, *The Foreign Policy of Iran: A Developing Nation in World Affairs, 1500–1941* (Charlottesville: University of Virginia Press, 1966), chs 8–12; George Lenzcowski, *Russia and the West in Iran, 1918–48* (Ithaca, NY: Cornell University Press, 1949), ch. 12; and Amin Banani, *The Modernization of Iran, 1921–41* (Stanford, CA: Stanford University Press, 1961).

[13] Mark J. Gasiorowski, 'US Foreign Policy and the Client State: Implications for Domestic Politics and Long-Term US Interests in Iran' (unpublished PhD dissertation, University of North Carolina, Chapel Hill, 1984), ch. 6. See also Barry Rubin, *Paved With Good Intentions* (New York: Oxford University Press, 1980); John D. Stempel, *Inside the Iranian Revolution* (Bloomington: Indiana

University Press, 1981), ch. 4; and Michael T. Klare, 'Arms and the Shah' in David H. Albert (ed), *Tell the American People* (Philadelphia: Movement for a New Society, 1980), pp. 44–57.

[14] United Nations, *Yearbook of International Trade Statistics* (New York: United Nations, 1954 and 1978); US Senate, Committee on Foreign Relations, *US Military Sales to Iran, Staff Report* (Washington: US Government Printing Office, 1976), p. 33.

[15] Cottam, *Nationalism in Iran*, ch. 16; Mohammed Reza Pahlavi, *Mission for my Country* (New York: McGraw-Hill, 1961), ch 6.

[16] On the National Front and related organizations after 1953, see Cottam, *Nationalism in Iran*, chs 17–8; Abrahamian, *Iran Between Two Revolutions*, pp. 457–73.

[17] Banani, *The Modernization of Iran*, pp. 52–61 and ch 7; Roger M. Savory, 'Social Development in Iran During the Pahlavi Era' in Lenczowski, *Iran Under the Pahlavis*, pp. 90–9; Ahmad Ashraf, 'Iran: Imperialism, Class, and Modernization from Above' (unpublished PhD dissertation, New School for Social Research, New York, 1971), chs 5–6.

[18] Ibid., pp. 153–9.

[19] An elaborate Tudeh network in the Iranian army was broken up in September 1954, severely damaging the party. See Farhad Kazemi, 'The Military and Politics in Iran: The Uneasy Symbiosis' in Elie Kedourie and Sylvia G. Haim (eds), *Towards a Modern Iran* (London: Frank Cass, 1980), pp. 217–40.

[20] *New York Times*, 29 December 1957, p. 6, col. 1; 1 March 1958, p. 4, col. 5 and 5 May 1960, p. 6, col. 5.

[21] Julian Bharier, *Economic Development in Iran, 1900–70* (London: Oxford University Press, 1971), pp. 95–9; Amin Saikal, *The Rise and Fall of the Shah* (Princeton, NJ: Princeton University Press, 1980), ch 3.

[22] Eric J. Hooglund, *Land and Revolution in Iran, 1960–80* (Austin: University of Texas Press, 1982), chs 4–6; Ervand Abrahamian, 'Structural Causes of the Iranian Revolution', *MERIP Reports*, vol. 86, March –April 1980, pp. 3–15; J. Amuzegar and A. Fekrat, *Iran: Economic Development Under Dualistic Conditions* (Chicago: University of Chicago Press, 1971), p. 123. See also Abol-Hassan Bani Sadr, 'Developpement de la Consommation du Futur et Misère' in Paul Vieille and Abol-Hassan Bani Sadr, *Petrole et Violence* (Paris: Anthropos, 1974), pp. 69–135; and Farhad Kazemi, *Poverty and Revolution in Iran* (New York: New York University Press, 1980).

[23] See Robert Graham, *Iran: The Illusion of Power* (New York: St

Martin's, 1980), chs 6–7; and Fred Halliday, *Iran: Dictatorship and Development* (Harmondsworth: Penguin, 1979), chs 5–6.

[24] Fereydoun Hoveyda, *The Fall of the Shah* (New York: Wyndham Books, 1979), p. 136.

[25] Pahlavi, *Mission for my Country*, pp. 54–5, 326.

[26] A gripping study of Third World secret police forces uses SAVAK as its primary example: see Thomas Plate and Andrea Darvi, *Secret Police* (New York: Doubleday, 1981). The best source on the structure and operation of SAVAK is National Front of Iran, 'A Portion of the Secrets of the Security Organization' (unpublished manuscript in the author's possession, May 1971). See also Reza Baraheni, *The Crowned Cannibals* (New York: Vintage Books, 1977); The Iran Committee, *Torture and Resistance in Iran* (nd); Committee Against Repression in Iran, *Iran: The Shah's Empire of Repression* (London: CARI, 1976), ch 7; and Ali-Reza Nobari (ed), *Iran Erupts* (Stanford, CA: Iran–America Documentation Group, 1978), ch 10.

[27] Amnesty International, *Annual Report, 1974–5* (London, 1975), p. 8.

[28] On the Fedayan-i-Islam, see Shahrough Akhavi, *Religion and Politics in Contemporary Iran: Clergy–State Relations in the Pahlavi Period* (Albany: State University of New York Press, 1980), pp. 66–9 and elsewhere. On the guerrilla groups of the 1970s, see Suroosh Irfani, *Iran's Islamic Revolution: Popular Liberation or Religious Dictatorship* (London: Zed Press, 1983).

[29] Mohammad Reza Pahlavi, *Answer to History* (New York: Stein and Day, 1980), pp. 14, 23.

[30] Ashraf Pahlavi, *Faces in a Mirror* (Englewood Cliffs, NJ: Prentice-Hall, 1980), ch 8.

[31] Graham, *Iran: The Illusion of Power*; Hooglund, *Land and Revolution in Iran*; Kazemi, *Poverty and Revolution in Iran*.

[32] Abrahamian, *Iran Between Two Revolutions*; Nikki R. Keddie, *Roots of Revolution: An Interpretive History of Modern Iran* (New Haven, CT: Yale University Press, 1981); Katouzian, *Political Economy of Modern Iran*; Hossein Bashiriyeh, *The State and Revolution in Iran, 1962–82* (New York: St Martin's, 1984).

[33] Michael M. J. Fischer, *Iran: From Religious Dispute to Revolution* (Cambridge, MA: Harvard University Press, 1980); Jerrold D. Green, *Revolution in Iran: The Politics of Countermobilization* (New York: Praeger, 1982).

[34] In Western languages, see *Islam and Revolution: Writings and Declarations of Imam Khomeini*, trans. Hamid Algar (Berkeley, CA:

Mizan Press, 1981); Seyyed Mahmood Taleqani, *Islam and Ownership* (Lexington, KY: Mazda Publishers, 1983); Ali Shariati, *On the Sociology of Islam* (Berkeley, CA: Mizan Press, 1979); Abol Hassan Bani Sadr, *Quelle Revolution pour l'Iran?* (Paris: Fayolle, 1980).

[35] Robert L. Rothstein, 'The "Security Dilemma" and the "Poverty Trap" in the Third World', p. 28.

# 10. Managing National Security: The American Experience and Lessons for the Third World

R. D. McLAURIN

The term 'national security' has crept gradually into usage in the aftermath of World War II. Since it first appeared, the term has been employed, much like other objective terms, as if it had a conceptually self-evident meaning, however difficult it might be to transform the concept into operational terms. The reality is quite otherwise, as this chapter shows.

'National security' gained acceptance as a symbol or concept without its supposed content having undergone any serious study or question, even though both the words that compose the symbol have been individually subjected to such scrutiny on an almost continuous basis. The purposes of this chapter are to open an inquest into the meaning of 'national security' and to apply some of the lessons drawn from this inquiry to the subject of national security in the Third World. We shall consider, first, the emergence of the circumstances giving rise to the birth, nurturing, and maturation of the symbol and concept, as well as those processes themselves; second, the essence or core of the concept; third, an assessment of its true meaning; fourth, how the concept and meaning can best be applied to the Third World; and, finally, the implications of this approach for decision-making and the 'national security process'.

## EMERGENCE OF THE NATIONAL SECURITY CONCEPT[1]

While the words 'national' and 'security', and their foreign-language counterparts, are both hoary terms, they have not been used together until quite recently. The context in which these two words were married arose during World War II.

Prior to World War II, the USA, while far from the marginal actor in world affairs many believe the country to have been,[2] took much less interest in and less responsibility for the course of international events than it has taken since 1945. Having rejected membership in the League of Nations and embarked on a course of limited involvement in foreign affairs, USA maintained only small, volunteer armed forces, employed largely passive diplomacy (except in Latin America), and generally eschewed foreign intelligence activities.

As Arnold Wolfers has suggested,[3] 'security' in the pre-World War II era might most immediately have evoked economic referents on the part both of the American public at large and of its leaders. The reasoning underlying this observation is crucial to our exploration as well.

'Security' is a concept devoid of operational meaning in the absence of some identification of threat. Security against what? In all discussions of security, from the personal to the international, there is an implicit or explicit determi-nation of threat. Security against recession, against illegal search and seizure, against military attack, against inflation, against erosion — security assumes threat.[4]

In this regard, it is hardly surprising, then, that 'national' security had a largely welfare orientation prior to World War II. The USA was just emerging from a massive economic crisis involving widespread social dislocation. The predominant sense of 'threat' throughout the 1930s was certainly socioeconomic in nature.

That the essence of perceived threat changed in the 1940s is certainly not a revelation. Europe was engulfed in war after 1939, and Americans joined the war fully at the end of 1941. Since 1941 the USA has been an active and influential participant in international affairs, and as leader of the Western powers she has provided the security umbrella for Europe and many other countries against what they and Americans perceive to be an imminent or eventual Soviet threat.

From the conceptual point of view, then, it is perfectly understandable that security has gained an increasingly military connotation. However, it is equally important to understand the *management* component in this concept. This, too, derives from the World War II and post-war experience.

Because the limited role of the USA in world affairs prior to the war (and the even greater limitation on American military activities world-wide) allowed the perpetuation of a relatively distinct line between diplomatic and military spheres, redundancies and conflicts over 'turf' were also limited in number and import and were therefore manageable. With the demands of the war, this situation changed abruptly and radically. Throughout the war years, political and military considerations interacted intensely both in terms of day-to-day policies and practices and in terms as well of planning for the post-war world.

As a result of the conflicting pressures institutions arose for the integration of political and military planning. The most important and well-known of these institutions was the State-War-Navy Coordinating Committee (SWNCC). It was inside such institutions that national security issues cutting across departmental responsibilities — in the war-time environment, issues of political and military strategy, tactics, and operations — were addressed and resolved.

It would be inaccurate to suggest the diplomatic/foreign policy participants enjoyed a voice equal to their military and naval counterparts during the war. It is not so much a question of the State Department's having been overcome by the combined efforts of the War and Navy Departments as it is a function, again, of the threat. In a war of the magnitude of World War II it is not surprising or undesirable that military and naval views assume an especially compelling force. This was particularly true in the USA where the professional military establishment had traditionally eschewed matters political and was seen as a body of technical experts commenting within their field of expertise. To these considerations must be added the fact that the secretary of state also adhered to rigidly compartmentalised views of 'political' responsibilities, so that he tended to avoid strategic issues and, in the face of the increasing deference shown to military planners during the war, essentially retreated from the field. A diverse set of circumstances therefore conduced to a dominant military and naval voice in national security during the war years.

Following World War II the USA did not re-embrace a policy of 'isolationism'. Quite the contrary, the decline in the relative strength of her Western European allies, France and Britain, left an increasing burden of responsibility for the security of the political independence and territorial integrity of other friendly governments on the USA. This continuing overseas involvement substantially exceeded in quantity and intensity anything envisaged by the active internationalists of the World War II period despite the expansiveness of their reaction to pre-World War II 'isolationism'. Neither the isolationalist converts nor those who had long been apostles of internationalism anticipated the degree of change. Particularly when the perception of a growing Soviet menace developed — when Soviet threats against Turkey, Soviet-supported instability in Greece, and Soviet activities in Eastern Europe raised the spectre of a large and imminent totalitarian threat to the values, the aspirations, and indeed the survival of the Western liberal democracies — the American government with a surprising degree of public support committed itself to a variety of programs actively to defend the West. In Greece and Turkey, in Western Europe, in East Asia, American policy did not hesitate to place the USA on the front line of the battle that was seen as the only means to save the Western democratic way of life.

Thus, the end of World War II did not see the return of American military, naval, and now air strategic thought to the narrow confines of intra-military debate and contingency planning. There are those, in fact, who claim — erroneously — that American foreign policy and diplomacy were militarised after the war — or not demilitarised.[5] They adduce as evidence the appointment of General George C. Marshall, former Army chief of staff, as Secretary of State; the assertive American position on Micronesia wherein military counsels clearly carried the day in inter-departmental debate and discussion; what they see as aggressive American behaviour in Greece; and many other elements of the strong posture Washington assumed *vis-à-vis* Moscow.

Others[6] have traced the rise of the American obsession with the political-military aspects of national security in the so-called 'cold war' period, and it seems unnecessary to treat the subject at length here. It is however important to note that the term 'national security' arose early during this period and perhaps therefore incidentally, as much as in any other way, became irrevocably associated with *military* security. The National Security Act (1947), for example, addressed the organization of the government for military and intelligence ativities.

Yet, in spite of the magnitude of substantive international issues, they constituted only *external* environment. The cluster of post-war politico-military issues in which the concept of 'national security' was born was heavily weighted toward administrative questions — but for economic as well as other reasons. These issues followed logically from the war years, and were to some extent independent from world issues. One of the most pressing and controversial was 'unification', the debate over the integration and organization of America's armed services. In this argument were found the services' competing views on priorities for budgetary outlays, the hotly debated question of universal military training, the emergence of the Air Force as a separate service, and many more. It was specifically in this context that the term 'national security' began to enjoy widespread conscious use.

It is worthy of note that the National Security Council (NSC), created by the National Security Act, was clearly — and, given the timing of its birth, not surprisingly — concerned with military, foreign policy, and related intelligence issues.[7] This new SWNCC brought together (although not all on an equal statutory basis) the key executive branch participants in these domains — the armed forces, the State Department, and the Central Intelligence Agency (CIA). (While the CIA was also created by the Act, many of its activities had been performed earlier by the Office of Strategic Services.) We have already indicated that the preoccupation with politico-military issues that characterized this period was the cause of this definition. Irrespective of the cause, however, the coincidence of this focus with the birth of the NSC and with the institutionalization of an apparatus associated with the term 'national security' operationally and functionally defined and to a greater extent than intended delimited that term not only for that period but for the future as well.

There is a school of thought among American diplomatic and economic historians that sees economic desiderata rather than political and military considerations at the base of American policy and activities in the post-war (and indeed even the war) years. Marxists and some revisionists have come (often along quite different, even opposing, paths) to their conclusions about the salience of economic drives on the basis of interesting, enlightening, and altogether quite acceptable evidence. Nevertheless, even the briefest interviews with the 'players', a cursory review of their memories and recollections, or any reading of the events of record in newspapers of the era will suffice to show that, at least at the conscious level, key decision-makers were acting primarily on political and military grounds, not economic. Similarly, review or content analysis of cable traffic, of memoranda and other documentary evidence of how decision-makers perceived events and their reactions at the time, would certainly disclose a similar concern with the political and military over the economic. This is not to deny the value of arguments of economic causation; it is to assert the primacy of the political and military domains as impetuses to action in the war and post-war years.

Since the 1940s and early 1950s, with the birth of the North Atlantic Treaty Organization and subsequent establishment of other military-based security pacts designed first to contain then to deter the Soviet Union; with the advent of sovereignty for the many new states of Africa, Asia, and Oceania; with the growing political and military competition between the superpowers in these areas; and with the growth of military assistance and arms transfers as policy tools, the already fuzzy line between the political and the military, between the realm of the State Department and that of the Defense Department, was hopelessly blurred.[8] Certainly, each institution, each activity, retained specific functions clearly its own: on only the rarest of occasions did State's consular functions (in those years) involve Defense, or Defense's military exercises or bases in the continental United States affect State, for example. Nevertheless, the dramatic growth was not in activities at the core of unique departmental responsibilities, but rather at the core of the intersection of interdepartmental ones. In arms control, overseas bases, treaties and security agreements, not to mention the broad outlines of national strategy and a myriad other areas, a clear distinction between State and Defense responsibilities became not only impossible to make but dangerously naive even to attempt.

Anyone who has worked in either State or Defence in the post-war years can be impressed, on the one hand, with the bureaucratic sameness of government work or, on the other — and this is the critical point — with the sharply divergent bureaucratic culture in these two federal departments. If their responsibilities and interests increasingly overlapped, Defence and State approaches to decision-making did not. Decisiveness on national security issues was characteristic of the Defence bureaucracy,[9] but much less so in State. Consequently, the more powerful the career staff of 'the Department' (State), the less clear-cut its policy guidance. This was less true of the Department of Defence. Note the issue is not one of sensitivity or prescience, not one of accuracy of analysis or appropriateness of recommendation. A president is simply more comfortable in accepting straightforward, concise, and pointed recommendations than in making decisions based on complex, arcane and guarded suggestions. The military decision-making 'style' tends to produce more compelling products than its civilian counterparts when policy questions are at stake.

This is not to say that the DoD was always the winner in inter-agency disputes, nor that Defence perpetually dominated the policy process. The role of personalities cannot be overlooked, whether they be Acheson, Marshall, Dulles, Rogers, Kissinger, or Shultz at the State Department, or Forrestal, Marshall, Wilson, McNamara, or Weinberger at Defence. Nevertheless, in the course of the four decades after World War II a concept of national security arose that certainly represented a high degree of concern with military power as its core.

The management of national security in fact evolved in accordance with the style of the president. The role of the NSC grew under some presidents, virtually passed into oblivion under others, and was reborn in the first Nixon term. Irrespective of the precise role of the NSC, the interdependence of the two policy departments of State and Defence and, in a different way, of the CIA was such that some institutional mechanism for inter-departmental co-ordination — and adjudication — was imperative. Thus, even in the periods of NSC somnolence other institutions emerged to facilitate such co-ordination. These institutions always had some connection with the White House, and can in fact be conceptually assimilated into the NSC role even if they were not organisationally or legally so assimilated at the time.

The restoration of the NSC under President Nixon and his first national security adviser, Henry Kissinger,[10] significantly reduced the inter-departmental power of the Defence Department.[11] So effectively inculcated was the regnant definition of national security that the shift in management brought about no fundamental change in that regard. The growth in the role of the national security adviser had been widely recognized for years, and the institutional innovations introduced by Kissinger consolidated, legalized, and increased that growth.

The term 'national security', then, arose in a prominent way as a result of the armed forces unification debates after World War II but against the critical backdrop of a continued significant American role in world affairs. 'National security' was conceptually and indissolubly linked to the new *Zeitgeist* of internationalism, but was first thoughtfully used in a specific military context. In fact, however, throughout the period of the 1940s the term was abstract and enjoyed only limited usage.

Through the 1950s and 1960s the phrase national security' was employed intermittently, but increasingly as a symbol, still abstract. Policies or actions were justified by reference to 'national security', and a wider array of executive branch organs (and hence activities) was seen to be related to national security. It may well be that the existence of the National Security Council pre-empted the name from usage for domestic issues relating to national security. By the 1960s, too, the components of the symbol had lost any specific, individual meaning. They took on an independent existence such that 'security' within the national security context necessarily and exclusively referred to foreign policy/defence issues. Economic or social concerns were relevant to national security only when and to the extent they impinged upon the foreign policy/defence domain. One leading textbook defined national security as 'the ability of a nation to protect its internal values from external threats'.[12]

The renaissance of the National Security Council system brought about by Henry Kissinger in 1969 increased the management component of the term 'national security'. Thenceforth, national security more often referred to or assumed reference to the process of integration of foreign and defence policy and national intelligence.

## THE CORE OF THE CONCEPT

It is against this evolutionary backdrop of the term 'national security' that we must work. As a symbol, 'national security' has accumulated a substantial amount of conceptual and processual baggage of some of which we should disembarrass ourselves.

Security, we have suggested, is a concept devoid of meaning except by reference to some idea, implicit or explicit, of threat. The increasing reliance on the management rather than the conceptual component of security has tended to blind us to the full breadth of threat inherent in the concept and to focus our attention instead upon who participates in identifying the manifestations and dimension of an a priori defined threat; how to adjudicate between alternative definitions; who will respond; and how to respond. (The inchoate agreement on the essential nature and source of threat has tended to restrict discussion of these issues.)

In his classic analysis of the 'national security' concept, Arnold Wolfers wrote that it was an outgrowth of the idea of national interest, and that in essence it represented a 'change from a welfare to a security interpretation of the symbol "national interest" '. He cites Walter Lippmann, and though putting words in Lippmann's mouth, in fact improves on Lippmann's language. Wolfers' formulation (of Lippmann) states that 'a nation is secure to the extent to which it is not in danger of having to sacrifice core values, if it wishes to avoid war, and is able, if challenged, to maintain them by victory in such a war'.[13]

Viewed conceptually rather than empirically, the contemporary American concentration on military aspects of national security stands in stark contrast to reality. No less a personage than Harry S. Truman, highly regarded for his determined posture against the growth of Soviet influence and for his readiness to use measured force in response, reminded the American people that 'National security does not consist only of an army, a navy, and an air force.... It depends on a sound economy ... on civil liberties and human freedoms'.[14] We have tried to provide some of the reasons why 'Since the . . . late 1940s, every administration in Washington has defined American national security in excessively narrow and excessively military terms'.[15] The truth is that bureaucratic, economic, and other reasons have played an equally significant role in this operationalization of the national security concept.[16]

If we are to consider national security outside the specific context of its development in the USA then we must truly consider 'national security' *per se*, i.e. move beyond a definition of threat that is limited in scope to military or power elements. We suggest that a threat to national security is any activity, phenomenon, or course of events that poses a danger to either the existence of a form of government or the welfare of the people of a sovereign state.

We believe a defence of the excessive focus on military aspects of national security in American thinking is related to the USA's role and responsibilities in the world, as well as to the fact that the principal near-term existential threat to the American government can arguably be said to derive from the American-Soviet rivalry. This argument is irrelevant to the historical evolution of the application of the term in the USA, since, as we have seen, that application did not grow from logic. Whether or not national security should be restricted in application to foreign policy and defence issues is certainly subject to some debate. In any case, there would appear to be no justification for the restriction when the context of national security is shifted to the Third World.


## SECURITY, THREAT AND THE THIRD WORLD

We have noted that the phrase 'national security' was in the right place at the right time. Its initial, limited usage (in the unification debates) was swiftly eclipsed, as the term came to be applied to the abstract concept of the nexus of foreign policy and defence issues. The maturation of the concept took place as the phrase was assimilated into the management questions related to formulating, integrating, coordinating, administering, and executing coherent policies in the conjoined foreign policy/defence arena.

These problems — both the conceptual and the management problems — are real and important challenges in the Third World, too. There is hardly a single developing country that does not attach great importance to both foreign relations and defence.[17] Nor do many Third World countries benefit from the margin of military security enjoyed by the USA (and the Soviet Union), a situation in which only one country constitutes an existential threat and that state would have to commit an act of national suicide to launch an attack.

Despite the salience of foreign policy and defence issues and problems to Third World states, it is reasonable and salutary to rethink the application of the term, the concept, and the employment of 'national security' in the Third World context. It has become fashionable in some circles to hold all that which is related to the military in opprobrium. Thus, many criticise American or European or Soviet or Third World elites for what is seen as obsessive concern with military security. This point of view and its logical conclusions lie outside the scope of the present chapter. Whether contemporary leaders *should* perceive threats differently or *should* place different priorities on national problems is an important question, but it is a very different question from the one we raise in the present chapter. For our purposes, we accept as inevitable a focus, even a high-priority focus, on military security and on foreign military or political threats. We leave to others the debate over the *most* proximate threat, the *most* significant, the *most* realistic. Military threats are perceived to be real, significant, and proximate by most if not all contemporary political elites — and by likely alternative elites.

Yet it is equally clear that social and economic vulnerabilities are directly related to national security throughout the Third World, and in most cases much more directly related than in the developed countries. Threat, we have pointed out, lies at the heart of the concept of security. 'The threat' in the Third World is economically and socially based at least as much as it is politically and militarily based.

Conceptually, national security *must* reflect the threat posed by economic and social problems, whether that threat is manifested, for example, in a purely internal erosion of legitimacy or, by contrast, in an external manipulation of social divisions or economic frustrations.

The convenient dichotomy so widely favoured between 'guns' and 'butter' entirely misses the point. Security is not a guns-or-butter choice, especially in the Third World. It is not a choice between resource allocation for social needs and resource allocation for 'destructive violence'. Those who so couch the dilemma of security in developing countries fail to understand even the most basic realities of these societies. It is often said in the West that without security there is no means to provide for social needs, but the margin of security is much more basic, much more immediate, much more vital in many developing countries.

Armed break-ins in many African countries are ubiquitous. Yet if the victim wishes to secure any kind of police response he had better be prepared to drive to the police station, pick up the police, and return them to the scene of the crime — not a particularly wise course if the robbers are in one's home, since he will have to leave his hiding place to get to his car. But the police in many countries have no cars at night. In two African countries the present author recently visited, the monthly police wage was approximately US$15. In another, armed bandits were generally better armed, better organized, and certainly more mobile than the police. These are national security resource allocation issues that destroy the fallacy of the guns-or-butter dichotomy.

Throughout a large number of Third World states, the disruptive forces of social change are reducing the social controls exercised by traditional identity groups (ethnic groups, religious groups, tribes, and so forth) without the effective substitution of alternative loci of such controls. Thus, one common result of urbanization is not nationalism, if by that we mean the reduction in identity with and loyalty to a tribe or other traditional identity group in favour of the newer statal institutions, but instead a tremendous growth in crime and violence. How does one manage or promote economic development in the midst of such pressures? How can one seriously consider addressing the pressing economic problems of countries like Lebanon or Nigeria or Peru without taking into consideration physical security and the causal political security issues that fundamentally shape economic developments there?

The security of the state and its government is a proper concern of that government. But who is to decide what 'security' means in operational terms? One problem faced by many developing countries across all domains of endeavour is the small and overtaxed reservoir of skilled manpower most must contend with. Given the inefficiency of government, the inevitable individual frustrations in even the most effective and representative political systems are not a strong inducement to 'the best and the brightest' to join government service. Realistically, most Third World political systems suffer from high levels of corruption, from low levels of public political articulation and participation, from poor public sector morale and motivation in infrastructural areas, and from decision-making behaviour that is at once necessarily and unnecessarily centralized. These and many other problems impede the recruitment, advancement, and retention of the most qualified personnel and prevent their making the kinds of contribution of which they are capable.

In a great many Third World countries, the military either directly or indirectly dominates the political process and exerts a heavy influence on the content of political rhetoric and interest articulation. In most developing countries, in fact, political institutions are young and fragile; they are not deeply rooted in the political culture of the society. Consequently, institutions that can bring to bear the instruments of force have a weight much more decisive than in societies and states where other elements of political culture may act as a counterpoise. The predominance of the military in national politics is often reflected in national decision-making. This may explain a bias towards an exclusively military concept of security. But the universality of this bias indicates there must be other reasons as well.

We suggest at least two additional explanations (doubtless, there are many more) — the effects of 'learning' and the impact of instability.

Just as most of the institutions and ideologies of government have been imported into the developing countries from the West, grafted, as it were, onto societies rather than emerging from their own dynamics and processes, so too the management of 'national security', which in its operational aspects is at base institutional, has been transplanted from the West with few modifications. There is no talk of 'appropriate technology' here. Those schooled or trained in the West have applied the fruits of that exposure to Western concepts and techniques of national security planning, but have not cared, or have not had the time, to query the relationship between the nature and environment of society and state, on the one hand, and the nature and environment of national security, on the other. In view of the vast differences between the developed and the developing worlds, it should be a matter of no little astonishment that the individuals and institutions charged with functions called 'national security' in the latter have responsibilities in areas virtually identical with those of their counterparts in the developed world.

The application of learning without knowledge is always dangerous. In numerous fields, Western 'experts' have studied and analyzed the problems of developing societies. Each succeeding generation of experts produces new insights into these problems; new concepts to understand, assess, and measure them; new techniques to manage or overcome the problems; and, of course, new disciples among both compatriots and Third World students. While this problem is interdisciplinary, it is best and most clearly exemplified in the study of economic development, where development 'solutions' have changed again and again and again over the several decades since this field exploded into prominence. Anyone who has spent time in the Third World over these years must come away impressed that notwithstanding the intellectual excitement generated by new theories and approaches, their concrete application has borne little fruit. Quite the contrary: despite impressive edifices and projects in most developing countries, the overall relative level of well-being of local populations may be declining. Indeed, in many of these states one must wonder whether the state is not becoming a marginal actor and the people are not returning to more basic activities to survive.

The development approaches, strategies, and policies of Western governments are, ironically, much less immediately or directly responsive to these shifting intellectual tides than are the minds of Third World students. Bureaucratic inertia in part explains this anomaly, and the influence of politics in government decision-making also plays a role. Academic experts understandably condemn these influences as pernicious, but they have at least served to insulate policy to some extent from the vagaries of intellectual enquiry.

The changing tides of Western expert judgement on how to address problems of development, or, indeed, even on the nature of these problems, reflect the vitality of thought and enquiry, but, even allowing for the disjunction between theory and practice, the resistance of developing societes to any of the strategies applied to date provides little room for pride and much for concern, both about the intractability of the problems and about the quality of analysis. Still, the prescriptions come forth, and with them new Third World disciples.

Is there any reason why the field of national security studies should show a career line different from other fields of academic and intellectual investigation? This is not to say that students from the Third World adopt every element of Western 'national security studies' without modification. They recognize the irrelevance of nuclear warfighting strategies and many other appurtenances of modern strategic thought to their own situation. Nor is the willingness to question the *definition* of national security, or in other words the inclusion and exclusion of potential component subject areas absent. Few indeed, it may be presumed, are the Third World students who do not recognize the salience of social and economic issues in their countries. Many pursue courses of instruction that integrate economics with the traditional 'national security' fields, primarily political science. Yet, despite the prevalence of scepticism (as gauged by questions) on the relative priority of issues while in American academic institutions the students once they return often seem to behave in a manner fully as compartmentalized as the curriculum they have just completed. They carry back to their own countries the American concept, a concept born, nurtured, and matured in circumstances wholly divergent from local experiences.

A second reason for the military focus of national security does reflect local conditions. Governments are political institutions — they depend upon and allocate power resources. True, they are also economic, social, and administrative institutions. However, the phenomenon of government is political. The economy may collapse, the society may fragment, the administration may deteriorate — all of this may occur while the government remains. By contrast, a government may be toppled while the economy is flourishing, the society is integrating, and public administration is functioning smoothly. Governments deal in political power and are principally concerned with their own power and security. Throughout the Third World, the fragility of these institutions, the shallowness of political legitimacy, the divisions of society, the disjunctions between real political culture and the new political institutions, and the inability of these institutions to meet popular aspirations and expectations (the so-called revolution of rising frustrations) create a state of constant political crisis. If there is no viable challenge to a specific government, it is all too often because that government has used violence or the threat of violence to suppress such a challenge.

Is it surprising then that national security is viewed in political terms and in terms that deal with the control of means of violence (means that may after all be turned against the government in power)? When the President of Lebanon established a national security adviser and set out to fashion an institution like the American National Security Council, his pre-eminent interests were political and military, despite the major religious divisions of the country, the then potential challenges to his legitimacy arising from internal divisions, and the state of a Lebanese economy historically vibrant but already increasingly paralyzed by the ceaseless violence and inability of government to control revenue sources and protect the population. Similarly, although many countries in Africa are reeling from levels of crime (particularly armed robbery) that imperil public order, public confidence, and foreign presence and support, there remains an almost appalling resistance to elevate the priority on the administration of justice — from police activities to the courts.

This set of conditions is not unlike the circumstances prevailing in the USA during and after World War II in the sense of the primacy of political and military issues, even if the nature of those issues is quite different. The multiplicity of political threats confronting Third World governments pre-empts the management experimentation. The threat, defined too narrowly, is met too narrowly, but it is met precisely as we met it. After all, it was the *State-War-Navy*, not the State-War-Navy-*Treasury*, Coordinating Committee. National security is operationally defined to include the political and military and to exclude the economic and social except as they impact on the other two. In the face of the perceived imminent threat by the Soviet Union, NATO took the same course. Only after that threat perception had changed did the organization take on a broader range of activities. (The Marshall Plan, still in retrospect an extraordinarily sensitive and sensible policy course, was initiated to strengthen the military effectiveness of its members as well as to outflank despair and dislocation. No matter its means, the Marshall Plan must be seen in a politico-military context.)

Certainly, it is understandable that political institutions (governments) and elites (leaders) see the 'threat' in political and military terms. And, as we have pointed out, the threat against them *as* governments and political leaders is most directly political (less often, but sometimes, military), even if the culture in which the threat develops and thrives is economic and social, as well as political. To overlook non-politico-military factors that provide the fuel on which political (and some types of military) challenges run is nevertheless a serious *political* error.

# THIRD WORLD NATIONAL SECURITY: FROM CONCEPT TO MANAGEMENT

We have indicated that the purpose of this chapter was *not* to depoliticize or demilitarize the concept of national security, nor even to alter the direction of national security thinking, which concentrates on political and military problems that threaten the political system or the state. However, even thus restricting the concept of national security, it is quite apparent that in the Third World social and economic problems are directly, immediately, and centrally relevant to the values whose preservation is sought.

The economic posture of developing societies is by definition less advanced than in that of their developed counterparts. As long as men were content to live their traditional lives, underdevelopment was not a political problem. The penetration of modern mass media into even the most traditional sectors and sections of developing countries has aroused aspirations — and demands — against which government performance, however unfairly, is judged. Moreover, the chasm between 'have' and 'have not' groups, between the poor and the wealthy, is extreme. In societies where political institutions, traditions, and culture are weak or new, these economic issues may become platforms for violent change.

Similarly, social divisions are often more meaningful points of individual identity and loyalty than the state. Ethnic, regional, religious, or tribal schisms characterize virtually all developing countries. The nation-state model is only rarely reflective of the political realities even in the developed world. How many truly 'national' states are there? Note that both superpowers and four of the five 'great powers' are characterized by either explicit or obvious national or sub-national identities. What distinguishes most advanced, industrialized countries from Third World countries is certainly not homogeneity; it is the *salience* of sub-state, supra-state, trans-state, or non-state identities. As important as religious feelings may be in the West, for example, few hesitate to subordinate any other identities to

that of the state, whether through a process of ration-
alization or otherwise. This is certainly less true in the Third
World, where other loyalties, frequently ascriptive loyalties,
often take precedence over identification with the state.

In view of these key distinctions between developed and
developing countries, the criticality of broadening the
concept of national security — or, more precisely, of
accurately reflecting the breadth of real national security —
is evident. Yet, this is not an intellectual exercise. How
analysts define national security does affect state behaviour,
but the relationship is certainly indirect. We are concerned
with the formulation and administration of national security
policy, and we suggest therefore that it is in the management of national security issues that the tone but also the
substance of national security thinking can best be assayed.

In the USA, the term 'national security' has been defined,
and the boundaries of the concept delineated, as we have
seen, not by events alone nor by experts or analysts, but
instead by the management processes established to deal
with issues that *post facto* came to be called 'national
security affairs'. The result has been institutional rigidity
and conceptual aridity, deficiencies that are significant but
survivable for the USA but could be (and in some cases
probably have been) lethal over the longer term in many
Third World states.

Ideally, all national security policy should reflect isomor-
phically the composite of 'threats' to the state and its
political order. National security policy should be designed
to co-ordinate policies and integrate strategies to achieve
balanced and optimum objectives measured against the
infinite range of the less-than-optimum. Looked at another
way, this is only to say that national security is an isomorph
of overall national policy and government behaviour.
Realistically, no small staff dealing with the infinite variety
of challenges confronting government is going to be able to
do what all of government itself cannot do. Therefore,
national security structures are and must be largely dedicated to the most critical threats.

In day-to-day terms, management of national security
cannot be seen as and is not principally an institutional

phenomenon. The realities of management are dictated by the realities in other concrete activities that are part of the national security process, activities such as manpower recruitment, selection, training, assignment, promotion; qualitative and other factors of intelligence collection, analysis, dissemination; overall organizational-administrative capability; research capabilities; communications support; and so forth.

Shortages of qualified manpower appropriate to national security management are known to be the rule rather than the exception in developing countries. However, it is not necessarily true that these shortages are a function of the scarce supply of skilled manpower in general. A large part of the shortage derives from the priority placed on political reliability. As a result, technically competent people are excluded, often because they come from the wrong tribe, religious group, or section of the country. In one effort (with which the author is personally familiar) to train and staff a national security apparatus, only three persons in the entire country were identified as 'qualified' for a certain key post, even though the country had a large body of competent, intellectually capable people. Of the three, none was really capable of handling the technical requirements of the position in question; all three were proposed because of their political reliability.

Other developing-country problems in the manpower area include turnover, competition, and isolation and in-service advancement. Turnover is a problem because it is unusual to be able to replace a rare competent employee with another equally competent. The bureaucracies are simply not deep enough. However, the alternative is to keep people in their jobs indefinitely, like Prince Saud al-Faisal, the long-time Foreign Minister of Saudi Arabia. While retention does limit the effects of the problems of continuity and assignment/reassignment, it tends to stultify the decision-making patterns and ossify what should be a dynamic process of constant reassessment of national requirements. Moreover, lacking in-service training and self-improvement programmes, time-in-grade can be a serious detriment rather than a major asset in developing states.

Whatever our conception of national security intelligence must play a capital role in it. Intelligence and research capabilities in widely diverse fields are critical to providing decision-makers with an accurate portrait of the world. Because much of the political world is not tangible, this potrait must be sensitive to the intangibles. For developing countries, intelligence does not generally mean satellite photography or long-distance listening devices. Instead, it refers to the ability to glean valuable insights from open sources; the ability to construct and communicate accurate and balanced assessments; the ability to update information and analysis in accordance with changed or changing circumstances; the ability to provide time-sensitive data on a timely basis; the ability to integrate diverse types of information from diverse sources into a 'finished' product. The poor quality of automated support, constraints on communications resources, restrictions on personnel inter-action resulting from political reliability questions, and the lack of systematic methods for updating — all seriously undermine the intelligence effort.

Isolation of qualified personnel in time and space also work against the employment of effective personnel. They are no longer able to keep up with professional develop-ments in their fields on a systematic or timely basis, they are unable to interact with their professional peers, their view of applications problems is overly restricted in view of the nature of the societies in which many find themselves. These problems affect bureaucrats in developed societies, as well, but overcoming them is far easier for the individual in those countries, should he choose to do so, than it is for his counterpart in the Third World.

Given the premium on well-trained, highly motivated, and competent personnel, it is exceedingly difficult for most developing states to retain them. Government salaries rarely compete with those of the private sector, where this is relevant, and even where it is not the employee can always consider employment outside the country. In a real sense, this problem is noticeably more pronounced in the econ-omics field than in political science. The demand for com-petent, technically sophisticated economists, for example, is such that few will stay in the government when faced with offers much greater than government can provide.

The 'bottom line' is still political and military security, but it is a bottom line that recognizes what is above the line, too — the substantial interdependence of political, economic, social, and military dimensions. The pay-off is still continued political tenure, and the intelligence and decision-making contributing to this end are so orientated. No butter-or-guns approach this — but it may be a means to avoid or minimize the need to choose guns over butter.

Better integration of social and economic factors into national security decision-making is realistic. It is realistic both in the sense that it is not based on anti-military or 'idealistic' chimera and in the sense that it is achievable. Greater attention to the plenitude of 'national security' considerations is achievable. For governments whose primary staffing criterion is loyalty, turning to opposition or new elements is *not* required. No sub-national group has a monopoly on wisdom or perspective. The initial step is simply to move backwards to greater generalization and away from greater specificity. National security planning must derive from a concept of what national security is all about. Current officials, if so directed, are quite capable of factoring in considerations now excluded. But the concept of the threat must first be taken out of its Western context and placed in a more realistic and more truly universalistic *national* framework. Such a framework is much more likely to correctly identify and move to overcome government and state vulnerabilities, and, in so doing, to make a significant and salutary contribution to the unity and progress of the society.

## NOTES

[1] See Chapter 3 in this volume, especially the section on the concept of national security.

[2] In retrospect, the American role in the inter-war period certainly appears to merit the 'isolationist' rubric. However, it is hardly fair to judge American inter-war behaviour by post-World War II

standards. By contrast with the period prior to World War I, the USA's activity level was considerable, and it is not at all clear that 'isolation', a term used originally in reference to certain specific policy options, paints an accurate portrait. Only perhaps in the psychological sense — which is certainly a crucial sense — was the USA 'isolationist'.

[3] Arnold Wolfers, ' "National Security" as an Ambiguous Symbol', *Political Science Quarterly*, vol. 67, no. 4 (December 1952), pp. 481–3.

[4] See Richard Ullman, 'Redefining Security', *International Security*, vol. 7, no. 1 (Summer 1983), p. 133.

[5] See, for example, Marcus G. Raskin, *The Politics of National Security* (New Brunswick, NJ: Transaction Books, 1979); Daniel Yergin's excellent *Shattered Peace: The Origins of the Cold War and the National Security State* (Boston: Little, Brown, 1977); or the many other so-called 'revisionist' histories of the war and post-war periods.

[6] Best treated by Yergin, *Shattered Peace*.

[7] See I.M. Destler, 'National Security Management: What Presidents Have Wrought', *Political Science Quarterly*, vol. 95, no. 4 (Winter 1980–1), pp. 573–88; John E. Endicott, 'The National Security Council' in John F. Reichart and Steven R. Strum (eds), *American Defence Policy* (5th edn, Baltimore, MD: Johns Hopkins University Press, 1982), pp. 521–7; Stanley L. Falk, 'The National Security Council Under Truman, Eisenhower, and Kennedy', *Political Science Quarterly*, LXXIX, no. 3 (September 1964), pp. 403–34; Paul Y. Hammond, 'The National Security Council: As a Device of Inter-departmental Coordination', *American Political Science Review*, LIV, (December 1960), pp. 899–910; Robert H. Johnson, 'The National Security Council: The Relevance of Its Past to Its Future', *Orbis*, vol. 13, no. 3 (Autumn 1969), pp. 709–35; *Report of the Commission on the Organization of the Government for the Conduct of Foreign Policy*.

[8] For a discussion of the evolution of the inter-departmental conflict resolution apparatus as an indicator of shortcomings in American national security management, see R. D. McLaurin, 'National Security Policy: New Problems and Proposals' in R. Gordon Hoxie *et al.*, *The Presidency and National Security Policy* (New York: Center for the Study of the Presidency, 1984), ch. 18. Useful discussions of inter-departmental conflict resolution techniques may be found in Graham Allison and Peter Szanton, *Remaking Foreign Policy: The Organizational Connection* (New

York: Basic Books, 1976); I. M. Destler, *Presidents, Bureaucrats, and Foreign Policy* (Princeton, NJ: Princeton University Press, 1974).

[9] The obvious exception, especially prior to the Defence reorganization of 1958, was on issues in which important interests of two or more of the armed services were affected in divergent ways.

[10] The literature on Kissinger is extraordinarily extensive. Interestingly, this literature is also quite diverse both in content and in substance. Although a number of theories have been advanced concerning the personal ambitions and objectives of Henry Kissinger and their relationship to the restoration of the NSC mechanism, it is clear that a more systematic means to centralize presidential control of foreign and defence policies was overdue. This is not to deny the importance of personality in politics and government, but it is to reassert the importance of trends and organization.

[11] For a useful treatment, see Geoffrey Piller, 'DOD's Office of International Security Affairs: The Brief Ascendancy of an Advisory System', *Political Science Quarterly*, vol. 98, no. 1 (Spring 1983), pp. 59–78. This article deals with what was then called 'little State', but numerous Defence institutions were involved in political-military affairs. J-5 (Plans and Policy) in the Organization of the Joint Chiefs of Staff, the political-military branches of each of the service staffs, and such offices as the Assistant Secretary of the Air Force for International Affairs were merely the most visible.

[12] Morton Berkowitz and P. G. Bock (eds), *American National Security: A Reader in Theory and Policy* (New York: Free Press, 1965), p. x. Emphasis added.

[13] Wolfers, " 'National Security,' " pp. 481–3 (Lippmann, *US Foreign Policy: Shield of the Republic* (Boston: Little, Brown, 1943) p. 51: 'A nation has security when it does not have to sacrifice its legitimate interests to avoid war and is able, if challenged, to maintain them by war.'(Brown, 1943), p. 51. We prefer Wolfers' change, but it *is* a change.) Cf. Walt W. Rostow, *The United States in the World Arena: An Essay in Recent History* (New York: Harper & Row, 1960), p. 543: 'It is the American interest to maintain a world environment for the United States within which American society can continue to develop in conformity with the humanistic principles which are its foundation'.

[14] Harry S. Truman, State of the Union Address, 6 January 1947.

[15] Ullman, 'Redefining', p. 129.

[16] Ibid. See also the classic book by Graham Allison, *Essence of*

*Decision: Explaining the Cuban Missile Crisis* (Boston: Little, Brown, 1971); and Morton C. Halperin and Arnold Kanter, *Bureaucratic Politics and Foreign Policy* (Washington, D.C., The Brooking Institute.)

[17] The few exceptions to this rule appear to be small, weak states that do not invest in military establishments either because the threat is impossible to deter, much less defend against, or because they already depend for their defence upon other countries to whose defence resources the sum of what they could add would be negligible.

# 11. Towards an Alternative Conceptualization

EDWARD E. AZAR and CHUNG-IN MOON

This book has dealt with the overall applicability of the Western concept of national security to the Third World setting. Contributors to this volume all agree that it has limited applicability. While the concept is narrowly defined, its operational meanings are rigidly fixed. Threats are unidimensionally treated, and management techniques suggested are by and large foreign to, and unfit for, Third World reality. Against the backdrop of these observations, and by way of conclusion, this chapter recasts security problems in the Third World by reviewing the concept, elucidating its multiple dimensions, and differentiating among complex threats and capabilities.

## THIRD WORLD NATIONAL SECURITY: CLARIFYING AMBIGUITIES

Three factors can be cited, which limit the application of the conventional approach. They are contextual differences, nation-state maturity, and variations in national values. The contextual differences stem from a set of internal and external conditions unique to developing nations.[1] Most analysts would agree with Buzan and Bobrow-Chan that the Third World is highly stratified and differentiated in terms of its resources, capabilities, and overall environment. Nevertheless, we can delineate common denominators characterizing the security context of developing countries. Most Third World countries, trapped in a complex vortex of local, regional and superpower rivalry are faced with a more precarious external security environment than their Western counterparts. This precarious situation is exacerbated by external weaknesses. Being poor in resources and often small in size, they are unable to accumulate the physical power needed to alter or protect themselves from external conditions. Such a setting makes Third World insecurity more real and pressing. External weakness is aggravated in part by economic backwardness. The perpetuation of one-crop or dual economies constrains the potential for industrialisation, and degrades the overall living conditions of the people. Furthermore, built-in structural rigidity and growing dependence on the international economic system impede opportunities for self-sustaining development.

Equally devastating is a pervasive domestic political fragility. Unlike developed Western countries, most developing countries suffer from eroding domestic political cohesion.[2] Failure to foster nation-building and to expedite institutionalisation has weakened the ability of the state authority to extract and mobilize resources and to coordinate the domestic political actors. In conditions of domestic fragmentation and where the legitimacy of the ruling élite is questioned, political unrest increases in frequency and intensity. Violent political changes occasioned by military coups or revolutions become frequent and pervasive, adding to political fragility and retarding the transition from 'traditional' to 'modern' political culture. Competing social groups pursue their own interests at the expense of the common good. In situations like this, the steering ability of the state machinery is severely undermined. In short, precarious security environments and external weaknesses, combined with economic backwardness and limited adaptive capabilities, clearly differentiate the Third World security context from that of the West. It is this difference that shapes the modalities by which national values are perceived and identified and policies determined and implemented.

Apart from the variation in contextual parameters, the applicability of the conventional approach is limited by a more substantive issue: 'security for whom?' Traditionally, the concept of national security is founded on two cardinal assumptions largely derived from the historical evolution of the modern European state system.[3] First, as evident in the billiard-ball model of the 'Realist' tradition, the nation-state is a unitary actor in which national security becomes automatically identical to state security. Second, as assumed by Western pluralist political tradition, the security of a nation state is the aggregration of homogeneous individual securities. National security in the West, therefore, is security for a nation-state which is composed of individual citizens who share a common destiny through extended nation-building and political socialisation.

Neither assumption applies readily or fully to the Third World setting. In most Third World countries, the link between state and nation (or state and society) is deformed, and is still in the process of formation. Very few countries in the Third World have completed the process of nation-building in a single political and territorial entity. Some are still 'state-nations' where the state incorporates a multitude of nationalities. In many cases, the nation is divided among two or more states. In such situations, the security of a 'nation' is quite a separate matter from the security of a 'state'. It is perhaps more accurate to argue that national security is equated with 'communal' security and state security with that of a ruling 'regime' that represents a segment of social or communal interests.

'Security of what?' is another perplexing question. More than three decades ago, Robert Osgood stated that 'national security, like danger, is an uncertain quality: it is relative, not absolute: it is largely subjective and takes countless forms'.[5] The question still remains unresolved. Ambiguity stems largely from multiple value contents. As Klaus Knorr noted, 'national security concerns arise when vital or core national values are threatened by external actions or events'.[6] Thus, there must be no single monolithic national value that would dominate national security concerns. Survival in terms of the physical protection of a homeland from external military threats is important, but does not exhaust the list of multiple national values. Rigid adherence to the survival value (i.e. political independence and territorial integrity) could result in a reductionist fallacy, seriously hindering the proper understanding of complex and dynamic Third World insecurity. Given the contextual parameters that condition the Third World security dilemma, several other values (e.g. economic well-being, prosperity, national integrity and communal harmony, domestic order and tranquillity, and prestige) may be almost as crucial as survival, but the hierarchy among these values is seldom rigidly fixed, and tends to vary across time and space. How core and peripheral national values are defined must be shaped chiefly by the political leadership's subjective judgement of the changing contexts and of domestic resources and capabilities.[1]

## MULTIPLE DIMENSIONS OF NATIONAL SECURITY

The multiplicity of national values, coupled with the precarious security context, produces security dimensions more diverse in the Third World than in the West.[8] Looked at in terms of a volatile security environment–the minimal military and security capabilities and the often bitter memories of colonial domination–the conventional conception of national security has a certain face validity across most developing countries. To many, political independence and territorial integrity are vital national values. Any threats to such values instantly invoke security concerns.

Nevertheless, physical security represents only one aspect of overall security. During periods of acute economic depression or external economic disturbances, economic issues may displace other core problems in the hierarchy of national values.[9] In the Western developed countries, economic threats may well be a 'matter of more or less',[10] because they seldom involve severe deprivation of basic economic welfare. Western economies are rich, well diversified, and resilient. In the Third World, however, economic security goes beyond a matter of 'more or less'; it is a life or death matter. Underdevelopment, chronic poverty, unemployment and deteriorating conditions of life are all pervasive. Escaping from the tenacious grip of underdevelopment and ensuring public welfare could certainly constitute important national values for many developing countries, to the extent that ruling élites perceive economic issues as national security concerns.[11]

The economic role in national security is vital because of its extensive spill-over effects on other national values. Persistent underdevelopment and deprivation of economic well-being degrade national morale and precipitate social unrest, thus furthering internal fragmentation. Such internal weakness can trigger hostile actions by potential or actual adversaries. As the author of the Argentine case in this book argues, an economic crisis may trigger a legitimacy crisis, tempting the ruling regime to create an imaginary enemy and to provoke a self-induced national security crisis in order to avert internal threats to the regime. Quite often such an artifical invocation of national security gravely endangers the entire nation. Moreover, a weak economy undermines the base of military power, which is essential for even conventional national security.

Another national security consideration is the growing ecological scarcity of resources and the implications of this phenomenon for the organic survival of a national population. Organic survival differs from political survival in that security of a nation-state could be more related to an organic dependence of its population on its physical environment than on the physical protection of a nation-state from external military threats. This reasoning derives from the reality that the national population constitutes the main component of the nation-state, and this population cannot survive without proper resource space to enable it to nourish itself and to expand. In this sense, keeping pace with rising domestic economic and resource demands either through external expansion of ecological space or by domestic adjustment is a crucial security issue. This ecological concern of national security has long been overshadowed by the anthropocentric paradigm that has dominated Western civilisation since the Renaissance, even though a number of historians have reminded us of the importance of ecology by documenting the rise and decay of national populations as an interface with environmental constraints.[12]

Organic survival as a national security concern is more relevant for the developing countries than for the West. Today's developing countries experience constant population growth, but lack domestic resources and technology to cope with the population pressures. Chronic food and energy shortages are often a daily reality in these states. In addition, the level of technological innovation is low, and technological dependence on the West is growing. So, as populations expand, resources become more scarce, and technological advancement remains elusive; the organic survival of a national population is, or should be, a vital national value.

As was stated, incomplete nation-building and its impact on domestic politics are pervasive in the Third World. Failure to ensure social and political integration amidst multi-communal fragmentation often undermines stability, order, and tranquillity. Communal conflicts are only the most obvious form of this instability. Traditionally, communal cleavages and attendant conflicts were not regarded in national security terms for two reasons. First, communal conflicts have been seen as primarily internal threats to congenial social order. Second, communal conflicts, being transitional by-products of modernization, were thought curable through effective nation-building and integrative programmes.[13]

More recent empirical examination of the role of the communalism in modernization and political and social change reveals that communal factors engender serious security vulnerabilities for most developing countries. First, communal conflicts often erupt when a certain group perceives that the country's modernization will disrupt communal tranquillity, thus threatening the traditional authority of the communal leaders. Coupled with this perceived threat to communal identity is the perception that progress and modernization are advancing at a disproportionate rate. Some communal groups are progressing and assimilating into the national modernization better than others. This perceived discrimination, warranted or not, polarizes the disenfranchised group to retract from society rather than to try and overcome the disparities. One result emerging from communal retraction is the demand for greater autonomy. In the most profound cases where friction between varying communal groups is most intense, one can witness a secessionist mentality developing, as the gap grows between communal groups enjoying wealth and prestige in the nation and other groups which have not been integrated by the modernization. The secessionist threat does not technically affect the survival or extinction of the state, but rather its disintegration. It is the type of threat which attacks the perceived 'vital' national values expressed in 'state' terms, because secessionist demands may produce territorial disintegration and political fragmentation. Second, in addition to internal fracture, communal conflicts have an immediate impact on the conventional notion of national security, which is more obvious. As the Lebanese, Sri Lankan and Kurdish cases among others indicate, such conflicts usually invite external intervention, which in turn jeopardizes the security of both nation and state. Finally, domestic fragmentation and the ensuing social unrest weaken a state both internally and externally. In the light of these threats, communal harmony is an essential national value for the ruling elites of many Third World countries.

We have delineated four distinctive national values directly associated with national security concerns in the Third World: political and territorial survival, preservation of economic well-being and prosperity, organic survival of the national population and communal harmony. These values, however, are not automatically translated into security concerns. Such translation is a function largely of the patterns of threats directed against these national values, which are nurtured and shared contextually. In this regard, the study of 'threat' becomes essential for understanding Third World national security.


## STRUCTURE OF MULTIPLE THREATS

Broadening the concept of security so that it accurately reflects its multiple dimensions necessarily entails an examination of the complex nature of threats associated with those dimensions. Like values, threat itself is highly complicated and ambiguous; behaviourally speaking it is a perceptual matter. The source, type and level of threat are mostly situational, reflecting the political leadership's subjective judgment. Buzan concisely describes such complexity:

> Each state exists, in a sense, at the hub of a whole universe of threats. These threats define its insecurity and set the agenda for national security as a policy problem. They do not, unfortunately, constitute a clear set of calculable and comparable risks like those faced by players of chess or bridge. Threats to the state come in diverse forms which cannot easily be weighed off against each other, and which are frequently in a state of constant evolution. They vary enormously in range and intensity, pose risks which cannot be assessed accurately, and depend on probabilities which cannot be calculated. Because threats are so ambiguous, and because knowledge of them is limited, national security policy-making is a highly imperfect art.[14]

Although the type, source and level of threat are subjectively determined by national security policy-makers, it is not impossible to elucidate some apparent forms of threat along each security dimension outlined above.

In the conventional approach, the type, source, and level of threat are considered easily identifiable as either overt, external or military, being imposed by actual or potential adversaries. Threats to economic well-being and prosperity, however, are less apparent, making perception and recognition more difficult and controversial. As recent experiences of Third World states demonstrates, some countries (such as Libya, Iran and Nicaragua) may face overt and behavioural threats such as interference in maritime trade, embargoes, restrictions on market access and positive or negative economic sanctions. Nevertheless, these types of threat are usually associated with political and military conflicts, and appear less salient in the Third World.

Subtle, structural threats to economic well-being are more pervasive. These problems are related to the pattern and degree of integration in the international economic system. One noticeable threat in this regard is systemic vulnerability, which arises from the concerns of developing countries, with limited domestic policy leverage, to the transmission of external economic disturbances originating from the international economic system *per se*. Recent debt crises and subsequent painful adjustments (often visible in sharp reductions of economic welfare) typify security concerns triggered by such vulnerabilities. Indeed, the international business cycle, the roller-coaster effects of commodity prices and worldwide inflationary pressures are identifiable forms of vulnerability that can be translated into vital security concerns.

While systemic vulnerability is of exogenous origin, some threats to economic well-being and even to economic sovereignty result from patterns of dependent development strategy, a product of both internal and external factors. The economic dependence of Third World countries usually takes two distinct forms. One is dyadic dependence, the other structural dependence.[15] Dyadic dependence, an asymmetric form of economic transaction between states or between a state and non-government actors such as multinational corporations, produces security concerns as a result of its intrinsic nature of domination and manipulation by the strong partner. Protectionist measures, economic sanctions and other kinds of discriminatory measures are threats associated with this. This dyadic dependence, manifested in the form of item concentration, is usually a function of structural dependence. Structural dependence is a source of important economic threat to the Third World nations because it deepens structural deformation of their economies and production activities. Some believe that poverty, growing income and wealth distribution gaps, and sectoral imbalances are seen as resulting from structural dependence, whose perpetuation often leads to the loss of economic sovereignty.

Altogether, these risks or threats not only affect economic welfare through diminishing income and wealth and worsening conditions of inflation and unemployment, in addition, vital values such as survival and prosperity are literally endangered by lack of accessibility to sources of raw materials, market outlets, and capital and technology inflows. In certain cases these risks become a direct threat to national sovereignty with the attendant loss of economic and political power to control the full range of economic policy instruments.'[16]

Threats to the organic survival of a national population may be much simpler to identify. The ecological threats can be easily understood by examining the relationship between resource availability and population dynamics, considering technology as an intervening variable. An analysis of vital resources such as energy, food, space, water, heat, and non-renewable resources within the territorial boundaries of a given space can reveal the overall gravity and direction of the ecological security concerns of a country.[17] Ecological security concerns arise from two major areas: first, domestic failure to cope with the combined pressure of demographic, economic and resource depletion and second, the tendency to cope with lateral pressure by expansion or other external actions. Domestic failure is most evident in cases where governments cannot satisfy resource demands internally, especially under circumstances of overpopulation. Refugees from areas of ecological disaster and mass starvation in India, Bangladesh and Ethiopia are cited as good examples of domestic failure. A lack of arable land, technology, and purchasing power, coupled with global food insecurity, caused severe security crises in these countries. The same can be said of economic hardships resulting from two waves of energy crises.

In the absence of domestic alternatives, some countries may seek solutions to ecological problems in the same way as they do to other problems–beyond their national boundaries. When domestic demands become intense in terms not only of resource scarcity *per se*, but also of its social consequences (including food riots), insecure regimes usually engage in internal consolidation practices which limit the activities of opposition groups in national policy affairs. Repression of opponents to the government are cited as precautionary measures to ensure national stability in times of crisis, the purpose being either to co-opt or coerce national opinion toward the government's policy goals. Included in this is the possibility of external military operations, which have the capability for giving psychological and strategic impetus to the faltering regime. Both domestic repression and external adventures increase the probability of military means as an answer to ecological problems. The militarization of ecological issues can become another security concern for all parties concerned. Ecological scarcity alters threat perception by linking lateral pressure with military concerns both for ecologically sound states and for those of lower carrying capacity.

Socially produced threats are difficult to detect as security concerns because they usually involve second-order causation. Societal factors are too often perceived to be purely internal. Nevertheless, communal fragmentation and resulting conflicts produce many security problems in the Third World. Threats emanating from communal elements are diverse because communal conflicts have different motives, intentions, goals, and contexts. Some communal conflicts are a by-product of domestic inequalities and discrimination which can be arrested once specific conditions are met by the national government, most notably, the allowance of ethnic and communal pluralism in government representation. Other communal movements pursue a secessionist direction through which new forms of political and territorial entities may be established. The types, sources and levels of threats stemming from communal problems may be best understood through the analytical paradigm of 'protracted social conflicts' (PSC).[18] PSCs are unique products of the inextricable intermeshing of all dynamics that constitute an individual identity, a group or a national identity. The dominant characteristics are: temporal protractedness, lack of clear demarcation between internal and external sources of conflict, fluctuation in intensity and frequency, spill-over into other realms of society, and the absence of explicit termination points. Communal conflicts ferment and emerge from a peculiar pattern of social structure in which a deep communal division coincides with structural inequality producing structural victimization of specific communal groups. Political and economic inequality across different communal identities within national boundaries and ideological domination of one communal group by another appear to be the primary causes of protracted conflict. In contrast with conventional threats, those associated with PSCs tend to be more mercurial since they are both behavioural and structural in cause; overt and covert in behaviour; and internal, external or both in their source.

Among many threats to national security originating from PSCs, the most serious is that of the eventual fragmentation or disintegration of the existing national entity through separation or partition. Although it does not imply the complete loss of sovereignty, and is therefore not a matter of national survival, this threat raises a spectre of territorial loss, always a severe blow to national pride. The bloody struggles to prevent secession in Pakistan (Bangladesh), Iraq, {Kurdistan}, and Nigeria (Biafra) are cases in point. In a limited sense, such threats perpetuate internal disorder and instability, fragment internal cohesiveness, exhaust national resources and morale, and may eventually incapacitate the state machinery. If the protection of the legitimate socio-political system from internal disorder can be regarded an important security concern, as Richard Smoke argues, then the presence of communal conflicts in the form of PSCs is an undeniable threat to the national security of many developing countries.[19] The Kurdish rebellion and its impact on Iran and Iraq, the Lebanese conflict, the Eritrean liberation movement, the Cyprus conflict, and even the Arab–Israeli conflict can perhaps be better understood in this context.

Arriving at an accurate threat perception and making appropriate decisions are difficult tasks for Third World national security policy-makers, even if a threat is overt. Economic, ecological and communal threats are often less acute, or at least less visible, and therefore difficult to detect.

The problem of the level of threat aside, the blurred demarcation line between internal and external sources of threat poses another barrier to effective threat recognition. Sources of threats to national security, as we have broadly defined, can be internal, external or both. As the Lebanese conflicts show, threats resulting from communal tensions involve dynamic interactions of internal and external events and actors. The security implications of the ecological dimensions also indicate that the source of threat is internal rather than external, although external conditions such as global food and energy insecurity affect the internal shaping of security concerns. Even in the economic dimension where threats are perceived as exogenous (i.e. the pattern and degree of integration into the system), internal factors such as economic mismanagement, the presence of a 'comprador' class allied with external forces, and an internal development logic of social formation play important roles in producing economic threats to national security. This blurred demarcation between the internal and external becomes more complicated when it is coupled with a multiplicity of actors. The state is not regarded as the exclusive source of threats. The source could be non-governmental actors such as multinational organizations or the IMF or non-actor specific, such as systemic disruptive factors related to the workings of the world economic system.

The four threat dimensions do not merely coexist as separate entities; they are closely intertwined, and generate spill-over effects. For example, a sharp decrease in external earnings for a certain developing country may create short- and medium-term uncertainties about its military strength through diminished allocations of resources for the military sector. It may also trigger social and political instabilities that provide momentum for neighbouring adversaries to instigate aggressive behaviour. Or it may tempt national leaders to engage in excessive internal repression to squash domestic anxiety over government policy. Along with this is the possibility of creating a climate of hostility towards a foreign adversary to rally public support, bolstering the regime by artificial means. These spill-over effects are quite salient in developing countries, necessitating the study of complex causal relationships among these threat dimensions.[20]

## CAPABILITY AND POLICY RESPONSES

Different threats require varying types of capability and policy response. Military security concerns, being overt, coercive, and behavioural, demand similarly coercive power to deter external threats or attack adversaries. Accumulation of power commodities (e.g. size, resources, industrial capability), along with effective policy infrastructure (e.g. strategic doctrine, force structure, intelligence and weapons system choice), is essential for a strong military security posture.[21] Given the multidimensional nature of Third World security, however, this behavioural capability alone may not solve or alleviate the security dilemma. Poor resource bases and diverse threats confronting Third World countries tend to make military capabilities both antinomial and inappropriate. For example, population size is usually regarded as one of the most important components of power. Thus, increasing population levels are seen as beneficial to a nation's security. For countries such as Egypt, India and Bangladesh, however, increasing population size is a crucial destabilizing factor. Population growth amid low domestic carrying capacity is a liability, not an asset, and this liability may eventually undermine the organic survival of national populations, as well as social and economic stability.

The maximization of coercive capability through a military build-up often engenders unanticipated disruptive results. In order to enhance military power and improve management capability, developing countries must mobilize all the resources available to society. In the economic realm, they must mobilize the labour force, capital, natural resources, and other economic capabilities for use by the military. Administratively, they have to design a future-orientated force structure to recruit and train officers and men, to develop and produce new and innovative weapons systems, and to maintain an effective, flexible military system along with stable logistics. Most importantly, all this must be accompanied by a new structuring of the political base so that resources from the civilian sector can be diverted to the military sector with the highest priority on military issues. Security capability in the conventional sense then, requires an interactive sum of economic, administrative, and political elements.[22]

In practice this seldom happens in the Third World. Pursuing this type of capability is often accompanied by unbearable social costs. Excessive allocation of resources to the military sector produces negative side-effects in terms of income shifts, productivity, investment, and the welfare distribution pattern.[23] For example, advanced developing countries such as Brazil and South Korea initiated extensive military industrialization in the 1970s in order to reduce dependence on dominant area suppliers. Enhancing military self-support through endogenous military industrialization dictated the concentration of scarce economic resources in the heavy industrial sector that has linkage effects to the defence industry. But these attempts resulted in the distorted allocation of resources and severe economic crises, which in turn precipitated political instabilities and undermined the basis of national security.

More serious are political costs associated with overall militarization. As the experiences of several Latin American and Middle Eastern countries illustrate, the process of militarization to enhance coercive capability often leads to a concentration of political power in the military sector. Such a trend precipitates military intervention in civil society, and eventually breeds a vicious circle of authoritarian military regimes. Likewise, preoccupation with behavioural capability, whether overt military threats exist or not, produces delicate trade-offs.[24]

Furthermore, military capability is inadequate for coping with other threats. In the case of economic security, for example, we have identified two types of threat, behavioural and structural, that could undermine economic welfare and autonomy. Military capability may be useful in coping with behavioural threats, but the very weakness of

Third World countries seldom allows the exercise of military options. On the other hand, military capabilities are inadequate for managing economic threats arising from structural sources. In this case, security management involves reconditioning of the pattern, rate, and degree of integration into the international economy that can reduce vulnerability and dependence. The reconditioning can be done either through an internal adjustment capable of altering development strategies, or through changing the existing international regime. For example, Third World countries may pursue a more self-sustaining development strategy that can reduce or eliminate external dependence and vulnerability through a diversified economic structure and expanded domestic demands. Strengthened collective bargaining or self-reliance, once manifested in global negotiations involving the new international economic order, could be another option that can alleviate structural sources of economic insecurity in the Third World.

Ensuring organic survival also necessitates both domestic and external adjustment. Domestic adjustment involves the expansion of carrying capacity, coupled with population and consumption control. Such adjustment, however, requires a realignment of production and consumption patterns as well as social reorganization. Undertaking alternative energy paths, pursuing food-first policies, or adopting appropriate technology are characteristics of this realignment.[25] By contrast, external adjustment in the wake of mounting lateral pressure can take several different forms. Territorial expansion, as was manifested in nineteenth century colonialism, could be an option.[25] However, this option seems the least feasible, not only because most Third World countries are inherently weak, but also because military conflicts resulting from it could increase, rather than lessen, insecurity. In this circumstance, regional cooperation or economic integration could be an option because it would allow countries to expand their resource bases beyond national boundaries in a peaceful and less risky manner.

Security concerns of communal origin are usually manifested in forms of domestic political instability, secessionist movements, and sometimes overt external military threats arising from linkages between domestic communal groups and their external patrons. National governments may reduce or eliminate such threats by taking an equally militant and violent course. But such a course of action tends to trigger a chain of violent behaviour, rather than to contain or quell the situation. Moreover, governments in multi-communal settings are usually too weak to pursue such a policy course. A viable option is to accelerate nation-building through the appeasement and co-optation of diverse communal groups. Recognizing communal identities, eliminating sectoral and regional imbalances forged along communal lines, and implementing balanced personnel recruitment constitute some examples of such a policy choice. Appeasing and co-opting communal groups in this way requires not only material and positional resources, but also the significant structural reform of society.[27] Given the inherent scarcity of positional and material resources in the Third World, communal threats require more effective political skill and leadership.

It is this diverse nature of physical capability and policy responses that places policy capacity at the centre of national security management.[28] Resources and physical capabilities are necessary, but not sufficient, conditions for a strong security posture. Indeed the Third World security dilemma lies more in rigid domestic policy capacity failing to serve as a crucial link between security environment, capabilities, and final security posture than anywhere else. Policy capacity is important because it reflects the perception, decision and implementation of security policies. It is through the policy capacity of a nation-state that national values are defined, threats and vulnerabilities are perceived and assessed, resources are allocated, and options are screened, selected and implemented. Altering development strategies for economic security, ensuring organic survival through social reorganization and value change, and achieving communal harmony through nation-building, all require effective, adaptive and flexible policy capacity. Even physical protection through military options cannot be successfully undertaken without appropriate policy capacity. Success or failure in coping with external threats depends not only on capability and hardware, but also on a policy capacity that determines the national will and the quality of government. Policy capacity is all the more important precisely because of acute resource scarcity, limits to building physical capability, and pervasive structural rigidities in the Third World.

Effective policy capacity demands a political atmosphere conducive to policy agreement, along with a comprehensive, coherent and flexible implementation scheme. Although the degree of policy capacity varies across countries, most countries suffer from a fragile and rigid security coping mechanism. Perpetual legitimacy crises and resulting regime insecurity quite often induce ruling élites to equate regime security with national security. Such political instrumentalization of national security undermines national consensus on ends and means, and weakens the ability to mobilize resources at time of real security crisis. Moreover, the existence of multiple communal and social groups and failure to integrate them into a unified political fabric brings about contradicting threat perceptions as well as a divided policy agenda. At the same time, bureaucratic diversity and confusion of accountability, coupled with arbitrary political governance, hinder comprehensive and coherent policy decisions. Even if coherent decisions are reached, very few developing countries are able to implement them speedily and flexibly. Rigid and compartmentalized, conflicting social forces weaken the internal strength of the state and deprive it of its ability to mobilize resources and implement decisions. It is this weak and rigid policy capacity common to Third World developing countries that makes policy capacity an important unit of analysis in the study of Third World national security.[29]

## SUMMARY

This book is intended to broaden the theoretical and empirical evaluation of national security to encompass economic, ecological and communal factors. In the Third

World security context, it is necessary to include domestic composition and diverse national values as active elements in Third World security discussions. Further, because Third World security concerns are distinctly different from the West, which has completed the task of nation-building, it necessitates the need for conceptual expansion or revision of the realist paradigm.

Security concerns in the Third World cannot be meaningfully understood without reference to the often fragile domestic political structure and policy capacity of these nations. Their ability to respond to crises and threats is often contingent upon the regime's capacity to consolidate multi-actor domestic concerns. In trying to elucidate Third World security needs, we have tried to delineate the structure of multiple threats and capabilities to correspond with diverse security measures.

We do not claim to have presented a brand new generalization of Third World national security, but we have identified old and new problems and suggested a set of guidelines with which to conduct inquiries and derive some prescriptions. We have avoided drawing conclusions and developing universal frameworks to identify the Third World security milieu because of the complex and ever-changing nature of Third World security needs. It is uncommonly difficult to formulate a strategy that can be uniformly applied across countries. It is from this vantage point that we suggest a contextual analysis focusing on policy capacity and on disaggregated empirical dimensions.

## NOTES

[1] See Robert Rothstein, *The Weak in the World of the Strong* (New York: Columbia University, 1977); Stephan Krasner, *Structural Conflict* (Berkeley: University of California Press, 1985), pp. 32–49; Barry Buzan, *People, State and Fear: The National Security Problem in International Relations* (Brighton: Wheatsheaf, and Chapel Hill: University of North Carolina Press, 1983), ch. 2.

[2] See Chapters 1 and 4 in this volume.

[3] See, for example, Hans Morgenthau, *Politics Among Nations*, 5th

edn (New York: Knopf, 1973); Kenneth H. Dyson, *The State Tradition in Western Europe* (Oxford: Martin Robertson, 1980).

[4] Buzan, *People, State and Fear* pp. 46–9.

[5] Robert Osgood, *Ideals and Self-Interest in America's Foreign Relations* (Chicago: University of Chicago Press, 1953), p. 443.

[6] Klaus Knorr and Frank N. Trager (eds), *Economic Issues and National Security* (Lawrence, KS: University Press of Kansas, 1977), p. 8.

[7] On the subjective value content of national security, see Chapter 3 in this volume; Robert Rothstein, 'The "Security Dilemma" and the "Poverty Trap" in the Third World', *Jerusalem Journal of International Relations*, vol. 8, no. 4 (1986), p. 13; Edward E. Azar and Chung-in Moon, 'Third World National Security: Toward a New Conceptual Framework', *International Interactions*, vol. 11, no. 2 (1984).

[8] Although national security concerns are a function of *subjective* threat perception and value judgement by ruling elites, it is possible to identify a set of *objective* conditions that are more likely to cause security threats than others.

[9] See Knorr and Trager, *Economic Issues*; and L. Krause and J. Nye, 'The Economics and Politics of International Economic Organizations' in C.F. Bergsten and L. Krause, *World Politics and International Economics* (Washington, DC: The Brookings Institution, 1975), pp. 323–42.

[10] Knorr and Trager, *Economic Issues*, p. 87.

[11] In reality, very few ruling elites would regard economic issues as national security concerns. Increasing military spending amidst poverty is evidence of this trend. See Rothstein, 'The "Security Dilemma" '.

[12] See Arnold Toynbee, *A Study of History* (London: Oxford University Press, 1961); William McNeil, *The Human Condition: An Ecological and Historical View* (Princeton, NJ: Princeton University Press, 1980).

[13] This view has been presented by both modernization and revisionist theorists. See S.M. Lipset, *Political Man* (New York: Doubleday, 1959); Karl Deutsch, *Nationalism and Social Communication* (New York: Wiley, 1953); Clifford Geertz, 'The Integrative Revolution: Primordial Sentiments and Civil Politics in the New States' in Clifford Geertz (ed), *Old Societies and New States* (New York: Free Press, 1963), pp. 105–57.

[14] Buzan, *People, State and Fear*, pp. 88–9.

[15] James Caporaso, 'Dependence, Dependency and Power in

Global System: A Structural and Behavioural Analysis', *International Organization*, vol. 32, no. 1 (1978), pp. 13–43; See also Buzan, *People, State and Fear*, chapter 5.

[16] C. Murdoch, 'Economic Factors as Objects of Security' in Knorr and Trager, *Economic Issues*.

[17] Dennis Pirages, *Global Ecopolitics* (North Scituate, MA: Duxbury Press, 1978); H. Sprout and M. Sprout, *Toward Planetary Earth* (Princeton, NJ: Princeton University Press, 1971); Lester Brown, *Redefining National Security* (Washington, DC: World Watch Institute, 1977); Nazli Choucri and Robert North, *Nations in Conflict* (San Francisco: Freeman Press, 1975).

[18] Edward E. Azar, 'Protracted International Conflicts: Ten Propositions' in Edward E. Azar and John Burton (eds), *International Conflict Resolution: Theory and Practice* (Brighton: Wheatsheaf, 1986), pp. 28–40; Edward E. Azar and Chung-in Moon, 'Managing Protracted Social Conflicts: Facilitation and Development Diplomacy', *Millennium: Journal of International Studies*, vol. 15, no. 3 (1986), pp. 393–408; Edward E. Azar and Steve Cohen, 'Peace as Crisis and War as Status Quo', *International Interactions*, vol. 6, no. 2 (1980), pp. 159–84; Edward E. Azar and Nadia Farah, 'Protracted Social Conflicts, Ethnicity, and Population' (mimeo, 1982).

[19] Richard Smoke, 'National Security Affairs' in Fred Greenstein and Nelson Polsby (eds), *Handbook of Political Science* (Reading, MA: Addison-Wesley, 1975), p. 248.

[20] A more serious difficulty comes from the lack of consensus on identifying the nature of threat. In many cases, each constituent (regime in power, opposition, communal actors, etc) of a nation-state tends to share divergent threat perceptions.

[21] See Ray Cline, *World Power Trends and the US Foreign Policy for the 1980s* (New York: Basic Books, 1976); Robert Art, 'The Role of Military Power in International Relations' in Thomas Trout and James E. Harf (eds), *National Security Affairs: Theoretical Perspectives and Contemporary Issues* (New Brunswick, NJ: Transaction Books, 1982), pp. 3–15.

[22] Klaus Knorr, *Power of Nations* (New York: Basic Books, 1976), ch. 3.

[23] See Emile Benoit, 'Growth Effects of Defence in Developing Countries', *International Development Review*, vol. 14, no. 2 (1972), pp. 2–15; Saadet Deger and Ron Smith, 'Military Expenditure and Growth in LDCs', *Journal of Conflict Resolution*, vol. 27, no. 2 (June 1983), pp. 335–53.

[24] See Andre Gunder Frank, *Crisis: In the Third World* (New York: Holmes and Meier, 1981), pp. 230–79; S.E. Finer, 'The Military and Politics in the Third World' in W. Scott Thompson (ed), *The Third World: Premises of US Policy* (San Francisco: Institute for Contemporary Studies, 1983).

[25] See Lester Brown, *Redefining*.

[26] See Choucri and North, *Nations*, ch. 1.

[27] Donald Rothchild, 'State and Ethnicity in Africa: A Policy Perspective', a paper presented at the annual convention of the American Political Science Association in Washington, DC, August 1984; Cynthia H. Enloe, *Ethnic Conflict and Political Development* (Boston: Little, Brown, 1973); Milton Esman, 'The Management of Communal Conflict', *Public Policy*, vol. 21, no. 1 (Winter 1973), pp. 49–78.

[28] See chapter 4 in this volume.

[29] For new interpretations of strength versus weakness in states, see Peter Katzenstein (ed), *Between Power and Plenty* (Madison: University of Wisconsin Press, 1978); Mancur Olson, *The Rise and Decline of Nations* (New Haven, CT: Yale University Press).

# Index

Acheson, Dean 146, 258
Achievers (Third World subcategory) 7, 61, 64–8, 72–4
Alfonsín, President 149
Allende, Salvadore 163
alliances 4, 10, 32, 85
ambiguities in national security 277–80
Amini, Ali 238–9
Amnesty International 241
anarchic states 22, 24, 28, 29
anarchy, international 27–8
Anglo-Iranian Oil Company 232, 242
Angola 29
anti-colonialism 107
anti-Semitism 211–13
Arab League 33
Arabs 90–91
Argentina 9, 83
  arms supplies 159, 174
  class war 206–209
  Dirty Wars 10, 189–92, 216–18
  economic downturn and radical change 203–6
  economic models 199–203
  human rights abuse 197–8
  labour movement 205–6, 214, 215
  security regimes 195, 199–203
  Socialist Party 214, 215
  Tragic Week 204, 205, 207, 211, 213, 215, 216
  World War I 203–4
Argentine Patriotic League (Liga) 207, 208, 213
arms acquisition 9, 152–80
  arms import option 154–6
  local production/import acquisition 176–8, 180
  military import substitution 166–80
  multiple source acquisition 164–6, 179
  single/predominant source acquisition 156–64, 179
  strategies 154, 179
arms embargoes 159, 166

arms import option 154–6
arms import by Third
   World 4
arms industries 67
arms race 37–8
arms supply 37–8
arms transfers 162–3, 169
ASEAN 32, 51, 73
Assad, President 83
atomic bomb 120
Azar, Edward 8, 88, 102

Baer, Werner 139
balance of power 22, 30,
   35
   asymmetrical 30, 35
   transnational 30, 32
Baldwin, David 145, 147
'bamboo curtain' 117
Benoit, Emile 142
Bobrow, Davis 7, 8, 278
Brazil 9, 138–41
   Air Force 171–2
   arms exports 173
   arms imports 173, 175
   arms production 171,
      291
   economic development
      139–40, 144
   national security 147
   Navy 172
   redemocratization 148,
      149
   role of army 139
   steel industry 139–41
   World War I 138–9, 141
   World War II 139, 141
Britain 157
Bucy, J. F. 170
Buenos Aires 205, 207,
   209
bureaucratic
   authoritarianism 202
Burns, Bradford 144

Buzan, Barry 6–8, 278,
   284

Cahn, Anne 168
capability, and policy
   responses 290–94
capital accumulation
   199–203
capitalism 190–92
   216–17
   crises 198
   dependent 10
Cardoso, Fernando 143
Caribbean 40
Carter, President J. 163,
   193
Castro, Fidel 143
Central Intelligence
   Agency (CIA) 256,
   258
Chan, Steve 7, 8, 278
charismatic leaders 111,
   115, 117, 118, 232
Chile 163, 188
China 38, 56
   atomic bomb 120
   Cultural Revolution
      (1966–76) 106,
      112, 114–17,
      120, 123
   foreign trade 127–30
   Great Leap Forward
      120
   ideology 8
   mass mobilization
      116
   militarization of
      politics 120–6
   military power 70,
      175
   politicization of the
      military 120–6
   population 61, 113
   self-reliance 112–34

trade surpluses 127
class interests 10
class war 191, 206–209
client relationships 5
Cline, R. S. 80
closed systems 110–11, 117
coalitions 4
cold war 2, 36, 142–3, 255
Colombia 190
colonial boundaries 34
colonialism 107
colonial ties 5
communal conflict 86–90, 282, 283, 287–8
communalism 282–3
Communism 144, 146
concept of national security 6, 7, 11, 39
  ambiguity 23
  American 45
  core 260–61
  development in USA 1, 11
  emergence 252–9
  generalized 44–53
  meaning 251–2
  Third World countries 14, 16
  Western 2, 14, 265
Connor, W. 86
Cordobazo 205
Coser, L. 91
Council for Mutual Economic Assistance 53
Cuba 36, 141, 149, 197
  revolution 143
Cultural Revolution (1966–76) 106, 112, 114–17, 120, 123
Cyprus 161, 288

Davids (Third World subcategory) 7, 61, 64–6, 72–4
decision-making 266
  centralization 92, 93, 95
decolonization 26, 33, 35
defence spending 60, 61
Defense Department, USA 257, 258
definition of national security 102–3, 266, 270
dependence 48, 64, 70, 71, 73, 105
  dyadic 285
  dynamic 170
  military 169–70, 175
  static 170
  structural 285
  technological 283
dependency theory 105
*desaparecidos* 188, 190
deterrence 102
developing countries 5
Dirty Wars (Argentina) 10, 189–92, 216–18
domestic conflicts 32
domestic failure 286
domestic threats 24–6
Druze community 87, 88

ecological determinism 4
ecological problems 287
ecology 282
economic development 9, 265
  and national security 136–49
economic linkage 66, 67

economic role in
    national security
    281
economic security 281
ecopolitical pressures 2
Ecuador 204
Egan, Carlos 9
Egypt 163, 165, 166,
    174, 178
elections 29
Embraer 171, 172
ethnocentrism 106, 108,
    115
external behaviour
    80–1

Falklands crisis 83, 159,
    174
foreign direct
    investment 171
Fourth World 59
fragmented states 28,
    29, 278, 282, 283,
    288
France 20, 157, 159

Galtieri, President 83
Gasiorowski, Mark 10
Ghana 157
Gilpin, Robert 137
goal attainment 47, 48,
    52
Goliaths (Third World
    subcategory) 7, 61,
    64, 65, 68–74
  accomplishments 69
  endowments 69, 72
government, weakness
    25
government service 264
graduation 58
Great Leap Forward 120
Greece 254, 255
Group of 77, 64

guerrilla movements 24
guns-or-butter
    dichotomy 263, 273

Haggard, Stephan 137
Haig, Alexander 193
Haiti 25
hardware dimension of
    national security
    policies 8
Ho Chi Minh 103
human rights abuse 10,
    163, 188–218
  Argentina 197–8
  cycles 198
  Latin America
    192–9

ideological education
    110
ideology 8, 15, 21, 104,
    108, 110
  China 8
  North Korea 8
'import substitution'
    model of
    industrialization
    200–202
independence 26
India 20, 38
  Air Force 173
  defence production
    171, 173, 175
  military power 70
  population 61
Indo-Pakistani War
    (1971) 159
industrialization 113,
    138, 200, 237, 239
inflation 83, 240, 286
information
    manipulation 117
insecurity 3, 7, 27, 278
instability 7, 54, 83

integration 78, 79
  and security
  dilemma 86–91
International Institute
  for Strategic Studies 169
Iran 10, 33, 36, 82, 227–46
  American military aid 235
  arms supplies 159
  Constitutional Revolution
    (1906) 231, 233, 234
  corruption 237–40
  coup (1953) 233
  economic development 228
  industrialization 239
  Majles 231–3
  monarchical tradition 230,
    233
  National Front 236, 239, 242,
    243
  nationalism 234
  oil industry 227, 235, 242
  regime legitimacy 241–4
  relationship with USA 235,
    245
  revolution (1979) 10, 82, 160,
    227, 236, 243–5
  Tudeh Party 232, 238, 242
  underdevelopment 237–40
  White Revolution 239
  World War I 231
  World War II 238
Iran-Iraq war 82
Iraq 10, 82, 87
  invasion of Iran 227, 229,
    244
Islam 21, 30
Israel,
  arms supplies 159, 162, 163,
    174, 178
  communal divisions 90
  GNP 61
  legitimacy 95
  policy capacity 94, 95
  policy mood 93

  security 91, 93–4
  unity 91
Italy 176

Japan, colonial policies 112
Jews 90–91, 211–12
Joint US Military Advisory
    Group (JUSMAG) 163
*Juche* ideology 8, 103, 115–19

Kapstein, Ethan 9
Kenya 157
Khomeini, Ayatollah 159, 236,
    239, 242–4
Kim II Sung 104, 112–18, 126,
    132
Kissinger, Henry 258, 259
Knorr, Klaus 280
Korea, liberation 112
Korean War (1950–3) 112, 116,
    141, 145, 163
Kuomintang 84–5
Kurds 87, 288
Kurian, George 113

Latin America 24, 66; *see also*
    *under names of countries*
  cold war 142–3
  human rights abuse 188,
    192–9
  militarization 291
  redemocratization 148
leadership 80
Lebanon 25, 28, 29, 58, 289
  army 90
  fragmentation 87, 267
  legitimacy 95
  policy capacity 95
legitimacy 21–4, 78–86, 95; *see*
    *also* regime legitimacy
  and national security 79
  nature 79
  and security management
    80–86

weak 84, 85
Lenin, V. I. 115
leverage 46–7, 49–53, 56, 58, 66, 74
  direct 50
  indirect 50
  limitations 49, 50, 56
linkage politics 80, 82
Lippmann, Walter 260
literature on Third World national security 1–2
Little, Richard 21, 22, 30, 35
Lock, Peter 169
Luckham, Robin 160

McLaurin, Ronald 10
Manchuria 112
Maoism 8, 103, 115, 118
Mao Zedong 84, 103, 104, 112–18, 122, 124
  death 117, 132
  Mass Line campaign 116
Marcos, President 84
Mares, David 137
Maronites 87, 88, 90
Marshall, General George 255, 258
Marshall Plan 268
Marxism-Leninism 114, 115
mass media 110, 117, 269
mass mobilization 35, 84, 109–10, 116
mass uprisings 24
mediation 34
medium-sized powers 5
Micronesia 255
micro-states 18
middle classes 141, 143, 147, 208
Middle East 38, 40, 41, 66, 291; *see also under*

*names of countries*
  arms supplies 163
middle powers 19
militarization of politics 120–26
military,
  capability 291–2
  coups 24, 82
  expenditure 4, 196
  government 32
  import substitution 166–80
  industry 119–20
  power 4, 9, 11–12, 153: measurement 106; primacy 4
  threats, external 3, 4, 11
mini-states 18
modernization 81, 86, 283
Mohammad Reza Pahlavi (Shah of Iran),
  installed on throne 232–4
  legitimacy 240–42
  nationalism 236
  overthrow 10, 82, 160, 244
  reforms 238–40
  relationship with USA 227, 228, 240
  White Revolution 239
Moodie, Michael 169
Moon, Chung-in 102, 228, 229
Morgenthau, H. 80
Morocco 84
Mossadeq, Mohammad 232, 233, 235, 236, 238
MPLA 29
multiple dimensions of national security 280–84

nationalism 26, 108, 112,
234
as legitimizing force
233–6
national security, and
imaginary foreign
threat 209–13
National Security Act,
USA (1947) 255
National Security
Council, USA 256,
258, 259, 267
national will 78, 80
nation state 279, 281
nature of states 17–27
neo-colonialism 105–6
Netherlands 15
Neuman, Stephanie 169
Nicaragua 25
Nigeria 157, 164–5
Nixon, President 258
Non-Aligned Movement 3
North Atlantic Treaty
Organization (NATO)
257, 268
North Korea,
arms supplies 175
ethnic composition 113
fear of South Korea 112
foreign trade 127, 131–3
ideology 8
mass media 117
mass mobilization 116
militarization of politics
120–26
military expenditure 121
politicization of the
military 120–26
self-reliance 112–34
trade deficits 127
North Vietnam 65
nuclear technology 67
nuclear threats 23
nuclear weapons 33, 34

OAS 33
OAU 33
October 1973 War 94
oil states 17
OPEC 51, 56
Opium War (1839) 112
organic survival 281–2,
286, 292
Organization for
Economic Cooperation
and Development 53
Osgood, Robert 279

Pakistan 19, 21, 30, 38,
41, 42
armed forces 70
arms supplies 159, 175,
177
break-up 28
Palestinians 33
Park,
Han-Sik 8
Kyung A. 8
President 142
partition movements 87
People's Liberation Army
124
people's militia 105
Persian Gulf 10
Peru 143, 144
Philippines 84, 87, 88,
163, 177
'Point Four' Programme
146
police state 111
policy,
capacity 78, 79, 84, 85,
88, 90, 94–8:
dynamics 79; and
security performance
91–5, 293–5
elites 49
goals 109
mood 91, 93

Polisario 84
political,
    cohesion 19
    factionalism 24
    institutions in Third
        World countries 264
    rights 192–3
    succession 82
politicization 110
    of military 120–26
population size 59–61,
    286, 290
Portugal 15, 162
power,
    commodities 103, 109,
        290
    differences 31
    distribution 17–18
    monopoly 21
Price, Jane 122
priority-focusing 48
protracted social conflicts
    287, 288

Qadhafi, Colonel 83

Rajaratnam, S. 158, 160
Reagan, President R. 193–4
recession 201
refugees 286
regime legitimacy 241–6
    and national security
        227–46
    sources 229–33
regime security 83–4, 294
regional politics 36
religion 110, 269
resources 5, 35, 138, 278,
    286
revolution 35
Reza Shah 229, 231–4
    legitimacy 237
    nationalism 234

reforms 237–8
Rhee, President Syngman
    142
Rio Pact (1945) 196
Roca, Julio 195
Rosenau, J.N. 60
Ross, Andy 9

Sadat, President 159, 163
Saudi Arabia 30, 160
    arms supplies 162
    GNP 61
    leverage 50
SAVAK 235, 241
scarcity 48, 64, 81
schools 110
secessionist movements
    24, 87, 283, 288
security community 15
security complexes 41, 42
security environment 8,
    27–40, 77, 96
self-defence 119–20
self-government 23
self-help 3
self-reliance 8
    China 102–4, 112–34
    conditions for 107–9
    and dependency 104–7
    economic 103, 105,
        106, 126–33
    and ideology 104
    as ideology 114–18
    military 168
    for national security
        104–11
    and national security
        119–20
    North Korea 102–4,
        112–34
    policy implications 109
Shah of Iran *see*
        Mohammad Reza Pahlavi

Sh'ia community 87, 88, 90
significance 50, 74
Sino-Soviet split 117, 124
Six Day War 159
skilled manpower 264, 271–2

Smoke, Richard 288
social divisions 269
social mobilization 81
sociopolitical cohesion
    18–22, 31
software dimension of
    national security policies
    8, 78–98
South Africa 19, 33, 157
    arms imports 173
South Asia 38
South Korea 9
    American economic
        assistance 142
    arms exports 174
    arms imports 174, 175
    arms production 171,
        173, 291
    economic policy 142, 174
    ethnic composition 113
    legitimacy 95
    policy capacity 94
    regime security 84
    security policy 94, 141–2
South-West Asia 41
sovereign states 16
Soviet Union 15, 19, 29,
    32, 34
    aid to insurgents 107–8
    arms supplies 157–61
    Middle East role 41
    military technicians
        161, 165
Spain 23
Spiegel, Steven 171
Sri Lanka 20, 87, 88
Staley, Eugene 146
Stalin, J. 115

State Department, USA
    256–8
'state nations' 279
state terrorism 217
State-War-Navy
    Coordinating
    Committee 253, 257
'statist' regimes 138
status discrepancy theory
    68
strikes 204–208
strong states 19, 20, 25,
    28–30
subgroupism 86
Sunni community 87, 88
superpower rivalry 85
superpowers 5, 10
    nuclear arms race 102
    rivalry 12, 257
Sweden 15, 176
systemic vulnerability
    285

Tamils 87, 88
territorial disputes 156
Thailand 70
Third World,
    and First and Second
        Worlds 52, 53
    identification 53–9
Third World countries,
    national profiles 62
Third World national
    security, typology 95–8
threats to national
    security 284–90
totalitarian regimes 16
trade unions 190
traditional approach to
    national security 11, 13
Truman, President Harry
    146, 260
Turkey 161, 254, 255

underdevelopment 269, 281
unemployment 204, 281, 286
Unión Cívica Radical (UCR) 206, 208, 212–16
UNITA 29
United Nations 33
United States 29, 34
  aid to insurgents 107–8
  arms supplies 157–63, 174
  foreign aid 146
  imports of raw materials 145
  isolationism 254
  national security before World War I 252–3
  policy-making 1
  presidency 1
  World War II 254
Uruguay 188, 204

Vietnam 70
Vietnam War 106, 163
Viola, General R. 189
violence 26
Volta Redonda 139–41

Wald, Pedro 210, 211
Waltz, K.N. 17
war 3, 27, 33, 34
Warsaw Pact 161
weakness of Third World countries 56, 58, 61, 278
weak states 18–35, 40
Weak (Third World subcategory) 7
weapons systems 37, 153, 159, 160, 167
Wirth, John 139
Wolfers, Arnold 23, 153, 252, 260
World War I 138–9, 141, 203–4, 231
World War II 139, 141, 238, 254
Wulf, Herbert 169

xenophobia 26

Yrigoyen, President 208, 212–14, 216

Zhou Enlai 132
Zionism 94